Famous Short Stories

Annotated with Editor's Notes

by

Na, Byung-Woo

Shinasa

Contents

Critical Introduction

I. 머리말

벌써 대학에서 강의를 한 지가 30년이 되었다. 그 동안에 단편 소설 과목을 맡을 때마다 늘 어떤 교재를 선택하며, 어떤 작가의 어떤 작품을 가르칠 것인가 하는 문제로 고심하며 편저자 나름대로 감동을 받고 의미 있었던 글들을 중심으로 책을 한 권 엮어야 하겠다는 생각을 해왔다.

멀티미디어 시대인 오늘날 일반 독자들이나 어문학과 학생들이 공통적으로 활자화된 혹은 책의 형태로 출간된 장편을 기피하려는 경향을 보인다. 밤을 세우며 독서할 수 있는 인내력이 사라지고 짧은 시간 시청각적 매체들을 통해서 사람들은 문학에 접근하려고 한다. 독자들은 원작 소설을 읽기보다는 한 두 시간이면 감상할 수 있는 분량으로 만든 영화를 보는 것이 요즘의 경향이다. 따라서 과거 그 어느 때보다 더 단편 소설 교재의 필요성이 커졌다고 하겠다. 한 자리에 앉아서 한 두 시간 안에 읽어낼 수 있는 분량에, 긴밀한 구성, 단일한 사건, 단일한 효과를 노리는 단편 소설의 집중성이 현대 독자의 기호에 딱 맞아떨어진다.

본서는 국내외에 이미 출판되어 있는 작품집들을 참고로 하였으나 많은 작가의 많은 작품을 백과사전식으로 나열하고 총망라하는 형식을 탈피하고 정말 좋은 작품을 선정하여 깊이 있는 연구를 하도록 하였다. 작품 선정에 있어서 어차피 편저자의 주관과 취향과 관심이 절대적인 기준이 될 수밖에 없으나, 이 책의 작품 선정에 있어서 기준으로 삼은 것은 우선 재미있는 작품이고, 그 다음으로 인생에 관한 의미있는 메시지를 담고 있어야 한다는 것이었다. 누구나 공감할 수 있는 명작들을 선정하여 독자들의 이해를 돕기 위하여 상세한 주석을 첨가하였다. 그리고 텍스트 말미에 참고 자료로서는, 단편 소설을 하나의 문학 형식으로 이론적 체계를 세운 Edgar Allan Poe의 글을 수록하였고, 단편 소설의 특징과 흐름에 관한 글도 몇 편 수록하였다. 모두 열 두 편의 단편

—미국 작품 여섯 편, 영국 작품 여섯 편—을 수록하였으나, 일일이 참고자료를 구하기도 어렵고, 분량도 너무 많아지는 것을 피하기 위해, 마지막 단편인 "The Dead"에 관한 비평만을 수록하였다.

아무쪼록 낭만과 상상력이 메말라 가는 세상을 우리가 살아가지만, 이 단편 소설 선집을 통하여 영혼과 정신에 흡족한 단비가 뿌려지기를 기대한다. 아울러 영어 독해 실력을 향상시키는 데에도 큰 도움이 될 것을 소망한다.

Ⅱ. 작품해설

첫 작품 "Rip Van Winkle"은 미국 문학의 아버지 혹은 순문학의 시조라고 할 수 있는 Washinton Irving의 유명한 단편이다. 주인공 립 밴 윙클은 엄처시하에서 고통받는 소박하고 착한 사람이다. 그는 마을 사람들에게 인기가 있었고 아이들이나 심지어 마을의 개까지도 그를 좋아하였다. 다른 사람들의 일은 잘 도와주나, 자기 집안일은 돌보지 않는 모순된 사람이었다. 물론 돈을 버는 일도 잘 하지 못했다. 그는 농장 노동의 고역과 아내의 잔소리를 벗어나기 위해 어느 날 총을 한 자루 메고 케츠킬 산 속을 헤매다가 우연히 만난 사람의 술을 얻어먹고 깊은 잠에 빠져든다. 깨어나니 20년이나 세월이 흐른 후였다. 아내는 이미 세상을 떠났고, 어린 자식들은 장성하였고, 세상 사람들도 변하여 온통 정치에 정신이 팔려 있다. 이 단편에서 어빙은 개성이 뚜렷한 한 인물을 창조하였고, 잠을 통하여 엄처시하의 고통이 얼마나 심한 것이고, 거기에서 벗어나고자 하는 립 밴 윙클의 염원이 얼마나 강력한 것이었는가 하는 사실을 여실히 보여준다. 미국의 꿈이라는 관점에서 해석하자면 영국의 식민 통치에서 해방되어 정치적 자유가 보장되는 독립국가가 되었으면 하는 꿈과 염원이 얼마나 큰 것인가 하는 점도 암시된 작품이다.

흔히들 단편 소설의 시조라고 하는 Edgar Allan Poe는 "The Tell-Tale Heart"에서 병을 앓고 난 후 감각이 매우 예민해진 1인칭 주인공 "I"를 그려낸다. 이웃에 부자 노인이 사는데 주인공은 그 노인에게 아무런 피해도 입지 않았고, 그 노인을 또한 사랑하지만 독수리의 눈을 닮은 그 노인의 눈 때문에 노인을 죽이고 눈을 빼기로 마음을 먹는다. 은밀하게 노인의 방에 접근하여 목적을 이룬 주인공은 방바닥 나무판자를 뜯어내고 시신을 은폐하였으나, 나중에 경찰의 조사 과정에서 그 나무판자 위에 의자를 놓고 앉아서 태연한척 하려고 했지만 결국 스스로 비밀을 털어놓게 됨으로써(tell-tale) 범행이 탄로 나게 된다. 무섭기도 하고 으스스한 분위기를 보여주는 이 단편을 통하여 작가는 인간 본성 속에 내재된 어둠과 악의 요소를 주목하며, 그러나 양심 앞에 죄악이 은폐될 수 없음을 암시한다.

"David Swan"에서 Nathaniel Hawthorne은 인간에게 닥치는 사건에는 두 가지 종류가 있다고 이야기한다. 하나는 직접적으로 현실 속에 발생하여 한 인간의 삶에 큰 영향을 미치는 사건들이다. 다른 하나는 우리도 모르게 가까이 다가왔다가 사라져버리는 사건, 어떤 면에서는 사건이라고 부를 수도 없는 사건이 있다. 그 예화로 작가는 20세 청년 데이빗 스완이 보스턴으로 가는 길에 고단하여 길가 숲속에서 잠이 든 사이에 벌어지는 몇 가지 사건을 제시한다. 마차를 타고 지나가던 노상인 부부가 마침 마차의 고장으로 인해 잠든 데이빗 스완을 보게 된다. 곤한 잠에서 깨어나면 양자로 삼고 재산의 절반이라도 주어야겠다고 생각하던 부자 상인 부부는 마차가 다 수리되고, 데이빗 스완은 잠에서 깨어나지 않자 그냥 그곳을 떠나간다. 이어서 부잣집 딸 예쁜 소녀가 가까이 다가왔으나 청년은 예쁜 연인을 만나고 그녀의 부친의 사업을 이어받을 수도 있는 기회도 모른 채 계속 잠을 잔다. 마지막으로 건달들에게 노상강도를 당할 위기도 만나기도 한다. 이렇게 하여 여러 가지 흥망성쇠의 기회들이 데이빗 스완의 삶에 직접적인 영향을 미치지 않은 채 그냥 지나가버린 것이다. 작가는 작품 말미에서 "눈으로 보이지도 않고 예상도 할 수 없는 많은 사건들이 끊임없이 우리의 인생길을 가로질러 밀려오는 와중에, 인생에 부분적으로라도 예측을 가능하게 해 줄 정도의 규칙성이 있어야 한다는 것은 신의 섭리가 작용하고 있다는 것을 주장하는 것이 아니겠는가?"하는 말로써 작품을 마무리한다. 즉 우리 인생에는 우연한 것도 많아 보이지만 여전히 신의 섭리 안에 영위되고 있음을 암시하는 결론으로 이해된다.

O. Henry는 "The Cop and the Anthem"에서 Soapy라는 주인공의 현재의 고달픈 삶과 유년 시절의 행복한 삶의 대비를 통하여 재미있는 구성을 보여준다. 사는 것이 힘들고 특히 추운 겨울나기가 쉽지 않은 소피는 으레 겨울이면 범행을 저지르고 감옥에 가서 숙식을 해결하는 밑바닥 인생을 살고 있다. 그는 찬바람과 함께 다가온 겨울을 블렉웰 형무소에 가서 지내기로 마음먹고 범행을 시도한다. 고급 레스토랑에 들어가서 음식을 먹고 지불 불능자임을 밝히기로 하고 식당에 들어가다가 초라한 옷차림 때문에 쫓겨나는 등 여러 차례 시도에도 불구하고 범인으로 체포되는 데 실패한다. 결국 그는 뉴욕의 번화가를 벗어나 조용한 골목길로 접어들게 되고 우연히 오래 된 교회당에서 울려 퍼지는 찬송가 연주를 듣게 된다. 그는 어린 시절의 행복과 꿈을 생각하게 되고, 지나간 실패한 인생을 돌아보게 되고, 이제 일 자리도 찾고 새사람이 되어야 하겠다고 결심하는 순간 경찰에 체포되는 의외의 결말로 소피의 겨울 준비가 끝이 난다. 작가의 주특기인 반전의 결말이 이 단편에서도 구사된 것이다.

미국의 건국 이후 줄곧 미국인들의 혈관 속에 관통하는 정신이 미국인의 꿈이라고 할 수 있다. American dream은 초기에는 순수한 민주와 자유에의 꿈, 정치 종교 등 모든 분야에서 새로운 에덴을 건설하려는 꿈이었으나, 나중에는 물질적 성공에 더 경도되는 세속화된 꿈으로 변질된다. 쇠퇴되어 부정적인 측면이 많이 노출된 미국인의 꿈이 Fitzgerald의 작품 속에 나온다. 그의 단편 "Winter Dreams"도 같은 맥락에서 볼 수 있다.

젊음과 사랑과 성공을 향한 낭만적인 꿈에 부푼 주인공 Dexter Green은 어린 시절, 골프장 캐디로 아르바이트를 하던 중, 부유한 집안 출신의 미인인 Judy Jones를 만나면서 꿈과 좌절과 성공과 실패를 경험하게 된다. 첫 만남에서 자존심에 큰 상처를 입은 그는 자신의 가난을 떨치고 그녀의 사랑을 얻기 위하여 부자가 되려고 노력하며 대학에 진학도 하고 23세에 여러 곳의 지점을 거느린 세탁업 경영권을 확보하여 사업가로서 성공을 거둔다. 그러나 삶에 뿌리를 내리지 못하고 환락과 쾌락을 추구하는 주디로 인하여 한없는 절망과 환멸을 경험한다. 덱스터는 주디를 향한, 미네소타의 추운 겨울에 무의식중에 품게 되었던 겨울 꿈의 지배로부터 벗어나지 못하고, 떠나갔던 주디가 돌아오면 다시 받아 주고 사랑하게 된다. 결국 주디는 불행한 결혼을 하게 되고, 그 소식을 뒤늦게 알게 된 덱스터는 심한 상실감과 인생의 비애를 맛보며, 더 잃을 것이 없어서 눈물이 마른 상태에 이르게 된다. 이 작품은 삶에 뿌리를 내리지 못하고 방황하는 현대인의 길 잃은 모습을 잘 보여주는 단편이다. 꿈은 아름답고 좋은 것이지만, 그 꿈이 초래하는 한없는 절망과 상실감과 비애를 이 작품은 담고 있다.

본 선집에 수록된 미국 단편 중 마지막 작품 "The First Seven Years"는 성경 속의 야곱과 외삼촌 라반 그리고 외사촌인 라헬, 레아 등과 관련된 사건에서 소재를 따온 작품이다. 유태계 작가인 Bernard Malamud는 유태인인 구둣방 주인 Feld와 역시 유태인인 구두 수선공 Sobel의 삶을 통하여 유태인의 고뇌를 보여주는 동시에 물질보다 정신이 우위에 있음을 재미있게 그리고 깊이 있게 감동적으로 그려내고 있다. 자수성가한 펠드는 외동딸 Miriam을 세속적으로 성공한 사람에게 결혼을 시키길 원한다. 그는 고객 중에 착실한 청년 Max를 사윗감으로 생각하고 여러 가지 노력을 해보지만, 소벨의 책에 심취한 딸 미리엄이 맥스를 거부하고 소벨을 선택한다. 결국 펠드도 소벨을 받아들이게 되는 작품의 결말은 앞에 말한 작가의 주제를 강력하게 뒷받침해준다. 펠드로서는 그것이 중요하고 올바른 것이지만 현실 속에서 받아들이기 어려운 결정이 아닐 수 없다.

다음으로 영국 단편 중에 Katherine Mansfield의 "The Fly"는 짧지만 인간의 깊은 감정을 담아낸다. 장래가 촉망되던 아들을 향한 아버지의 기대와 사랑, 뜻하지 않게 전사당한 아들의 죽음이 주는 고통, 그로 인해 신 앞에 선 인간의 존재 의미에 대한 성찰이 이어진다. 자식을 잃은 아픔이 세월이 흐르면 잊힐 줄 알았는데, 어느 날 친구의 방문과 그 친구의 딸로부터 전해들은 아들의 묘지에 관한 언급으로 인해 사장은 끝없는 절망 속으로 빠져든다. 책상 위에 등장한 파리는 신 앞의 무력한 인간의 모습으로 겹쳐온다. 그 파리는 잉크의 무게를 견디지 못하고 죽고 만다.

영국의 작가 중에 아마 제일 많은 단편을 쓴 작가가 "Red"를 쓴 Somerset Maugham일 것이다. 그는 특히 이국적 환경에 사는 백인들의 행태를 즐겨 다룬다. 미국의 오 헨리처럼 작품 끝에 가서 의외의 결말(surprise ending)을 짓는 경우도 많다. 널리 읽히는 그의 단편이 많이 있지만, 본 선집에 수록된 "Red"는 첫 사랑의 강렬함과 끈질김, 인간 운명의 무자비함 등을 다룬다. 30년 전에 레드가 원주민 여자 Sally와 강렬한 사랑을 나누었다. 자연 속에서 두 젊은이들 사이에 피어나는 순수한 사랑이 무척 아름답게 그려지고 있다. 그들의 사랑은 레드가 그곳을 방문한 포경선을 방문했다가 납치당함으로써 비극이 되고 만다. 레드의 귀환을 기다리던 샐리는 애기를 사산하고, 3년이 지난 후 새로운 백인인 스웨덴 출신 Neilson과 결혼하게 된다. 그는 폐병으로 사형 선고를 받고 이곳에 요양하러 왔으나 온화한 기후와 사랑의 기쁨으로 인하여 점차 건강이 회복되고 결국 결혼까지 하게 된 것이다. 30년의 세월이 흐른 후 레드가 선장이 되어 이곳에 다시 방문한다. 자신의 신분을 밝히지도 못하고, 젊은 날의 사랑의 현장을 찾은 레드는 샐리의 현재의 남편 닐슨을 만나게 되고, 샐리도 잠시 조우하게 되지만 샐리는 옛 사랑을 알아보지 못한다. 닐슨은 긴 세월 샐리와 살았지만 결국 그녀의 마음과 사랑을 소유하지 못하고 살아온 셈이다. 모두가 가슴 아픈 삶을 산 것이다.

"Shooting an Elephant"에서 George Orwell은 식민지에서 근무했던 경험을 심도 있게 그려내고 있다. 식민지에서 피식민자들에게 식민통치 관리들은 공포와 두려움의 대상인 동시에 경멸과 비난의 대상이기도 하다. 주인공은 심정적으로 식민통치가 옳은 것이 아니라고 느끼고 식민 지배를 받는 주민들을 이해한다. 그러나 식민지의 경찰관 1인칭 주인공은 공인으로서 자신의 직위에 맞는 처신을 해야 한다. 코끼리를 죽여야 하는 문제에 직면하여 그는 첨예한 갈등과 고뇌를 느낀다. 거대한 동물인 코끼리에 대한 두려움도 느끼는 동시에 현지인 앞에서 비굴하거나 나약한 모습을 보일 수도 없다는 생각도 한다. 결국 인간적 고뇌에도 불구하는 주인공은 코끼리를 총으로 쏘고, 식민지 관리로서의 직무를 행한다.

황폐하고 허무한 현대인의 삶에 관능적 사랑으로 그 돌파구를 찾은 D. H. Lawrence의 "The Horse Dealer's Daughter"는 그의 장편 소설에 등장하는 중요한 문제를 다룬다. Joseph Pervin의 죽음 이후, Pervin가는 파산상태에 이르고, 형제자매는 뿔뿔이 흩어져 각자 자기의 길을 찾아가야 한다. 막내 딸 Mabel은 모친이 돌아가신 이후 집안 살림을 맡아왔고 살아있는 사람보다는 죽은 어머니의 세계와 더 깊은 교감 속에 살다가 이제는 자살을 결심하고 연못 속으로 걸어 들어간다. 이 광경을 목격한 의사 Jack Fergusson은 그녀를 구출하고 집으로 데리고 와서 간호하여 소생시킨다. 다시 살아난 메이블의 육체적 마력 앞에 잭 퍼거슨은 이성적 통제력을 상실하고 결국 무너지게 된다. 로렌스의 이상적 남녀관계는 상호간에 개체성과 타자성을 인정하는 가운데 의지의 충돌과 긴장관계를 보여주나 관능적 사랑으로 굳게 맺어져있는 있는 관계라고 생각할 때 이 단편에 나타난 두 주인공의 관계는 단편의 속성상 충분히 형상화되어 있지는 않고, 서로 어울릴 것 같지 않지만 육체적 사랑 속에 갈등과 긴장의 관계 속에서도 로렌스식 남녀관계를 잘 형성해 갈 것으로 판단된다.

Virginia Woolf의 “The Mark on the Wall”은 최근 출판된 울프의 단편 전집에서 단편 소설로 분명하게 분류하고 있는 단편이다. 이 작품은 작가의 장편 소설의 기법과 주제를 여실히 보여주는 소품이다. 자유연상법이 사용되고, 의식의 흐름이 뚜렷하게 실험된다. 짧은 글 속에서 인생과, 진리와, 인위적 서열과 질서가 지배하는 사회를 향한 도전과, 소설가의 모습 등 여러 가지 주제를 다룬다. 한 부인이 책상 앞 의자에 앉아서 벽 위에 있는 어떤 점 혹은 흔적을 주목한다. 그것이 무엇일까 궁금해 하면서 주인공의 의식의 흐름이 이어진다. 끝없이 흘러가는 상념 가운데 벽 위의 점을 주목하면서 현실로 돌아오곤 한다. 끝에 가서 누군가 말을 걸어오고 그의 말을 통해 결국 벽 위에 있는 것이 무엇인가를 알게 된다.

이 선집의 마지막 작품은 James Joyce의 “The Dead”이다. 이 작품은 그의 첫 장편 소설인 *Dubliners*에 수록된 15편의 작품 중 마지막 작품이기도 하다. 종교가 구원을 목적으로 하듯이 문학도 우리 인간이 성숙해가고 구원을 얻게 하는 하나의 방법이라고 생각할 때 주인공의 구원을 다룬 이 단편은 세계의 모든 단편 소설 중에 최고 걸작이라고 생각된다. 참으로 단편 중의 대작이라고 평가를 하면서도 분량이 많기 때문에 단편 선집에 수록하기가 망설여지는 작품이지만, 본 선집에 결론적인 작품으로 수록하게 되었다. 그리고 말미에 참고 자료도 특별히 선정하여 싣게 되었다.

편집자가 가장 주목하는 이 작품의 매력은 주인공이 이기적 인간에서 이타적 인간으로 변모하는 데에 있다. 세상 경험을 많이 하고, 학문을 많이 배우고, 글을 많이 읽으면 자기중심적인 유아적 인간에서 다른 사람들을 배려하고 사랑하고 이해하는 이타적인 인간으로 성숙해가야 한다. 그러나 이 과정이 얼마나 힘들고 어려운 것인지 모른다.

이 단편은 주인공이 자아를 분명하게 보게 되는 epiphany의 순간을 경험하고, 좁은 이기적 자아를 극복하고 모든 사람을 사랑하고 용서하고 포용할 수 있는 성숙한 인간으로 변모하는 감동적인 내용을 담고 있다. 배경으로 등장하는 눈(snow)이 이야기의 흐름과 유기적으로 연결되어 주제를 더욱 부각시킨다. 작품 서두에서는 차갑고 귀찮은 눈으로 작용하다가, 끝부분에 내리는 눈은 인간의 더럽고 추한 모든 것을 덮어주고 하나로 만드는 천상의 사랑과 같은 따뜻한 눈으로 바뀐다. "The Dead"는 다소 긴 작품이고 읽기가 쉽지 않은 작품이지만, 뒤에 수록한 비평을 참고로 하여 수고의 땀을 흘린다면 충분한 보상과 보람을 가져다 줄 작품이다.

2009년 8월 편저자

나 병 우

Rip Van Winkle

by Washington Irving

Introduction to the Author

Washington Irving (1783-1859)

Born and brought up in New York City, the eleventh child of a well-to-do merchant. When his family business failed in 1818, he resolved to live by writing. Literary historians sometimes credit Irving writing the first modern stories. Certainly he popularized this genre and improved with his own peculiar emphasis on setting, tone, and finish. "Rip Van Winkle"(1819) and "The Legend of Sleepy Hollow"(1820) are famous stories in *The Sketch Book.*

The following Tale was found among the papers of the late Diedrich Knickerbocker, an old gentleman of New York, who was very curious in the Dutch history of the province, and the manners of the descendants from its primitive settlers. His historical researches, however, did not lie so much among books as among men; for the former are lamentably scanty on his favorite topics; whereas he found the old burghers, and still more their wives, rich in that legendary lore, so invaluable to true history. Whenever, therefore, he happened upon a genuine Dutch family, snugly shut up in its low-roofed farmhouse, under a spreading sycamore, he looked upon it as a little clasped volume of black-letter, and studied it with the zeal of a book-worm.

The result of all these researches was a history of the province during the reign of the Dutch governors, which he published some years since. There have been various opinions as to the literary character of his work, and, to tell the truth, it is not a whit better than it should be. Its chief merit is its scrupulous accuracy, which indeed was a little questioned on its first appearance, but has since been completely established; and it is now admitted into all historical collections, as a book of unquestionable authority.

The old gentleman died shortly after the publication of his work, and now that he is dead and gone, it cannot do much harm to his memory to say that his time might have been better employed in weightier labors. He, however, was apt to ride his hobby his own way; and though it did now and then kick up the dust a little in the eyes of his neighbors, and grieve the spirit of some friends, for whom he felt the truest deference and affection; yet his errors and follies are remembered "more in sorrow than in anger," and it begins to be suspected, that he never intended to injure or offend. But however his memory may be appreciated by critics, it is still held dear by many folks, whose good opinion is well worth having; particularly by certain biscuit-bakers, who have gone so far as to imprint his likeness on their new-year cakes; and have thus given him a chance for immortality, almost equal to the being stamped on a Waterloo Medal,[1] or a Queen Anne's Farthing.[2]

---

1) Waterloo Medal: a silver medal presented by the British crown to all participants in the Battle of Waterloo(June 18, 1815).

2) Queen Anne's Farthing: In the reign of Queen Anne(1702-1714) farthings (bronze coins worth a quarter of a penny) bearing her image were minted.

Rip Van Winkle

Whoever has made a voyage up the Hudson[1] must remember the Kaatskill mountains. They are a dismembered branch of the great Appalachian family, and are seen away to the west of the river, swelling up to a noble height, and lording it over the surrounding country. Every change of season, every change of weather, indeed, every hour of the day, produces some change in the magical hues and shapes of these mountains, and they are regarded by all the good wives, far and near, as perfect barometers. When the weather is fair and settled, they are clothed in blue and purple, and print their bold outlines on the clear evening sky, but, sometimes, when the rest of the landscape is cloudless, they will gather a hood of gray vapors about their summits, which, in the last rays of the setting sun, will glow and light up like a crown of glory.

At the foot of these fairy mountains, the voyager may have descried[2] the light smoke curling up from a village, whose shingle-roofs[3] gleam among the trees, just where the blue tints of the upland melt away into the fresh green of the nearer landscape. It is a little village of great antiquity, having been founded by some of the Dutch colonists, in the early times of the province, just about the beginning of the government of the good Peter Stuyvesant,[4] (may he rest in peace!) and there were some of the houses of the original settlers standing within a few years, built of small yellow bricks brought from Holland, having latticed windows and gable fronts, surmounted

---

1) the Hudson: 허드슨 강. 미국 뉴욕 주 동부를 남쪽으로 흘러 뉴욕만(灣)으로 흘러든다. 길이 493km이다.

2) descry: 찾아내다. 발견하다.

3) shingle-roofs: 판자 지붕.

4) Peter Stuyvesant(1592-1672): 화란 식민지 최후의 총독(the autocratic governor of New Amsterdam)인 피터 스타이브슨트. 1647년부터 1664년까지 재직. 그는 1655년 스웨덴으로부터 델라웨어의 Fort Christina를 빼앗았다.

with weather-cocks.

In that same village, and in one of these very houses (which, to tell the precise truth, was sadly time-worn and weather-beaten), there lived many years since, while the country was yet a province of Great Britain, a simple good-natured fellow of the name of Rip Van Winkle. He was a descendant of the Van Winkles who figured so gallantly[5)] in the chivalrous days of Peter Stuyvesant, and accompanied him to the siege of Fort Christina. He inherited, however, but little of the martial character[6)] of his ancestors. I have observed that he was a simple good-natured man; he was, moreover, a kind neighbor, and an obedient hen-pecked husband.[7)] Indeed, to the latter circumstance might be owing that meekness of spirit which gained him such universal popularity; for those men are most apt to be obsequious[8)] and conciliating abroad, who are under the discipline of shrews[9)] at home. Their tempers, doubtless, are rendered pliant and malleable in the fiery furnace of domestic tribulation; and a curtain lecture[10)] is worth all the sermons in the world for teaching the virtues of patience and long-suffering. A termagant[11)] wife may, therefore, in some respects, be considered a tolerable blessing; and if so, Rip Van Winkle was thrice blessed.

Certain it is, that he was a great favorite among all the good wives of the village, who, as usual, with the amiable sex,[12)] took his part in all family squabbles; and never failed, whenever they talked those matters over in their evening gossipings, to[13)] lay all the blame on Dame Van Winkle. The children of the village, too,

---

5) gallantly: gallant. 용감한.
6) the martial character: 군인 정신, 용감한 성품.
7) hen-pecked husband: 공처가.
8) obsequious: 순종하는, 고분고분 하는.
9) shrew: 엄처. 잔소리 심한 여자.
10) a curtain lecture: 침실 설교. 아내가 남편에게 하는 잔소리.
11) termagant: 잔소리 심한, 몹시 거친.
12) the amiable sex: 여성.
13) never fail to: 반드시 ~했다.

would shout with joy whenever he approached. He assisted at their sports, made their playthings, taught them to fly kites and shoot marbles, and told them long stories of ghosts, witches, and Indians. Whenever he went dodging about the village, he was surrounded by a troop of them, hanging on his skirts, clambering on his back, and playing a thousand tricks on him with impunity;[14] and not a dog would bark at him throughout the neighborhood.[15]

The great error in Rip's composition was an insuperable aversion to all kinds of profitable labor. It could not be from the want of assiduity[16] or perseverance; for he would sit on a wet rock, with a rod as long and heavy as a Tartar's lance,[17] and fish all day without a murmur, even though he should not be encouraged by a single nibble.[18] He would carry a fowling-piece[19] on his shoulder for hours together, trudging through woods and swamps, and up hill and down dale, to shoot a few squirrels or wild pigeons. He would never refuse to assist a neighbor even in the roughest toil, and was a foremost man at all country frolics[20] for husking Indian corn, or building stone-fences; the women of the village, too, used to employ him to run their errands, and to do such little odd jobs as their less obliging[21] husbands would not do for them. In a word Rip was ready to attend to anybody's business but his own; but as to doing family duty, and keeping his farm in order, he found it impossible.

In fact, he declared it was of no use to work on his farm; it was the most pestilent[22] little piece of ground in the whole country; every thing about it went wrong, and would go wrong, in spite of him.

---

14) with impunity: 벌 받지 않고. 무사히.
15) 이웃의 개에게까지도 인기가 많았다.
16) assiduity: 부지런함. 근면성. 꾸준함. 끈기.
17) Tartar's lance: 타르타르족의 창. 타르타르 족은 몽고계 터키계 종족을 총칭.
18) nibble: 물고기의 입질.
19) fowling-piece: 엽총.
20) frolic: 유쾌한 모임. 놀이. 친목회.
21) obliging: 친절한.
22) pestilent: 귀찮은, 성가신, 유해한.

His fences were continually falling to pieces; his cow would either go astray, or get among the cabbages; weeds were sure to grow quicker in his fields than anywhere else; the rain always made a point of[23] setting in just as he had some out-door work to do; so that though his patrimonial[24] estate had dwindled away under his management, acre by acre, until there was little more left than a mere patch of Indian corn and potatoes, yet it was the worst conditioned farm in the neighborhood.

His children, too, were as ragged and wild as if they belonged to nobody. His son Rip, an urchin[25] begotten in his own likeness, promised to inherit the habits, with the old clothes of his father. He was generally seen trooping like a colt at his mother's heels, equipped in a pair of his father's cast-off galligaskins,[26] which he had much ado to hold up with one hand, as a fine lady does her train[27] in bad weather.

Rip Van Winkle, however, was one of those happy mortals, of foolish, well-oiled dispositions, who take the world easy, eat white bread or brown, whichever can be got with least thought or trouble, and would rather starve on a penny than work for a pound. If left to himself, he would have whistled life away in perfect contentment; but his wife kept continually dinning[28] in his ears about his idleness, his carelessness, and the ruin he was bringing on his family. Morning, noon, and night, her tongue was incessantly going, and everything he said or did was sure to produce a torrent of household eloquence. Rip had but one way of replying to all lectures of the kind, and that, by frequent use, had grown into a habit. He shrugged his shoulders, shook his head, cast up his eyes, but said nothing. This, however, always provoked a fresh volley[29] from his

23) make a point of~: 꼭 ~하다.
24) patrimonial: 조상으로부터 물려받은.
25) urchin: 개구쟁이. 장난꾸러기.
26) cast-off galligaskins: 버려진 바지, 각반.
27) train: 옷자락.
28) din: 큰 소리로 말하다.

wife; so that he was fain to draw off his forces, and take to the outside of the house-the only side which, in truth, belongs to a hen-pecked husband.

Rip's sole domestic adherent was his dog Wolf, who was as much hen-pecked as his master; for Dame Van Winkle regarded them as companions in idleness, and even looked upon Wolf with an evil eye, as the cause of his master's going so often astray. True it is, in all points of spirit befitting an honorable dog, he was as courageous an animal as ever scoured[30] the woods—but what courage can withstand the ever-doing and all-besetting[31] terrors of a woman's tongue? The moment Wolf entered the house his crest fell,[32] his tail drooped to the ground, or curled between his legs, he sneaked about with a gallows air,[33] casting many a sidelong glance at Dame Van Winkle, and at the least flourish of a broom-stick or ladle, he would fly to the door with yelping precipitation.

Times grew worse and worse with Rip Van Winkle as years of matrimony rolled on; a tart[34] temper never mellows with age, and a sharp tongue is the only edged tool that grows keener with constant use. For a long while he used to console himself, when driven from home, by frequenting a kind of perpetual club of the sages, philosophers, and other idle personages of the village; which held its sessions on a bench before a small inn, designated by a rubicund portrait of His Majesty George the Third.[35] Here they used to sit in the shade through a long lazy summer's day, talking listlessly over village gossip, or telling endless sleepy stories about nothing. But it would have been worth any statesman's money to have heard the profound discussions that sometimes took place, when by chance

---

29) volley: 일제 사격. 연발.
30) scour: 좇아다니다. 뛰어다니다.
31) all-besetting: 항상 붙어 다니는.
32) his crest fell: 기가 꺾였다. 풀이 죽었다.
33) with a gallows air: 교수형을 받을 상을 하고서.
34) tart: 톡 쏘는. 신랄한.
35) George the Third: 조지 3세(1738-1820). 재위 기간은 1760년부터 1820년까지.

an old newspaper fell into their hands from some passing traveller. How solemnly they would listen to the contents, as drawled out by Derrick Van Bummel, the schoolmaster, a dapper learned little man, who was not to be daunted[36] by the most gigantic word in the dictionary; and how sagely they would deliberate upon[37] public events some months after they had taken place.

The opinions of this junto[38] were completely controlled by Nicholas Vedder, a patriarch of the village, and landlord of the inn, at the door of which he took his seat from morning till night, just moving sufficiently to avoid the sun and keep in the shade of a large tree; so that the neighbors could tell the hour by his movements as accurately as by a sundial. It is true he was rarely heard to speak, but smoked his pipe incessantly. His adherents, however (for every great man has his adherents), perfectly understood him, and knew how to gather his opinions. When anything that was read or related displeased him, he was observed to smoke his pipe vehemently, and to send forth short, frequent and angry puffs; but when pleased, he would inhale the smoke slowly and tranquilly, and emit it in light and placid[39] clouds; and sometimes, taking the pipe from his mouth, and letting the fragrant vapor curl about his nose, would gravely nod his head in token of perfect approbation.

From even this stronghold[40] the unlucky Rip was at length routed[41] by his termagant wife, who would suddenly break in upon the tranquillity of the assemblage and call the members all to naught;[42] nor was that august personage, Nicholas Vedder himself, sacred from the daring tongue of this terrible virago, who charged him outright with encouraging her husband in habits of idleness.

---

36) daunt: 위압하다. 기세를 꺾다.
37) deliberate upon: consider carefully.
38) junto: 비밀결사. 도당. 여기서는 마을 남자들의 모임.
39) placid: quiet, calm, peaceful.
40) stronghold: 성채. 요새. 근거지.
41) rout: 패주하다(=defeat).
42) call ~ to naught: 깎아내리다.

Poor Rip was at last reduced almost to despair; and his only alternative, to escape from the labor of the farm and clamor of his wife, was to take gun in hand and stroll away into the woods. Here he would sometimes seat himself at the foot of a tree, and share the contents of his wallet with Wolf, with whom he sympathized as a fellow-sufferer in persecution. "Poor Wolf," he would say, "thy mistress leads thee a dog's life of it;[43] but never mind, my lad, whilst I live thou shalt never want a friend to stand by thee!" Wolf would wag his tail, look wistfuly in his master's face, and if dogs can feel pity I verily believe he reciprocated[44] the sentiment with all his heart.

In a long ramble of the kind on a fine autumnal day, Rip had unconsciously scrambled to one of the highest parts of the Kaatskill mountains. He was after his favorite sport of squirrel shooting, and the still solitudes had echoed and re-echoed with the reports[45] of his gun. Panting and fatigued, he threw himself, late in the afternoon, on a green knoll,[46] covered with mountain herbage, that crowned the brow of a precipice. From an opening between the trees he could overlook all the lower country for many a mile of rich woodland. He saw at a distance the lordly Hudson, far, far below him, moving on its silent but majestic course, with the reflection of a purple cloud, or the sail of a lagging bark, here and there sleeping on its glassy bosom, and at last losing itself in the blue highlands.

On the other side he looked down into a deep mountain glen, wild, lonely, and shagged, the bottom filled with fragments from the impending cliffs, and scarcely lighted by the reflected rays of the setting sun. For some time Rip lay musing on this scene; evening was gradually advancing; the mountains began to throw their long

---

43) 여편네 때문에 너도 고생한다.
44) reciprocate: 교환하다. 보답하다.
45) report: 총성. 포성.
46) knoll: 작은 산. 둔덕.

blue shadows over the valleys; he saw that it would be dark long before he could reach the village, and he heaved a heavy sigh when he thought of encountering the terrors of Dame Van Winkle.

As he was about to descend, he heard a voice from a distance, hallooing, "Rip Van Winkle! Rip Van Winkle!" He looked round, but could see nothing but a crow winging its solitary flight across the mountain. He thought his fancy must have deceived him, and turned again to descend, when he heard the same cry ring through the still evening air: "Rip Van Winkle! Rip Van Winkle!"—at the same time Wolf bristled[47] up his back, and giving a low growl, skulked to his master's side, looking fearfully down into the glen. Rip now felt a vague apprehension stealing over him; he looked anxiously in the same direction, and perceived a strange figure slowly toiling up the rocks, and bending under the weight of something he carried on his back. He was surprised to see any human being in this lonely and unfrequented place, but supposing it to be some one of the neighborhood in need of his assistance, he hastened down to yield it.[48]

On nearer approach he was still more surprised at the singularity of the stranger's appearance. He was a short square-built[49] old fellow, with thick bushy hair, and a grizzled beard. His dress was of the antique Dutch fashion–a cloth jerkin strapped round the waist–several pair of breeches, the outer one of ample volume, decorated with rows of buttons down the sides, and bunches at the knees. He bore on his shoulder a stout keg, that seemed full of liquor, and made signs for Rip to approach and assist him with the load. Though rather shy and distrustful of this new acquaintance, Rip complied with his usual alacrity;[50] and mutually relieving one another, they clambered up a narrow gully,[51] apparently the dry

---

47) bristle: 털을 곤두세우다.
48) to yield it: 그 청에 응하려고.
49) square-built: 어깨가 떡 벌어진.
50) with his usual alacrity: 예의 그 민첩한 태도로.
51) gully: 협곡. 도랑.

bed of a mountain torrent. As they ascended, Rip every now and then heard long rolling peals, like distant thunder, that seemed to issue out of a deep ravine, or rather cleft, between lofty rocks, toward which their rugged path conducted. He paused for an instant, but supposing it to be the muttering of one of those transient thunder-showers which often take place in mountain heights, he proceeded. Passing through the ravine, they came to a hollow, like a small amphitheatre, surrounded by perpendicular[52] precipices, over the brinks of which impending trees shot their branches, so that you only caught glimpses of the azure sky and the bright evening cloud. During the whole time Rip and his companion had labored on in silence; for though the former marvelled greatly what could be the object of carrying a keg of liquor up this wild mountain, yet there was something strange and incomprehensible about the unknown, that inspired awe and checked familiarity.

On entering the amphitheatre, new objects of wonder presented themselves. On a level spot in the centre was a company of odd-looking personages playing at nine-pins.[53] They were dressed in a quaint outlandish[54] fashion; some wore short doublets,[55] others jerkins,[56] with long knives in their belts, and most of them had enormous breeches, of similar style with that of the guide's. Their visages, too, were peculiar: one had a large beard, broad face, and small piggish eyes: the face of another seemed to consist entirely of nose, and was surmounted by a white sugar-loaf hat set off with a little red cock's tail. They all had beards, of various shapes and colors. There was one who seemed to be the commander. He was a stout old gentleman, with a weather-beaten countenance; he wore a laced doublet, broad belt and hanger,[57] high-crowned hat and feather, red stockings,

52) perpendicular: 가파른, 수직의.
53) nine-pins: 볼링과 비슷한 놀이.
54) outlandish: strange, exotic.
55) doublets: 허리가 잘록한 남자의 웃옷.
56) jerkins: 남자용의 짧은 상의.
57) hanger: 단검.

and high-heeled shoes, with roses in them. The whole group reminded Rip of the figures in an old Flemish painting, in the parlor of Dominie Van Shaick, the village parson, and which had been brought over from Holland at the time of the settlement.

What seemed particularly odd to Rip was, that though these folks were evidently amusing themselves, yet they maintained the gravest faces, the most mysterious silence, and were, withal,[58] the most melancholy party of pleasure he had ever witnessed. Nothing interrupted the stillness of the scene but the noise of the balls, which, whenever they were rolled, echoed along the mountains like rumbling peals of thunder.[59]

As Rip and his companion approached them, they suddenly desisted from their play, and stared at him with such fixed statue-like gaze, and such strange, uncouth, lack-lustre countenances, that his heart turned within him,[60] and his knees smote together.[61] His companion now emptied the contents of the keg into large flagons,[62] and made signs to him to wait upon the company. He obeyed with fear and trembling; they quaffed[63] the liquor in profound silence, and then returned to their game.

By degrees Rip's awe and apprehension subsided. He even ventured, when no eye was fixed upon him, to taste the beverage, which he found had much of the flavor of excellent Hollands.[64] He was naturally a thirsty soul, and was soon tempted to repeat the draught. One taste provoked another; and he reiterated his visits to the flagon so often that at length his senses were overpowered, his eyes swam in his head, his head gradually declined, and he fell into a deep sleep.

---

58) withal: 게다가. 또한.
59) rumbling peals of thunder: 울려 퍼지는 뇌성.
60) his heart turned within him: 깜짝 놀라다. 용기가 꺾이다.
61) smite together: 맞부딪치다.
62) flagon: 병.
63) quaff: 들이키다. 마시다.
64) excellent Hollands: 고급 네덜란드 술.

On waking, he found himself on the green knoll whence he had first seen the old man of the glen. He rubbed his eyes–it was a bright sunny morning. The birds were hopping and twittering among the bushes, and the eagle was wheeling[65] aloft, and breasting the pure mountain breeze. "Surely," thought Rip, "I have not slept here all night." He recalled the occurrences before he fell asleep. The strange man with a keg of liquor—the mountain ravine—the wild retreat among the rocks–the woe-begone[66] party at ninepins—the flagon—"Oh! that flagon! that wicked flagon!" thought Rip—"what excuse shall I make to Dame Van Winkle!"

He looked round for his gun, but in place of the clean well-oiled fowling-piece, he found an old firelock[67] lying by him, the barrel incrusted[68] with rust, the lock falling off, and the stock worm-eaten. He now suspected that the grave roysterers[69] of the mountain had put a trick upon him, and having dosed him with liquor, had robbed him of his gun. Wolf, too, had disappeared, but he might have strayed away after a squirrel or partridge. He whistled after him and shouted his name, but all in vain; the echoes repeated his whistle and shout, but no dog was to be seen.

He determined to revisit the scene of the last evening's gambol,[70] and if he met with any of the party, to demand his dog and gun. As he rose to walk, he found himself stiff in the joints, and wanting in his usual activity. "These mountain beds do not agree with me," thought Rip; "and if this frolic should lay me up with a fit of the rheumatism,[71] I shall have a blessed time with Dame Van Winkle." With some difficulty he got down into the glen: he found the gully up which he and his companion had ascended the preceding eve-

---

65) wheel: 선회하다. 맴돌다.
66) woe-begone: 우수에 찬.
67) firelock: 화승총.
68) incrusted: covered.
69) roysterer: 술꾼. 술 마시며 떠드는 사람(=roisterer).
70) gambol: 유희.
71) if this ~ rheumatism: 놀고 다닌 탓으로 관절염에 걸려 눕게 된다면.

ning; but to his astonishment a mountain stream was now foaming down it, leaping from rock to rock, and filling the glen with babbling murmurs. He, however, made shift to scramble up its sides, working his toilsome way through thickets of birch, sassafras, and witch-hazel, and sometimes tripped up or entangled by the wild grapevines that twisted their coils or tendrils[72] from tree to tree, and spread a kind of network in his path.

At length he reached to where the ravine had opened through the cliffs to the amphitheatre; but no traces of such opening remained. The rocks presented a high impenetrable wall over which the torrent came tumbling in a sheet of feathery foam, and fell into a broad deep basin, black from the shadows of the surrounding forest. Here, then, poor Rip was brought to a stand. He again called and whistled after his dog; he was only answered by the cawing of a flock of idle crows, sporting high in air about a dry tree that overhung a sunny precipice; and who, secure in their elevation, seemed to look down and scoff at[73] the poor man's perplexities. What was to be done? The morning was passing away, and Rip felt famished for want of his breakfast. He grieved to give up his dog and gun; he dreaded to meet his wife; but it would not do to starve among the mountains. He shook his head, shouldered the rusty firelock, and, with a heart full of trouble and anxiety, turned his steps homeward.

As he approached the village he met a number of people, but none whom he knew, which somewhat surprised him, for he had thought himself acquainted with every one in the country round. Their dress, too, was of a different fashion from that to which he was accustomed. They all stared at him with equal marks of surprise, and whenever they cast their eyes upon him, invariably stroked their chins. The constant recurrence of this gesture induced Rip, involuntarily, to do the same, when to his astonishment, he found his beard had grown a foot long!

72) tendril: 덩굴.
73) scoff at: 비웃다. 조롱하다.

He had now entered the skirts of the village. A troop of strange children ran at his heels, hooting after him, and pointing at his gray beard. The dogs, too, not one of which he recognized for an old acquaintance, barked at him as he passed. The very village was altered; it was larger and more populous. There were rows of houses which he had never seen before, and those which had been his familiar haunts had disappeared. Strange names were over the doors — strange faces at the windows—every thing was strange. His mind now misgave[74] him; he began to doubt whether both he and the world around him were not bewitched. Surely this was his native village, which he had left but the day before. There stood the Kaatskill mountains—there ran the silver Hudson at a distance—there was every hill and dale precisely as it had always been—Rip was sorely perplexed—"That flagon last night," thought he, "has addled[75] my poor head sadly!"

It was with some difficulty that he found the way to his own house, which he approached with silent awe, expecting every moment to hear the shrill voice of Dame Van Winkle. He found the house gone to decay—the roof fallen in, the windows shattered, and the doors off the hinges. A half-starved dog that looked like Wolf was skulking about it. Rip called him by name, but the cur snarled, showed his teeth, and passed on. This was an unkind cut[76] indeed —"My very dog," sighed poor Rip, "has forgotten me!"

He entered the house, which, to tell the truth, Dame Van Winkle had always kept in neat order. It was empty, forlorn, and apparently abandoned. This desolateness overcame all his connubial[77] fears—he called loudly for his wife and children—the lonely chambers rang for a moment with his voice, and then all again was silence.

---

74) misgive: (불안, 걱정, 의심)을 일으키다. 갖게 하다. His mind misgave him: 그는 지금 마음이 불안해졌다.
75) addle: confuse.
76) cut: 감정을 상하게 하는 행위. 무정한 처사. an unkind cut: 배은망덕한 행위.
77) connubial: 결혼의, 부부의.

He now hurried forth, and hastened to his old resort, the village inn—but it too was gone. A large rickety wooden building stood in its place, with great gaping windows, some of them broken and mended with old hats and petticoats, and over the door was painted, "the Union Hotel, by Jonathan Doolittle." Instead of the great tree that used to shelter the quiet little Dutch inn of yore, there now was reared a tall naked pole, with something on the top that looked like a red night-cap,[78)] and from it was fluttering a flag, on which was a singular assemblage of stars and stripes—all this was strange and incomprehensible. He recognized on the sign, however, the ruby face of King George, under which he had smoked so many a peaceful pipe; but even this was singularly metamorphosed.[79)] The red coat was changed for one of blue and buff, a sword was held in the hand instead of a sceptre,[80)] the head was decorated with a cocked hat,[81)] and underneath was painted in large characters, GENERAL WASHINGTON.[82)]

There was, as usual, a crowd of folk about the door, but none that Rip recollected. The very character of the people seemed changed. There was a busy, bustling, disputatious tone about it, instead of the accustomed phlegm[83)] and drowsy tranquillity. He looked in vain for the sage Nicholas Vedder, with his broad face, double chin, and fair long pipe, uttering clouds of tobacco-smoke instead of idle speeches; or Van Bummel, the schoolmaster, doling forth the contents of an ancient newspaper. In place of these, a lean, bilious-looking fellow, with his pockets full of handbills, was haranguing[84)] vehemently about rights of citizens—elections—members of congress—liberty—

---

78) a red night-cap: the "liberty cap," familiar symbol of the French revolution, was often displayed in the United States.

79) metamorphose: 변형되다. 변화되다. transform.

80) sceptre(=scepter): 왕의 홀(笏). 왕권의 상징으로 손에 쥐는 것.

81) a cocked hat: 위로 젖혀진 삼각모.

82) General Washington(1732-1799): 미국 초대 대통령. 1789-1797년 재직함.

83) phlegm: 무감각.

84) harangue: 열변을 토하다.

Bunker's Hill[85]' heroes of seventy-six' and other words, which were a perfect Babylonish jargon[86] to the bewildered Van Winkle.

The appearance of Rip, with his long grizzled beard, his rusty fowling-piece, his uncouth dress, and an army of women and children at his heels, soon attracted the attention of the tavern politicians. They crowded round him, eyeing him from head to foot with great curiosity. The orator bustled up to him, and, drawing him partly aside, inquired "on which side he voted?" Rip stared in vacant stupidity. Another short but busy little fellow pulled him by the arm, and, rising on tiptoe, inquired in his ear, "Whether he was Federal or Democrat?" Rip was equally at a loss to comprehend the question; when a knowing, self-important old gentleman, in a sharp cocked hat, made his way through the crowd, putting them to the right and left with his elbows as he passed, and planting himself before Van Winkle, with one arm akimbo, the other resting on his cane, his keen eyes and sharp hat penetrating, as it were, into his very soul, demanded in an austere tone, "what brought him to the election with a gun on his shoulder, and a mob at his heels, and whether he meant to breed a riot in the village?"—"Alas! gentlemen," cried Rip, somewhat dismayed, "I am a poor quiet man, a native of the place, and a loyal subject of the king, God bless him!"

Here a general shout burst from the by-standers—"A tory! a tory! a spy! a refugee! hustle him! away with him!" It was with great difficulty that the self-important man in the cocked hat restored order; and, having assumed a tenfold austerity of brow, demanded again of the unknown culprit,[87] what he came there for, and whom he was seeking? The poor man humbly assured him that he meant no harm, but merely came there in search of some of his neighbors, who used to keep about the tavern.

85) Bunker's Hill: Boston 만 머리에 있는 구릉. 1775년 6월 17일에 영국과 미국의 격전지.

86) the Babylonish jargon: The "confusion of tongues" occurred at Babel. cf. Genesis 11: 1-9.

87) culprit: 범죄자. 피고.

"Well—who are they?—name them."

Rip bethought himself a moment, and inquired, "Where's Nicholas Vedder?"

There was a silence for a little while, when an old man replied, in a thin piping voice, "Nicholas Vedder! why, he is dead and gone these eighteen years! There was a wooden tombstone in the church-yard that used to tell all about him, but that's rotten and gone too."

"Where's Brom Dutcher?"

"Oh, he went off to the army in the beginning of the war; some say he was killed at the storming of Stony Point—others say he was drowned in a squall at the foot of Antony's Nose.[88] I don't know —he never came back again."

"Where's Van Bummel, the schoolmaster?"

"He went off to the wars too, was a great militia[89] general, and is now in congress."

Rip's heart died away at hearing of these sad changes in his home and friends, and finding himself thus alone in the world. Every answer puzzled him too, by treating of such enormous lapses of time, and of matters which he could not understand: war—congress—Stony Point;—he had no courage to ask after any more friends, but cried out in despair, "Does nobody here know Rip Van Winkle?"

"Oh, Rip Van Winkle!" exclaimed two or three, "Oh, to be sure! that's Rip Van Winkle yonder, leaning against the tree."

Rip looked, and beheld a precise counterpart of himself, as he went up the mountain: apparently as lazy, and certainly as ragged. The poor fellow was now completely confounded. He doubted his own identity, and whether he was himself or another man. In the midst of his bewilderment, the man in the cocked hat demanded who he was, and what was his name?

"God knows," exclaimed he, at his wit's end;[90] "I'm not myself

---

88) Antony's Nose: 허드슨 강변에 있는 곳.
89) militia: 시민군. 국민군.

—I'm somebody else—that's me yonder—no—that's somebody else got into my shoes—I was myself last night, but I fell asleep on the mountain, and they've changed my gun, and every thing's changed, and I'm changed, and I can't tell what's my name, or who I am!"

The by-standers began now to look at each other, nod, wink significantly, and tap their fingers against their foreheads. There was a whisper also, about securing the gun, and keeping the old fellow from doing mischief, at the very suggestion of which the self-important man in the cocked hat retired with some precipitation. At this critical moment a fresh comely woman pressed through the throng to get a peep at the gray-bearded man. She had a chubby[91] child in her arms, which, frightened at his looks, began to cry. "Hush, Rip," cried she, "hush, you little fool; the old man won't hurt you." The name of the child, the air of the mother, the tone of her voice, all awakened a train of recollections in his mind. "What is your name, my good woman?" asked he.

"Judith Gardenier."

"And your father's name?"

"Ah, poor man, Rip Van Winkle was his name, but it's twenty years since he went away from home with his gun, and never has been heard of since—his dog came home without him; but whether he shot himself, or was carried away by the Indians, nobody can tell. I was then but a little girl."

Rip had but one question more to ask; but he put it with a faltering voice:

"Where's your mother?"

"Oh, she too had died but a short time since; she broke a blood-vessel in a fit of passion[92] at a New-England peddler."

There was a drop of comfort, at least, in this intelligence. The honest man could contain himself no longer. He caught his daughter

---

90) at his wit's end: 진퇴양난에 처해.
91) hubby: 통통한, 토실토실한.
92) a fit of passion: 노발대발.

and her child in his arms. "I am your father!" cried he—"Young Rip Van Winkle once—old Rip Van Winkle now!—Does nobody know poor Rip Van Winkle?"

All stood amazed, until an old woman, tottering out from among the crowd, put her hand to her brow, and peering under it in his face for a moment, exclaimed, "Sure enough! it is Rip Van Winkle —it is himself! Welcome home again, old neighbor—Why, where have you been these twenty long years?"

Rip's story was soon told, for the whole twenty years had been to him but as one night. The neighbors stared when they heard it; some were seen to wink at each other, and put their tongues in their cheeks:[93] and the self-important man in the cocked hat, who, when the alarm was over, had returned to the field, screwed down the corners of his mouth, and shook his head—upon which there was a general shaking of the head throughout the assemblage.

It was determined, however, to take the opinion of old Peter Vanderdonk, who was seen slowly advancing up the road. He was a descendant of the historian[94] of that name, who wrote one of the earliest accounts of the province. Peter was the most ancient inhabitant of the village, and well versed in[95] all the wonderful events and traditions of the neighborhood. He recollected Rip at once, and corroborated[96] his story in the most satisfactory manner. He assured the company that it was a fact, handed down from his ancestor, the historian, that the Kaatskill mountains had always been haunted by strange beings. That it was affirmed that the great Hendrick Hudson,[97] the first discoverer of the river and country, kept a kind of vigil there every twenty years, with his crew of the Half-moon;

---

93) put their tongues in their cheeks: 빈정대며 말하다. 불성실한 말을 하다.

94) Adriaen Van der Donck(1620-1655): Dutch lawyer and founder of Yonkers, wrote a description of New Netherlands, published in Dutch(Amsterdam, 1655).

95) versed in: 정통한, 조예가 깊은.

96) corroborate: 확증하다. 확실하게 하다.

97) Hendrick Hudson(1576-1611): 허드슨 강을 탐험하여(1609), 허드슨 만을 발견(1611). Hendrick은 Henry의 화란식 이름.

being permitted in this way to revisit the scenes of his enterprise,[98] and keep a guardian eye upon the river, and the great city called by his name. That his father had once seen them in their old Dutch dresses playing at nine-pins in a hollow of the mountain; and that he himself had heard, one summer afternoon, the sound of their balls, like distant peals of thunder.

To make a long story short, the company broke up,[99] and returned to the more important concerns of the election. Rip's daughter took him home to live with her; she had a snug, well-furnished house, and a stout cheery farmer for a husband, whom Rip recollected for one of the urchins that used to climb upon his back. As to Rip's son and heir, who was the ditto[100] of himself, seen leaning against the tree, he was employed to work on the farm; but evinced a hereditary disposition to attend to anything else but his business.

Rip now resumed his old walks and habits; he soon found many of his former cronies,[101] though all rather the worse for the wear and tear[102] of time; and preferred making friends among the rising generation, with whom he soon grew into great favor.

Having nothing to do at home, and being arrived at that happy age when a man can be idle with impunity, he took his place once more on the bench at the inn door, and was reverenced as one of the patriarchs of the village, and a chronicle of the old times "before the war." It was some time before[103] he could get into the regular track of gossip, or could be made to comprehend the strange events that had taken place during his torpor.[104] How that there had been a revolutionary war—that the country had thrown off the yoke of

---

98) the scenes of his enterprise: 그가 전에 탐험했던 곳.
99) broke up: 해산했다.
100) ditto: 복제. 꼭 닮은 것. close copy.
101) crony: 친구. 벗.
102) the wear and tear: 소모. 마멸. the damage or change that is caused to something when it is being used normally.
103) It was some time before: 곧. 얼마 안 가서.
104) torpor: 휴면. 무기력. 무감각.

old England—and that, instead of being a subject of his Majesty George the Third, he was now a free citizen of the United States. Rip, in fact, was no politician; the changes of states and empires made but little impression on him; but there was one species of despotism under which he had long groaned, and that was—petticoat government.[105] Happily that was at an end; he had got his neck out of the yoke of matrimony,[106] and could go in and out whenever he pleased, without dreading the tyranny of Dame Van Winkle. Whenever her name was mentioned, however, he shook his head, shrugged his shoulders, and cast up his eyes; which might pass either for an expression of resignation to his fate, or joy at his deliverance.

He used to tell his story to every stranger that arrived at Mr. Doolittle's hotel. He was observed, at first, to vary on some points every time he told it, which was, doubtless, owing to his having so recently awaked. It at last settled down precisely to the tale I have related, and not[107] a man, woman, or child in the neighborhood, but knew it by heart. Some always pretended to doubt the reality of it, and insisted that Rip had been out of his head, and that this was one point on which he always remained flighty.[108] The old Dutch inhabitants, however, almost universally gave it full credit. Even to this day they never hear a thunderstorm of a summer afternoon about the Kaatskill, but they say Hendrick Hudson and his crew are at their game of nine-pins; and it is a common wish of all hen-pecked husbands in the neighborhood, when life hangs heavy on their hands,[109] that they might have a quieting draught out of Rip Van Winkle's flagon.

---

105) petticoat government: 내주장. 여인천하. 부인정치.

106) matrimony: 결혼.

107) not: there was not.

108) this was one ~ flighty: 이 이야기를 할 때만은 제 정신이 아니다. flighty: 들뜬, 경솔한.

109) when life hangs heavy on their hands: 세상살이가 힘에 겨울 때.

The Tell-Tale Heart

by Edgar Allan Poe

Introduction to the Author

Edgar Allan Poe (1809-1849)

One of the world's best known writers. His short stories are among the most famous ever written. He is credited with being the "father of the short story but this is not exactly correct. There is no question, however, that Poe's influence on this art form was tremendous.

Poe was a fine poet also. His poem "The Raven" has interested school children for over a century. To some people, Poe is best remembered as the founder of stories illustrating how crimes could be solved through the use of man's intelligence. He called these tales of ratiocination.

Poe had a very unhappy life. His actor-father died when Poe was only two and he was raised by Mr. and Mrs. John Allan whose name he took as a middle name. Mr. Allan did seem to understand the boy's needs and Edgar's childhood was a sad one. Poe had several unhappy love affairs, was thrown out of Point, the army school, and in 1826 married his thirteen-year-old cousin, Virginia. Her early death and Poe's poverty, in addition to his illness due to alcoholism, all contributed to the tragic aspect of his life. Poe died at the age of forty leaving many volumes of writings, including stories of terror like the one included here.

The Tell-Tale[1)] Heart

True!—nervous—very, very dreadfully nervous I had been and am: but why will you say that I am mad? The disease had sharpened my senses—not destroyed—not dulled them. Above all was the sense of hearing acute. I heard all things in the heaven and in the earth. I heard many things in hell. How, then, am I mad? Hearken![2)] and observe how healthily—how calmly I can tell you the whole story.

It is impossible to tell how first the idea entered my brain; but once conceived, it haunted me day and night. Object there was none. Passion there was none. I loved the old man. He had never wronged me. He had never given me insult. For his gold I had no desire. I think it was his eye! Yes, it was this! One of his eyes resembled that of a vulture—a pale blue eye, with a film over it. Whenever it fell upon me, my blood ran cold; and so by degrees—very gradually —I made up my mind to take the life of[3)] the old man, and thus rid myself of[4)] the eye forever.

Now this is the point. You fancy me mad. Madmen know nothing. But you should have seen me. You should have seen how wisely I proceeded—with what caution—with what foresight—with what dissimulation[5)] I went to work!

I was never kinder to the old man than during the whole week before I killed him. And every night, about midnight, I turned the latch[6)] of his door and opened it—oh, so gently! And then, when I had made an opening sufficient for my head, I put in a dark lantern,

---

1) tell-tale: 비밀을 드러내는.
2) hearken: listen carefully.
3) take the life of: 살해하다, 생명을 빼앗다.
4) rid~of: 없애다, 제거하다.
5) dissimulation: 시치미 뗌, 위장. pretence. deception.
6) latch: 걸쇠, 빗장.

all closed, closed, so that no light shone out, and then I thrust in my head. Oh, you would have laughed to see how cunningly I thrust it in! I moved it slowly—very, very slowly, so that I might not disturb the old man's sleep. It took me an hour to place my whole head within the opening so far that I could see him as he lay upon his bed. Ha!—would a madman have been so wise as this? And then, when my head was well in the room, I undid[7)] the lantern cautiously—oh, so cautiously—cautiously (for the hinges creaked)—I undid it just so much that a single thin ray fell upon the vulture eye. And this I did for seven long nights—every night just at midnight—but I found the eye always closed; and so it was impossible to do the work; for it was not the old man who vexed me, but his Evil Eye. And every morning, when the day broke, I went boldly into the chamber, and spoke courageously to him, calling him by name in a hearty tone, and inquiring how he had passed the night. So you see he would have been a very profound old man, indeed, to suspect that every night, just at twelve, I looked in upon him while he slept.

Upon the eighth night I was more than usually cautious in opening the door. A watch's minute hand moves more quickly than did mine. Never before that night had I felt the extent of my own powers of my sagacity.[8)] I could scarcely contain my feelings of triumph. To think that there I was, opening the door, little by little, and he not even to dream of my secret deeds or thoughts. I fairly chuckled at the idea; and perhaps he heard me; for he moved on the bed suddenly, as if startled. Now you may think that I drew back—but no. His room was as black as pitch with the thick darkness (for the shutters were close fastened, through fear of robbers), and so I knew that he could not see the opening of the door, and I kept pushing it on steadily, steadily.

I had my head in, and was about to open the lantern, when my thumb slipped upon the tin fastening,[9)] and the old man sprang up

---

7) undid: 끌렀다. 벗겼다.
8) sagacity: 현명함, 영리함. shrewdness. keen judgment.

in bed, crying out: "Who's there?"

I kept quite still and said nothing. For a whole hour I did not move a muscle, and in the meantime I did not hear him lie down. He was still sitting up in the bed listening;—just as I have done, night after night, hearkening to the death watches[10] in the wall.

Presently I heard a slight groan, and I knew it was the groan of mortal terror. It was not a groan of pain or grief—oh, no!—it was the low stifled sound that arises from the bottom of the soul when overcharged with awe.[11] I knew the sound well. Many a night, just at midnight, when all the world slept, it has welled up from my own bosom, deepening, with its dreadful echo, the terrors that distracted me. I say I knew it well. I knew what the old man felt, and pitied him, although I chuckled at heart. I knew that he had been lying awake ever since the first slight noise, when he had turned in the bed. His fears had been ever since growing upon him. He had been trying to fancy them causeless, but could not. He had been saying to himself: "It is nothing but the wind in the chimney—it is only a mouse crossing the floor," or "it is merely a cricket which has made a single chirp." Yes, he has been trying to comfort himself with these suppositions; but he had found all in vain. All in vain; because Death, in approaching him, had stalked[12] with his black shadow before him, and enveloped the victim. And it was the mournful influence of the unperceived shadow that caused him to feel—although he neither saw nor heard—to feel the presence of my head within the room.

When I had waited a long time, very patiently, without hearing him lie down, I resolved to open a little—a very, very little crevice

---

9) fastening: 빗장, 걸쇠, 자물쇠.

10) death watches: 죽음을 예고하는 풍뎅이. various insects, especially certain wood beetles, that make a ticking sound superstitiously regarded as an omen of death.

11) it was the low stifled sound~with awe: 그것은 두려움에 사로잡힐 때 영혼 깊은 곳에서 나오는 나직한 목이 메는 소리였다.

12) stalk: 몰래 접근하다. approach silently.

in the lantern. So I opened it—you cannot imagine how stealthily, stealthily—until, at length, a single dim ray, like the thread of the spider, shot from out the crevice and full upon the vulture eye.

It was open—wide, wide open—and I grew furious as I gazed upon it. I saw it with perfect distinctness—all a dull blue, with a hideous veil over it that chilled the very marrow in my bones; but I could see nothing else of the old man's face or person; for I had directed the ray, as if by instinct, precisely upon the damned spot.[13)]

And now—have I not told you that what you mistake for madness is but over-acuteness of the senses?—now, I say, there came to my ears a low, dull, quick sound, such as a watch makes when enveloped in cotton. I knew that sound well too. It was the beating of the old man's heart. It increased my fury, as the beating of a drum stimulates the soldier into courage.

But even yet I refrained and kept still. I scarcely breathed. I held the lantern motionless. I tried how steadily I could to maintain the ray upon the eye. Meantime the hellish tattoo of the heart increased. It grew quicker and quicker, and louder and louder every instant. The old man's terror must have been extreme! It grew louder, I say, louder every moment!—do you mark me well? I have told you that I am nervous: so I am. And now at the dead hour of night,[14)] amid the dreadful silence of that old house, so strange a noise as this excited me to uncontrollable terror. Yet, for some minutes longer I refrained and stood still. But the beating grew louder, louder! I thought the heart must burst. And now a new anxiety seized me—the sound would be heard by a neighbor! The old man's hour had come! With a loud yell, I threw open the lantern and leaped into the room. He shrieked once—once only. In an instant I dragged him to the floor, and pulled the heavy bed over him. I then smiled gaily, to find the deed so far done. But, for many minutes, the heart beat on with a muffled sound. This, however, did not vex me; it would

---

13) the damned spot: 독수리 눈같은 노인의 눈.
14) at the dead hour of the night: 한밤중에.

not be heard through the wall. At length it ceased. The old man was dead. I removed the bed and examined the corpse. Yes, he was stone, stone dead. I placed my hand upon the heart and held it there many minutes. There was no pulsation. He was stone dead. His eye would trouble me no more.

If still you think me mad, you will think so no longer when I describe the wise precautions I took for the concealment[15] of the body. The night waned, and I worked hastily, but in silence. First of all I dismembered the corpse. I cut off the head and the arms and the legs.

I then took up three planks from the flooring of the chamber, and deposited all between the scantlings.[16] I then replaced the boards so cleverly, so cunningly, that no human eye—not even his—could have detected anything wrong. There was nothing to wash out—no stain of any kind—no blood-spot whatever. I had been too wary for that. A tub had caught all—ha! ha!

When I had made an end to these labors, it was four o'clock—still dark as midnight. As the bell sounded the hour, there came a knocking at the street door. I went down to open it with a light heart—for what had I now to fear? There entered three men, who introduced themselves, with perfect suavity,[17] as officers of the police. A shriek had been heard by a neighbor during the night: suspicion of foul play had been aroused; information had been lodged at the police office, and they (the officers) had been deputed[18] to search the premises.

I smiled—for what had I to fear? I bade the gentlemen welcome. The shriek, I said, was my own in a dream. The old man, I mentioned, was absent in the country. I took my visitors all over the house. I bade them search—search well. I led them, at length, to his

---

15) concealment: 은폐.
16) scantling: 각재(角材), 켜낸 재목.
17) suavity: 정중한 태도. 예의(politeness).
18) depute: 위임하다. 임명하다.

chamber. I showed them his treasures, secure, undisturbed. In the enthusiasm of my confidence, I brought chairs into the room, and desired them here to rest from their fatigues, while I myself, in the wild audacity of my perfect triumph, placed my own seat upon the very spot beneath which reposed the corpse of the victim.

The officers were satisfied.[19)] My manner had convinced them. I was singularly at ease. They sat, and while I answered cheerily, they chatted familiar things. But, ere long, I felt myself getting pale and wished them gone. My head ached, and I fancied a ringing in my ears: but still they sat and still chatted. The ringing became more distinct:—it continued and became more distinct: I talked more freely to get rid of the feeling: but it continued and gained definitiveness—until, at length, I found that the noise was not within my ears.

No doubt I now grew very pale;—but I talked more fluently, and with a heightened voice. Yet the sound increased—and what could I do? It was a low, dull, quick sound—much such a sound as a watch makes when enveloped in cotton. I gasped for breath—and yet the officers heard it not. I talked more quickly—more vehemently; but the noise steadily increased. Why would they not be gone? I paced the floor to and fro with heavy strides, as if excited to fury by the observation of the men—but the noise steadily increased. Oh, God; what could I do? I foamed—I raved—I swore! I swung the chair upon which I had been sitting, and grated it upon the boards, but the noise arose over all and continually increased. It grew louder—louder—louder! And still the men chatted pleasantly, and smiled. Was it possible they heard not? Almighty God!—no, no! They heard!—they suspected!—they knew!—they were making a mockery of my horror! —this I thought, and this I think. But anything was better than this agony! Anything was more tolerable than this derision![20)] I could

---

19) The officers were satisfied: The officers thought that the search was thorough and complete. 또는 After all their thorough investigation they could not find any strange things, so they were sure that there had not been any foul play.

bear those hypocritical smiles no longer! I felt that I must scream or die! and now—again!—hark! louder! louder! louder! louder!—

"Villains!" I shrieked, "dissemble no more! I admit the deed!—tear up the planks!—here, here!—it is the beating of his hideous heart!"

20) derision: 비웃음. 조소.

David Swan

by Nathaniel Hawthorne

Introduction to the Author
Nathaniel Hawthorne (1804-1864)

American novelist and short-story writer who was a master of the allegorical and symbolic tale. He came from an old New England family, a fact that accounts for the strong sense of past and place in his work. While he took some pride in the accomplishments of his Puritan forebears, his writing also reveals an acute awareness of their misdeed. Salem, Massachusetts, was Hawthorne's birthplace and for many years his home. He graduated from Bowdoin College in 1825. In 1837 his shorter narratives and sketches were collected in a volume called *Twice-Told Tales*. After he and Sophia Peabody were married(1842), they lived at the Old Manse, where Hawthorne enjoyed the friendship of such literary figures as Emerson and Thoreau. He is best known for *The Scarlet Letter*(1850) and *The House of the Seven Gables*(1851).

David Swan

We can be but partially acquainted even with the events which actually influence our course through life, and our final destiny. There are innumerable other events, if such they may be called, which come close upon us, yet pass away without actual results, or even betraying[1] their near approach, by the reflection of any light or shadow across our minds. Could we know all the vicissitudes of our fortunes, life would be too full of hope and fear, exultation or disappointment, to afford us a single hour of true serenity. This idea may be illustrated by a page from the secret of David Swan.

We have nothing to do with David until we find him, at the age of twenty, on the high road from his native place to the city of Boston, where his uncle, a small dealer in the grocery line, was to take him behind the counter.[2] Be it enough to say, that he was a native of New Hampshire, born of respectable parents, and had received an ordinary school education, with a classic finish[3] by a year at Gilmanton Academy. After journeying on foot from sunrise till nearly noon of a summer's day, his weariness and the increasing heat determined him to sit down in the first convenient shade, and await the coming up of the stage-coach. As if planted on purpose for him, there soon appeared a little tuft of maples, with a delightful recess in the midst, and such a fresh bubbling spring, that it seemed never to have sparkled for any wayfarer[4] but David Swan. Virgin or not, he kissed it with his thirsty lips, and then flung himself along the brink, pillowing his head upon some shirts and a pair of pantaloons,[5] tied up in a striped cotton handkerchief. The sun-

1) betray: 배반하다, 누설하다; 보여주다.
2) take one behind the counter: 누구를 점원으로 쓰다.
3) classic finish: 정규과정 수료.
4) wayfarer: 나그네.
5) pantaloons(pl): 바지(pants).

beams could not reach him; the dust did not yet rise from the road, after the heavy rain of yesterday; and his grassy lair[6] suited the young man better than a bed of down.[7] The spring murmured drowsily beside him; the branches waved dreamily across the blue sky overhead; and a deep sleep, perchance hiding dreams within its depths, fell upon David Swan. But we are to relate events which he did not dream of.

While he lay sound asleep in the shade, other people were wide awake, and passed to and fro, afoot, on horseback, and in all sorts of vehicles, along the sunny road by his bed chamber. Some looked neither to the right hand nor to the left, and knew not that he was there; some merely glanced that way, without admitting the slumberer among their busy thoughts; some laughed to see how soundly he slept; and several, whose hearts were brimming full of scorn, ejected their venomous superfluity[8] on David Swan. A middle-aged widow, when nobody else was near, thrust her head a little way into the recess, and vowed that the young fellow looked charming in his sleep. A temperance[9] lecturer saw him, and wrought poor David into the texture[10] of his evening's discourse, as an awful instance of dead drunkenness by the road-side. But censure, praise, merriment, scorn, and indifference, were all one, or rather all nothing, to David Swan.

He had slept only a few moments when a brown carriage, drawn by a handsome pair of horses, bowled easily along, and was brought to a standstill nearly in front of David's resting-place. A linchpin[11] had fallen out, and permitted one of the wheels to slide off. The damage was slight, and occasioned[12] merely a momentary alarm to an eld-

---

6) lair: (야수의) 굴, 보금자리, 잠자리.
7) down: 솜털, 깃털.
8) venous superfluity: 지나친 악의.
9) temperance: 절제, 자제, 금주.
10) texture: 피륙, 천; 구조, (이야기의) 줄거리.
11) linchpin: 바퀴 멈추개(바퀴가 빠지지 않도록 박아 놓은 핀).
12) occasion: 야기시키다.

erly merchant and his wife, who were returning to Boston in the carriage. While the coachman and a servant were replacing the wheel, the lady and gentleman sheltered themselves beneath the maple-trees and there espied the bubbling fountain, and David Swan asleep beside it. Impressed with the awe which the humblest sleeper usually sheds around him, the merchant trod as lightly as the gout[13] would allow; and his spouse took good heed not to rustle her silk gown, lest David should start up, all of a sudden.

"How soundly he sleeps!" whispered the old gentleman. "From what a depth he draws that easy breath! Such sleep as that, brought on without an opiate, would be worth more to me than half my income, for it would suppose health and an untroubled mind."

"And youth besides," said the lady. "Healthy and quiet age does not sleep thus. Our slumber is no more like his than our wakefulness."

The longer they looked the more did this elderly couple feel interested in the unknown youth, to whom the wayside and the maple shade were as a secret chamber, with the rich gloom of damask curtains brooding over him. Perceiving that a stray sunbeam glimmered down upon his face, the lady contrived to twist a branch aside, so as to intercept it. And having done this little act of kindness, she began to feel like a mother to him.

"Providence seems to have laid him here," whispered she to her husband, "and to have brought us hither to find him, after our disappointment in our cousin's son. Methinks[14] I can see a likeness to our departed Henry. Shall we waken him?"

"To what purpose?" said the merchant, hesitating. "We know nothing of the youth's character."

"That open countenance!" replied his wife, in the same hushed voice, yet earnestly. "This innocent sleep!"

While these whispers were passing, the sleeper's heart did not throb, nor his breath become agitated, nor his features betray the

---

13) gout: 통풍(팔, 다리 따위에 염증이 생겨 아픔).
14) methinks: (고어)나는 생각한다(=it seems to me).

least token of interest. Yet Fortune was bending over him, just ready to let fall[15)] a burthen of gold.[16)] The old merchant had lost his only son, and had no heir to his wealth, except a distant relative, with whose conduct he was dissatisfied. In such cases, people sometimes do stranger things than to act the magician,[17)] and awaken a young man to splendour, who fell asleep in poverty.

"Shall we not waken him?" repeated the lady, persuasively.

"The coach is ready, sir," said the servant, behind.

The old couple started, reddened, and hurried away, mutually wondering that they should ever have dreamed of doing anything so very ridiculous. The merchant threw himself back in the carriage, and occupied his mind with the plan of a magnificent asylum[18)] for unfortunate men of business. Meanwhile, David Swan enjoyed his nap.

The carriage could not have gone above a mile or two, when a pretty young girl came along with a tripping pace, which showed precisely how her little heart was dancing in her bosom. Perhaps it was this merry kind of motion that caused—is there any harm in saying it?—her garter to slip its knot. Conscious that the silken girth, if silk it were, was relaxing its hold, she turned aside into the shelter of the maple-trees, and there found a young man asleep by the spring! Blushing as red as any rose, that she should have intruded into a gentleman's bedchamber, and for such a purpose[19)] too, she was about to make her escape on tiptoe. But there was peril near the sleeper. A monster of a bee had been wandering overhead—buzz, buzz, buzz—now among the leaves, now flashing through the strips of sunshine, and now lost in the dark shade, till finally he appeared to be settling on the eyelid of David Swan. The sting of a bee is sometimes deadly. As freehearted as she was innocent, the

---

15) let fall: 떨어뜨리다, 엎지르다.
16) burthen of gold: 금 덩어리(burthen은 burden의 고어).
17) act the magician: 요술쟁이 노릇을 하다.
18) asylum: 수용소, 은신처.
19) for such a purpose: 풀린 복대(腹帶)를 매려고 한 의도 때문에.

girl attacked the intruder with her handkerchief, brushed him soundly,[20] and drove him from the maple shade. How sweet a picture! This good deed accomplished, with quickened breath, and a deeper blush, she stole a glance at the youthful stranger, for whom she had been battling with a dragon in the air.

"He is handsome!" thought she, blushed redder yet.

How could it be that no dream of bliss grew so strong within him, that, shattered by its very strength, it should part asunder and allow him to perceive the girl among its phantoms? Why, at least, did no smile of welcome brighten upon his face? She was come, the maid whose soul, according to the old and beautiful idea, had been severed from his own, and whom, in all his vague but passionate desires, he yearned to meet. Her only could he love with a perfect love—him only could she receive into the depths of her heart—and now her image was faintly blushing in the fountain by his side;[21] should it pass away, its happy lustre would never gleam upon his life again.

"How sound he sleeps!" murmured the girl.

She departed, but did not trip along the road so lightly as when she came.

Now, this girl's father was a thriving country merchant in the neighbourhood, and happened, at that identical time, to be looking out for just such a young man as David Swan. Had David formed a wayside acquaintance with the daughter, he would have become the father's clerk, and all else in natural succession. So here, again, had good fortune—the best of fortunes—stolen so near that her garments brushed against him, and he knew nothing of the matter.

The girl was hardly out of sight when two men turned aside beneath the maple shade. Both had dark faces, set off by cloth caps, which were drawn down aslant over their brows. Their dresses were shabby, yet had a certain smartness. These were a couple of rascals,[22]

---

20) soundly: 완전하게, 심히, 호되게.

21) by one's side: 곁에.

who got their living by whatever the devil sent them, and now, in the interim of other business, had staked the joint profits[23] of their next piece of villainy on a game of cards, which was to have been decided here under the trees. But finding David asleep by the spring, one of the rogues whispered to his fellow.

"Hist!—Do you see that bundle under his head!"

The other villain nodded, winked, and leered.

"I'll bet you a horn of brandy," said the first, "that the chap has either a pocket-book or a snug little hoard of small change,[24] stowed away amongst his shirts. And if not there, we shall find it in his pantaloons' pocket.

"But how if he wakes?" said the other.

His companion thrust aside his waistcoat, pointed to the handle of dirk, and nodded.

"So be it!" muttered the second villain.

They approached the unconscious David, and, while one pointed the dagger towards his heart, the other began to search the bundle beneath his head. Their two faces, grim, wrinkled, and ghastly with guilt and fear, bent over victim, looking horribly enough to be mistaken for fiends, should he suddenly awake. Nay, had the villains glanced aside into the spring, even they would hardly have known themselves, as reflected there. But David Swan had never worn a more tranquil aspect, even when asleep on his mother's breast.

"I must take away the bundle," whispered one.

"If he stirs, I'll strike," muttered the other.

But, at this moment, a dog, scenting along the ground, came in beneath the maple trees, and gazed alternately at each of these wicked men, and then at the quiet sleeper. He then lapped[25] out of the fountain.

---

22) rascal(=rogue): 악당, 부랑배.
23) joint profit: 공동 이익금, 공동 몫.
24) a snug little hoard of small changes: 적잖게 모아둔 잔돈.
25) lap: 핥다.

"Pshaw!" said one villain. "We can do nothing now. The dog's master must be close behind."

"Let's take a drink, and be off," said the other.

The man with the dagger thrust back the weapon into his bosom, and drew forth a pocket-pistol,[26] but not of that kind which kills by a single discharge. It was a flask of liquor, with a block-tin tumbler[27] screwed upon the mouth. Each drank a comfortable dram,[28] and left the spot, with so many jests and such laughter at their unaccomplished wickedness that they might be said to have gone on their way rejoicing. In a few hours they had forgotten the whole affair, nor once imagined that the recording angel[29] had written down the crime of murder against their souls in letters as durable as eternity. As for David Swan, he still slept quietly, neither conscious of the shadow of death when it hung over him, nor of the glow of renewed life when that shadow was withdrawn.

He slept, but no longer so quietly as at first. An hour's repose had snatched from his elastic frame the weariness with which many hours of toil had burthened it. Now he stirred—now moved his lips, without a sound—now talked in an inward tone to the noonday spectres of his dream. But a noise of wheels came rattling louder and louder along the road, until it dashed through the dispersing mist of David's slumber—and there was the stage-coach. He started up, with all his ideas about him.[30]

"Halloo, driver!—Take a passenger?" shouted he.

"Room on top!" answered the driver.

Up mounted David, and bowled away merrily towards Boston without so much as a parting glance at that fountain of dreamlike vicissitude. He knew not that a phantom of Wealth had thrown a golden hue upon its waters—nor that one of Love had sighed softly

---

26) pocket-pistol: 소형 권총; 회중 술병.
27) block-tin tumbler: 주석 지금(地金)으로 만든 술잔 겸용 병마개.
28) dram: (술 따위의) 한 잔.
29) recording angel: 기록의 천사(인간계에서 일어나는 일들을 기록함).
30) with all his ideas about him: 완전히 제 정신을 차리고.

to their murmur—nor that one of Death had threatened to crimson them with his blood—all, in the brief hour since he lay down to sleep. Sleeping or waking, we hear not the airy[31] footsteps of the strange things that almost happen. Does it not argue a superintending Providence, that, while viewless and unexpected events thrust themselves continually athwart our path, there should still be regularity enough in mortal life to render[32] foresight even partially available?

31) airy: 공기의; 가벼운; 환상적인.
32) render: ~이 되게 하다; 주다(give).

The Cop and the Anthem

by O. Henry

Introduction to the Author

O. Henry (1862-1910)

William Sydney Porter. American short story writer whose tales romanticized the commonplace—in particular the life of ordinary people in New York City. His stories often had surprise endings, a device that became identified with his name.

The Cop and the Anthem

On his bench in Madison Square[1)] Soapy moved uneasily. When wild geese honk high of nights, and when women without sealskin coats grow kind to their husbands, and when Soapy moves uneasily on his bench in the park, you may know that winter is near at hand.

A dead leaf fell in Soapy's lap. That was Jack Frost's[2)] card. Jack is kind to the regular denizens of Madison Square, and gives fair warning of his annual call. At the corners of four streets he hands his pasteboard to the North Wind, footman of the mansion of All Outdoors, so that the inhabitants thereof may make ready.

Soapy's mind became cognizant of the fact that the time had come for him to resolve himself into a singular Committee of Ways and Means[3)] to provide against the coming rigour. And therefore he moved uneasily on his bench.

The hibernatorial ambitions of Soapy were not of the highest. In them there were no considerations of Mediterranean cruises, of soporific[4)] Southern skies or drifting in the Vesuvian Bay. Three months on the Island[5)] was what his soul craved. Three months of assured board and bed and congenial company, safe from Boreas[6)] and blue-coats, seemed to Soapy the essence of things desirable.

For years the hospitable Blackwell's had been his winter quarters. Just as his more fortunate fellow New Yorkers had bought their tickets to Palm Beach and the Riviera each winter, so Soapy had made his humble arrangements for his annual hegira[7)] to the

---

1) Madison Square: 뉴욕 시내에 있는 공원.
2) Jack Frost: 동장군(冬將軍). 서리. 엄동설한.
3) a singular Committee of Ways and Means: 단독 월동 대책 위원회.
4) soporific: 나른한, 최면 상태의.
5) the Island: Blackwells Island를 가리키며, 거기에 형무소가 있다.
6) Boreas: 그리이스 신화에 나오는 보레아스 신. 북풍. 삭풍.
7) hegira: 헤지라. 도피.

Island. And now the time was come. On the previous night three Sabbath newspapers, distributed beneath his coat, about his ankles and over his lap, had failed to repulse the cold as he slept on his bench near the spurting fountain in the ancient square. So the Island loomed[8)] big and timely in Soapy's mind. He scorned the provisions made in the name of charity for the city's dependents. In Soapy's opinion the Law was more benign[9)] than Philanthropy.[10)] There was an endless round of institutions, municipal[11)] and eleemosynary,[12)] on which he might set out and receive lodging and food accordant with the simple life. But to one of Soapy's proud spirit the gifts of charity are encumbered.[13)] If not in coin you must pay in humiliation of spirit for every benefit received at the hands of philanthropy. As Caesar had his Brutus, every bed of charity must have its toll[14)] of a bath, every loaf of bread its compensation of a private and personal inquisition. Wherefore it is better to be a guest of the law, which though conducted by rules, does not meddle unduly with a gentleman's private affairs.

Soapy, having decided to go to the Island, at once set about accomplishing his desire. There were many easy ways of doing this. The pleasantest was to dine luxuriously at some expensive restaurant; and then, after declaring insolvency, be handed over quietly and without uproar to a policeman. An accommodating[15)] magistrate would do the rest.

Soapy left his bench and strolled out of the square and across the level sea of asphalt, where Broadway and Fifth Avenue flow together. Up Broadway he turned, and halted at a glittering café,

---

8) loom: 어렴풋이 나타나다. 생각이 나다.
9) benign: 친절한. 인자한.
10) philanthropy: 박애. 자선. 자선행위.
11) municipal: 시립의.
12) eleemosynary: 자선의.
13) encumbered: 방해가 되다. (책임이나 부담)을 지우다. burdened.
14) toll: fare. tax.
15) accommodating: 친절한, 남의 일을 잘 돌보는.

where are gathered together nightly the choicest products of the grape, the silkworm and the protoplasm.[16)]

Soapy had confidence in himself from the lowest button of his vest upward. He was shaven, and his coat was decent and his neat black, ready-tied four-in-hand had been presented to him by a lady missionary on Thanksgiving Day. If he could reach a table in the restaurant unsuspected success would be his. The portion of him that would show above the table would raise no doubt in the waiter's mind. A roasted mallard duck, thought Soapy, would be about the thing—with a bottle of Chablis, and then Camembert, a demi-tasse and a cigar. One dollar for the cigar would be enough. The total would not be so high as to call forth any supreme manifestation of revenge[17)] from the café management; and yet the meat would leave him filled and happy for the journey to his winter refuge.

But as Soapy set foot inside the restaurant door the head waiter's eye fell upon his frayed[18)] trousers and decadent shoes. Strong and ready hands turned him about and conveyed him in silence and haste to the sidewalk and averted the ignoble[19)] fate of the menaced mallard.

Soapy turned off Broadway. It seemed that his route to the coveted island was not to be an epicurean[20)] one. Some other way of entering limbo[21)] must be thought of.

At a corner of Sixth Avenue electric lights and cunningly displayed wares behind plate-glass made a shop window conspicuous. Soapy took a cobblestone and dashed it through the glass. People came running around the corner, a policeman in the lead. Soapy stood still, with his hands in his pockets, and smiled at the sight

---

16) the choicest ~ protoplasm: 최고급 포도주와 비단옷을 입은 사람들. protoplasm은 원형질이란 뜻.
17) any supreme manifestation of revenge: 극단적인 복수심의 표출.
18) frayed: worn.
19) ignoble: 비천한. shameful, dishonourable.
20) epicurean: 유쾌한, 향락적인.
21) limbo: 구치소, 교도소.

of brass buttons.

"Where's the man that done that?" inquired the officer excitedly.

"Don't you figure out that I might have had something to do with it?" said Soapy, not without sarcasm, but friendly, as one greets good fortune.

The policeman's mind refused to accept Soapy even as a clue. Men who smash windows do not remain to parley with[22] the law's minions.[23] They take to their heels. The policeman saw a man half way down the block running to catch a car. With drawn club he joined in the pursuit. Soapy, with disgust in his heart, loafed along, twice unsuccessful.

On the opposite side of the street was a restaurant of no great pretensions.[24] It catered to[25] large appetites and modest purses. Its crockery[26] and atmosphere were thick;[27] its soup and napery thin. Into this place Soapy took his accusive shoes and telltale trousers without challenge. At a table he sat and consumed beefsteak, flapjacks,[28] doughnuts and pie. And then to the waiter he betrayed the fact that the minutest coin and himself were strangers.[29]

"Now, get busy and call a cop," said Soapy. "And don't keep a gentleman waiting."

"No cop for youse,"[30] said the waiter, with a voice like butter cakes[31] and an eye like the cherry in a Manhattan cocktail. "Hey, Con!"[32]

---

22) parley with: 협상하다.
23) minion: (권력자의) 앞잡이, 추종자. 하급 관리. 여기서 law's minion은 순경을 지칭함.
24) pretensions: 겉치레. 허식.
25) cater to: 만족시키다.
26) crockery: 사기 그릇. 도기.
27) thick: 투박한.
28) flapjack(=griddlecake): 철판으로 구운 얇은 반죽 과자. 핫 케이크류. 팬케이크.
29) 그에게는 돈이 한 푼도 없다.
30) youse: you의 복수 또는 단수로 쓰인 말. 교양 없는 사람의 말.
31) a voice like butter cakes: 너글너글한 목소리.
32) con: 사기꾼. 협잡꾼.

Neatly upon his left ear on the callous pavement two waiters pitched Soapy. He arose, joint by joint, as a carpenter's rule opens, and beat the dust from his clothes. Arrest seemed but a rosy dream. The Island seemed very far away. A policeman who stood before a drug store two doors away laughed and walked down the street.

Five blocks Soapy travelled before his courage permitted him to woo capture again. This time the opportunity presented what he fatuously[33)] termed to himself a "cinch."[34)] A young woman of a modest and pleasing guise[35)] was standing before a show window gazing with sprightly interest at its display of shaving mugs[36)] and inkstands, and two yards from the window a large policeman of severe demeanour leaned against a water plug.

It was Soapy's design to assume the role of the despicable and execrated[37)] "masher."[38)] The refined and elegant appearance of his victim and the contiguity of the conscientious cop encouraged him to believe that he would soon feel the pleasant official clutch upon his arm that would insure his winter quarters on the right little, tight little isle.[39)]

Soapy straightened the lady missionary's ready-made tie, dragged his shrinking cuffs[40)] into the open, set his hat at a killing cant and sidled toward the young woman. He made eyes at her, was taken with sudden coughs and "hems," smiled, smirked and went brazenly through the impudent and contemptible litany of the "masher." With half an eye Soapy saw that the policeman was watching him fixedly. The young woman moved away a few steps, and again bestowed her absorbed attention upon the shaving mugs. Soapy fol-

---

33) fatuously: 어리석게. 멍청하게.
34) cinch: 틀림없는 것. something that is certain.
35) guise: 외관. 옷차림.
36) shaving mug: 면도용 큰 컵.
37) execrated: 미움 받는, 저주 받는.
38) masher: 호색한(好色漢). 난봉꾼.
39) the right little, tight little isle: 적절하게 아담하고 작은 섬.
40) cuffs: 소매.

lowed, boldly stepping to her side, raised his hat and said:

"Ah there, Bedelia! Don't you want to come and play in my yard?"

The policeman was still looking. The persecuted young woman had but to beckon a finger and Soapy would be practically en route for his insular haven.[41] Already he imagined he could feel the cozy warmth of the station-house.[42] The young woman faced him and, stretching out a hand, caught Soapy's coat sleeve.

"Sure, Mike," she said joyfully, "if you'll blow me to a pail of suds.[43] I'd have spoke to you sooner, but the cop was watching."

With the young woman playing the clinging ivy to his oak[44] Soapy walked past the policeman overcome with gloom. He seemed doomed to liberty.

At the next corner he shook off his companion and ran. He halted in the district where by night are found the lightest streets, hearts, vows and librettos.[45] Women in furs and men in greatcoats moved gaily in the wintry air. A sudden fear seized Soapy that some dreadful enchantment had rendered him immune to arrest. The thought brought a little of panic upon it, and when he came upon another policeman lounging grandly in front of a transparent[46] theatre he caught at the immediate straw of "disorderly conduct."

On the sidewalk Soapy began to yell drunken gibberish at the top of his harsh voice. He danced, howled, raved and otherwise disturbed the welkin.[47]

The policeman twirled his club, turned his back to Soapy and remarked to a citizen.

" 'Tis one of them Yale lads celebratin' the goose egg they give

---

41) insular haven: 섬에 있는 안식처.
42) station-house: 경찰서.
43) blow me to a pail of suds: 나에게 술을 한 잔 사다.
44) playing the clinging ivy to his oak: 떡갈나무에 달라붙은 담장이처럼 굴다.
45) hearts, vows and librettos: 연인들과 사랑의 맹세와 오페라의 가사.
46) transparent: 빛나는, 번쩍거리는. 두명한.
47) welkin: sky. 하늘. 창공.

to the Hartford College. Noisy; but no harm. We've instructions to lave[48] them be."

Disconsolate,[49] Soapy ceased his unavailing racket.[50] Would never a policeman lay hands on him? In his fancy the Island seemed an unattainable Arcadia. He buttoned his thin coat against the chilling wind.

In a cigar store he saw a well-dressed man lighting a cigar at a swinging light. His silk umbrella he had set by the door on entering. Soapy stepped inside, secured the umbrella and sauntered off with it slowly. The man at the cigar light followed hastily.

"My umbrella," he said, sternly.

"Oh, is it?" sneered Soapy, adding insult to petit larceny.[51] "Well, why don't you call a policeman? I took it. Your umbrella! Why don't you call a cop? There stands one on the corner."

The umbrella owner slowed his steps. Soapy did likewise, with a presentiment that luck would again run against him. The policeman looked at the two curiously.

"Of course," said the umbrella man—"that is—well, you know how these mistakes occur—I—if it's your umbrella I hope you'll excuse me—I picked it up this morning in a restaurant—If you recognize it as yours, why—I hope you'll—"

"Of course it's mine," said Soapy, viciously.

The ex-umbrella man retreated. The policeman hurried to assist a tall blonde in an opera cloak across the street in front of a street car that was approaching two blocks away.

Soapy walked eastward through a street damaged by improvements.[52] He hurled the umbrella wrathfully into an excavation. He muttered against the men who wear helmets and carry clubs. Because he wanted to fall into their clutches, they seemed to regard him as a

---

48) lave: leave.
49) disconsolate: 우울한, 서글픈.
50) racket: 소란. 소동.
51) petit larceny: 좀도둑.
52) improvement: 개발(사업).

king who could do no wrong.

At length Soapy reached one of the avenues to the east where the glitter and turmoil was but faint. He set his face down this[53] toward Madison Square, for the homing instinct survives even when the home is a park bench.

But on an unusually quiet corner Soapy came to a standstill. Here was an old church, quaint and rambling[54] and gabled. Through one violet-stained window a soft light glowed, where, no doubt, the organist loitered over the keys, making sure of his mastery of the coming Sabbath anthem.[55] For there drifted out to Soapy's ears sweet music that caught and held him transfixed against the convolutions of the iron fence.[56]

The moon was above, lustrous and serene; vehicles and pedestrians were few; sparrows twittered sleepily in the eaves—for a little while the scene might have been a country churchyard. And the anthem that the organist played cemented Soapy to the iron fence, for he had known it well in the days when his life contained such things as mothers and roses and ambitions and friends and immaculate[57] thoughts and collars.

The conjunction of Soapy's receptive state of mind and the influences about the old church wrought a sudden and wonderful change in his soul. He viewed with swift horror the pit into which he had tumbled, the degraded days, unworthy desires, dead hopes, wrecked faculties and base motives that made up his existence.

And also in a moment his heart responded thrillingly to this novel mood. An instantaneous and strong impulse moved him to battle with his desperate fate. He would pull himself out of the mire;[58] he would make a man of himself again; he would conquer the evil

---

53) this: this avenue.
54) rambling: 짜임새 없이 넓은.
55) Sabbath anthem: 주일날(안식일날) 부를 찬송가.
56) the convolutions of the iron fence: 철조망 울타리.
57) immaculate: 청순한, 깨끗한, (도덕적, 정신적으로) 더렵혀지지 않은.
58) mire: 수렁.

that had taken possession of him. There was time; he was comparatively young yet; he would resurrect his old eager ambitions and pursue them without faltering. Those solemn but sweet organ notes had set up a revolution in him. Tomorrow he would go into the roaring downtown district and find work. A fur importer had once offered him a place as driver. He would find him tomorrow and ask for the position. He would be somebody in the world. He would —

Soapy felt a hand laid on his arm. He looked quickly around into the broad face of a policeman.

"What are you doin' here?" asked the officer.

"Nothin'," said Soapy.

"Then come along," said the policeman.

"Three months on the Island," said the Magistrate[59] in the Police Court[60] the next morning.

---

59) the Magistrate: 즉결 재판소 판사.
60) the Police Court: 경범죄 즉결 재판소.

Winter Dreams

by F. Scott Fitzgerald

Introduction to the Author

F. Scott Fitzgerald(1896-1940)

He was born in St. Paul, Minnesota, and graduated from Princeton University. In 1917, he joined the army, soon after the United States entered World War I. He was commissioned a lieutenant in the infantry but was not sent overseas. In 1920, he married Zelda Sayre of Montgomery, Alabama. He often lived aborad—in Paris, in Italy, and on the French Riviera. Fitzgerald is admired particularly for capturing the spirit of the 1920's—both the recklessness and the fear and cynicism that colored its gaiety. This story first appeared in the December edition of Metropolitan Magazine in 1922. It was later collected in the volume *All the Sad Young Men* in 1926.

Winter Dreams

I

Some of the caddies were poor as sin and lived in one-room houses with a neurasthenic[1] cow in the front yard, but Dexter Green's father owned the second best grocery-store in Black Bear—the best one was "The Hub," patronized by the wealthy people from Sherry Island—and Dexter caddied only for pocket-money.

In the fall when the days became crisp and gray, and the long Minnesota winter shut down like the white lid of a box, Dexter's skis moved over the snow that hid the fairways[2] of the golf course. At these times the country gave him a feeling of profound melancholy—it offended him that the links should lie in enforced fallowness, haunted by ragged sparrows for the long season. It was dreary, too, that on the tees where the gay colors fluttered in summer there were now only the desolate sand-boxes knee-deep in crusted ice. When he crossed the hills the wind blew cold as misery, and if the sun was out he tramped with his eyes squinted up against the hard dimensionless glare.

In April the winter ceased abruptly. The snow ran down into Black Bear Lake scarcely tarrying[3] for the early golfers to brave the season with red and black balls. Without elation, without an interval of moist glory, the cold was gone.

Dexter knew that there was something dismal about this Northern spring, just as he knew there was something gorgeous about the fall. Fall made him clinch his hands and tremble and repeat idiotic

---

1) neurasthenic: 신경쇠약의.

2) fairway: (골프)페어웨이. the mowed and tended area between the tee and putting green.

3) tarry: 늦어지다. 늦장 부리다. 체제하다, 기다리다.

sentences to himself, and make brisk abrupt gestures of command to imaginary audiences and armies. October filled him with hope which November raised to a sort of ecstatic triumph, and in this mood the fleeting brilliant impressions of the summer at Sherry Island were ready grist to his mill.[4] He became a golf champion and defeated Mr. T. A. Hedrick in a marvellous match played a hundred times over the fairways of his imagination, a match each detail of which he changed about untiringly—sometimes he won with almost laughable ease, sometimes he came up magnificently from behind.[5] Again, stepping from a Pierce-Arrow automobile, like Mr. Mortimer Jones, he strolled frigidly into the lounge of the Sherry Island Golf Club—or perhaps, surrounded by an admiring crowd, he gave an exhibition of fancy diving[6] from the spring-board of the club raft....Among those who watched him in open-mouthed wonder was Mr. Mortimer Jones.

And one day it came to pass that Mr. Jones—himself and not his ghost—came up to Dexter with tears in his eyes and said that Dexter was the—best caddy in the club, and wouldn't he decide not to quit if Mr. Jones made it worth his while,[7] because every other caddy in the club lost one ball a hole for him—regularly—

"No, sir," said Dexter decisively, "I don't want to caddy any more." Then, after a pause: "I'm too old."

"You're not more than fourteen. Why the devil did you decide just this morning that you wanted to quit? You promised that next week you'd go over to the State tournament with me."

"I decided I was too old."

Dexter handed in his "A Class" badge, collected what money was due him[8] from the caddy master, and walked home to Black Bear

---

4) ready grist to his mill. 그에게 알맞은 꿈을 제공했다.
5) came up magnificently from behind: 지다가 따라잡았다.
6) fancy diving: 곡예 다이빙.
7) wouldn't he ~ his while: 보수를 넉넉히 줄 것이니 캐디를 그만 두지 않겠다고 결심하지 않겠는가.
8) what money was due him: amount of money to be paid to him.

Village.

"The best—caddy I ever saw," shouted Mr. Mortimer Jones over a drink that afternoon. "Never lost a ball! Willing! Intelligent! Quiet! Honest! Grateful!"

The little girl who had done this was eleven—beautifully ugly as little girls are apt to be who are destined after a few years to be inexpressibly lovely and bring no end of misery to a great number of men. The spark, however, was perceptible. There was a general ungodliness[9] in the way her lips twisted down at the corners when she smiled, and in the—Heaven help us!—in the almost passionate quality of her eyes. Vitality is born early in such women. It was utterly in evidence now, shining through her thin frame in a sort of glow.

She had come eagerly out on to the course at nine o'clock with a white linen nurse and five small new golf-clubs in a white canvas bag which the nurse was carrying. When Dexter first saw her she was standing by the caddy house, rather ill at ease and trying to conceal the fact by engaging her nurse in an obviously unnatural conversation graced by startling and irrelevant grimaces from herself.

"Well, it's certainly a nice day, Hilda," Dexter heard her say. She drew down the corners of her mouth, smiled, and glanced furtively around, her eyes in transit falling for an instant on Dexter.

Then to the nurse:

"Well, I guess there aren't very many people out here this morning, are there?"

The smile again—radiant, blatantly artificial[10]—convincing.

"I don't know what we're supposed to do now," said the nurse, looking nowhere in particular.

"Oh, that's all right. I'll fix it up.

Dexter stood perfectly still, his mouth slightly ajar. He knew that if he moved forward a step his stare would be in her line of

---

9) ungodliness: 신앙심이 없음. 사악함, 부정함.
10) blatantly artificial: 아주 부자유스러운.

vision—if he moved backward he would lose his full view of her face. For a moment he had not realized how young she was. Now he remembered having seen her several times the year before in bloomers.[11)]

Suddenly, involuntarily, he laughed, a short abrupt laugh—then, startled by himself, he turned and began to walk quickly away.

"Boy!"

Dexter stopped.

"Boy—"

Beyond question he was addressed. Not only that, but he was treated to that absurd smile, that preposterous smile[12)]—the memory of which at least a dozen men were to carry into middle age.

"Boy, do you know where the golf teacher is?"

"He's giving a lesson."

"Well, do you know where the caddy-master is?"

"He isn't here yet this morning."

"Oh." For a moment this baffled her. She stood alternately on her right and left foot.

"We'd like to get a caddy," said the nurse. "Mrs. Mortimer Jones sent us out to play golf, and we don't know how without[13)] we get a caddy."

Here she was stopped by an ominous glance from Miss Jones, followed immediately by the smile.

"There aren't any caddies here except me," said Dexter to the nurse, "and I got to stay here in charge until the caddy-master gets here."

"Oh."

Miss Jones and her retinue now withdrew, and at a proper distance from Dexter became involved in a heated conversation, which was concluded by Miss Jones taking one of the clubs and hitting it on the ground with violence. For further emphasis she raised it

---

11) bloomers: 블루우머. 짧은 바지. 골프 바지.
12) he was ~ smile: 그는 터무니없는 어리석은 웃음의 대상이 되었다.
13) without: outside.

again and was about to bring it down smartly upon the nurse's bosom, when the nurse seized the club and twisted it from her hands.

"You damn little mean old thing!" cried Miss Jones wildly.

Another argument ensued. Realizing that the elements of the comedy were implied in the scene, Dexter several times began to laugh, but each time restrained the laugh before it reached audibility. He could not resist the monstrous conviction that the little girl was justified in beating[14] the nurse.

The situation was resolved by the fortuitous[15] appearance of the caddy-master, who was appealed to immediately by the nurse.

"Miss Jones is to have a little caddy, and this one says he can't go."

"Mr. McKenna said I was to wait here till you came," said Dexter quickly.

"Well, he's here now." Miss Jones smiled cheerfully at the caddy-master. Then she dropped her bag and set off at a haughty mince[16] toward the first tee.

"Well?" The caddy-master turned to Dexter. "What you standing there like a dummy for? Go pick up the young lady's clubs."

"I don't think I'll go out to-day," said Dexter.

"You don't—"

"I think I'll quit."

The enormity of his decision frightened him. He was a favorite caddy, and the thirty dollars a month he earned through the summer were not to be made elsewhere around the lake. But he had received a strong emotional shock, and his perturbation required a violent and immediate outlet.

It is not so simple as that, either. As so frequently would be the case in the future, Dexter was unconsciously dictated to by his winter dreams.

---

14) was justified in beating: 때리는 것도 당연하다.

15) fortuitous: accidental, lucky.

16) at a haughty mince: 거만하게 종종걸음으로.

II

Now, of course, the quality and the seasonability of these winter dreams varied, but the stuff of them remained. They persuaded Dexter several years later to pass up[17] a business course at the State university—his father, prospering now, would have paid his way—for the precarious advantage of attending an older and more famous university in the East, where he was bothered by his scanty funds. But do not get the impression, because his winter dreams happened to be concerned at first with musings on the rich, that there was anything merely snobbish in the boy. He wanted not association with glittering things and glittering people—he wanted the glittering things themselves. Often he reached out for the best without knowing why he wanted it—and sometimes he ran up against the mysterious denials[18] and prohibitions in which life indulges. It is with one of those denials and not with his career as a whole that this story deals.

He made money. It was rather amazing. After college he went to the city from which Black Bear Lake draws its wealthy patrons. When he was only twenty-three and had been there not quite two years, there were already people who liked to say: "Now there's a boy—" All about him rich men's sons were peddling bonds precariously, or investing patrimonies[19] precariously, or plodding through the two dozen volumes of the "George Washington Commercial Course," but Dexter borrowed a thousand dollars on his college degree and his confident mouth, and bought a partnership in a laundry.

It was a small laundry when he went into it but Dexter made a specialty of learning how the English washed fine woollen golf-stockings without shrinking them, and within a year he was catering to the trade that wore knickerbockers. Men were insisting that their Shetland hose and sweaters go to his laundry just as they

---

17) pass up: give up.
18) denial: 이루지 못한 일. 거부당하고 실패한 일.
19) patrimony: 세습재산, 유산.

had insisted on a caddy who could find golf-balls. A little later he was doing their wives' lingerie as well—and running five branches in different parts of the city. Before he was twenty-seven he owned the largest string of laundries in his section of the country. It was then that he sold out and went to New York. But the part of his story that concerns us goes back to the days when he was making his first big success.

When he was twenty-three Mr. Hart—one of the gray-haired men who like to say "Now there's a boy"—gave him a guest card to the Sherry Island Golf Club for a week-end. So he signed his name one day on the register, and that afternoon played golf in a foursome[20] with Mr. Hart and Mr. Sandwood and Mr. T. A. Hedrick. He did not consider it necessary to remark that he had once carried Mr. Hart's bag over this same links, and that he knew every trap and gully with his eyes shut—but he found himself glancing at the four caddies who trailed them, trying to catch a gleam or gesture that would remind him of himself, that would lessen the gap which lay between his present and his past.

It was a curious day, slashed abruptly with fleeting, familiar impressions. One minute he had the sense of being a trespasser—in the next he was impressed by the tremendous superiority he felt toward Mr. T. A. Hedrick, who was a bore and not even a good golfer any more.

Then, because of a ball Mr. Hart lost near the fifteenth green, an enormous thing happened. While they were searching the stiff grasses of the rough there was a clear call of "Fore!" from behind a hill in their rear. And as they all turned abruptly from their search a bright new ball sliced abruptly over the hill and caught Mr. T. A. Hedrick in the abdomen.

"By Gad!" cried Mr. T. A. Hedrick, "they ought to put some of these crazy women off the course. It's getting to be outrageous."

A head and a voice came up together over the hill:

---

20) foursome: (골프) 포섬. 네 사람이 2 조로 나누어서 각각 자기의 공을 치는 경기.

"Do you mind if we go through?"

"You hit me in the stomach!" declared Mr. Hedrick wildly.

"Did I?" The girl approached the group of men. "I'm sorry. I yelled 'Fore!"

Her glance fell casually on each of the men—then scanned the fairway for her ball.

"Did I bounce into the rough?"

It was impossible to determine whether this question was ingenuous[21] or malicious. In a moment, however, she left no doubt, for as her partner came up over the hill she called cheerfully:

"Here I am! I'd have gone on the green except that I hit something."

As she took her stance for a short mashie[22] shot, Dexter looked at her closely. She wore a blue gingham dress, rimmed at throat and shoulders with a white edging that accentuated her tan. The quality of exaggeration, of thinness, which had made her passionate eyes and down-turning mouth absurd at eleven, was gone now. She was arrestingly beautiful. The color in her cheeks was centered like the color in a picture—it was not a "high" color, but a sort of fluctuating and feverish warmth, so shaded that it seemed at any moment it would recede and disappear. This color and the mobility of her mouth gave a continual impression of flux, of intense life, of passionate vitality—balanced only partially by the sad luxury of her eyes.

She swung her mashie impatiently and without interest, pitching the ball into a sand-pit on the other side of the green. With a quick, insincere smile and a careless "Thank you!" she went on after it.

"That Judy Jones!" remarked Mr. Hedrick on the next tee, as they waited—some moments—for her to play on ahead. "All she needs is to be turned up and spanked[23] for six months and then

---

21) ingenuous: 솔직한, 순진한.
22) mashie: 짧은 골프채.
23) spank: (볼기짝 등을) 손바닥으로 찰싹 때리다.

to be married off to an old-fashioned cavalry captain."

"My God, she's good-looking!" said Mr. Sandwood, who was just over thirty.

"Good-looking!" cried Mr. Hedrick contemptuously, "she always looks as if she wanted to be kissed! Turning those big cow-eyes on every calf[24] in town!"

It was doubtful if Mr. Hedrick intended a reference to the maternal instinct.

"She'd play pretty good golf if she'd try," said Mr. Sandwood.

"She has no form," said Mr. Hedrick solemnly.

"She has a nice figure," said Mr. Sandwood.

"Better thank the Lord she doesn't drive a swifter ball," said Mr. Hart, winking at Dexter.

Later in the afternoon the sun went down with a riotous swirl of gold and varying blues and scarlets, and left the dry, rustling night of Western summer. Dexter watched from the veranda of the Golf Club, watched the even overlap of the waters[25] in the little wind, silver molasses under the harvest-moon. Then the moon held a finger to her lips[26] and the lake became a clear pool, pale and quiet. Dexter put on his bathing-suit and swam out to the farthest raft, where he stretched dripping on the wet canvas of the springboard.

There was a fish jumping and a star shining and the lights around the lake were gleaming. Over on a dark peninsula a piano was playing the songs of last summer and of summers before that—songs from "Chin-Chin" and "The Count of Luxemburg" and "The Chocolate Soldier"—and because the sound of a piano over a stretch of water had always seemed beautiful to Dexter he lay perfectly quiet and listened.

The tune the piano was playing at that moment had been gay and new five years before when Dexter was a sophomore at college.

---

24) calf: 풋내기. 순진한 남자.
25) the even overlap of the waters: 거듭 겹치는 수면의 잔물결.
26) held a finger to her lips: a signal to be silent.

They had played it at a prom[27] once when he could not afford the luxury of proms, and he had stood outside the gymnasium and listened. The sound of the tune precipitated in him a sort of ecstasy and it was with that ecstasy he viewed what happened to him now. It was a mood of intense appreciation, a sense that, for once, he was magnificently attune to life and that everything about him was radiating a brightness and a glamour he might never know again.

A low, pale oblong[28] detached itself suddenly from the darkness of the Island, spitting forth the reverberate sound of a racing motor-boat. Two white streamers of cleft water rolled themselves out behind it and almost immediately the boat was beside him, drowning out the hot tinkle of the piano in the drone of its spray. Dexter raising himself on his arms was aware of a figure standing at the wheel, of two dark eyes regarding him over the lengthening space of water—then the boat had gone by and was sweeping in an immense and purposeless circle of spray round and round in the middle of the lake. With equal eccentricity one of the circles flattened out and headed back toward the raft.

"Who's that?" she called, shutting off her motor. She was so near now that Dexter could see her bathing-suit, which consisted apparently of pink rompers.[29]

The nose of the boat bumped the raft, and as the latter tilted rakishly he was precipitated toward her. With different degrees of interest they recognized each other.

"Aren't you one of those men we played through this afternoon?" she demanded.

He was.

"Well, do you know how to drive a motor-boat? Because if you do I wish you'd drive this one so I can ride on the surfboard behind.

---

27) prom: 대학의 무도회.
28) oblong: 장방형(의)
29) romper: 롬퍼어즈. 아이들의 놀이옷. a one-piece garment combining a shirt and short.

My name is Judy Jones"—she favored him with an absurd smirk[30)] —rather, what tried to be a smirk, for, twist her mouth as she might, it was not grotesque, it was merely beautiful—"and I live in a house over there on the Island, and in that house there is a man waiting for me. When he drove up at the door I drove out of the dock because he says I'm his ideal."

There was a fish jumping and a star shining and the lights around the lake were gleaming. Dexter sat beside Judy Jones and she explained how her boat was driven. Then she was in the water, swimming to the floating surfboard with a sinuous crawl. Watching her was without effort to the eye, watching a branch waving or a sea-gull flying. Her arms, burned to butternut,[31)] moved sinuously among the dull platinum[32)] ripples, elbow appearing first, casting the forearm back with a cadence of falling water, then reaching out and down, stabbing a path ahead.

They moved out into the lake; turning, Dexter saw that she was kneeling on the low rear of the now uptilted surfboard.

"Go faster," she called, "fast as it'll go."

Obediently he jammed the lever forward and the white spray mounted at the bow. When he looked around again the girl was standing up on the rushing board, her arms spread wide, her eyes lifted toward the moon.

"It's awful cold," she shouted. "What's your name?"

He told her.

"Well, why don't you come to dinner to-morrow night?"

His heart turned over like the fly-wheel[33)] of the boat, and, for the second time, her casual whim gave a new direction to his life.

---

30) smirk: 능글능글하게 웃는 웃음.
31) burned to butternut: 호두 빛깔로 탄.
32) platinum: 백금. 하얀.
33) fly-wheel: 엔진의 회전 속도를 고르게 하는 조절 바퀴.

III

Next evening while he waited for her to come downstairs, Dexter peopled[34] the soft deep summer room and the sun-porch that opened from it with the men who had already loved Judy Jones. He knew the sort of men they were—the men who when he first went to college had entered from the great prep schools with graceful clothes and the deep tan of healthy summers. He had seen that, in one sense, he was better than these men. He was newer and stronger. Yet in acknowledging to himself that he wished his children to be like them he was admitting that he was but the rough, strong stuff from which they eternally sprang. When the time had come for him to wear good clothes, he had known who were the best tailors in America, and the best tailors in America had made him the suit he wore this evening. He had acquired that particular reserve peculiar to his university, that set it off[35] from other universities. He recognized the value to him of such a mannerism and he had adopted it; he knew that to be careless in dress and manner required more confidence than to be careful. But carelessness was for his children. His mother's name had been Krimelich. She was a Bohemian of the peasant class and she had talked broken English to the end of her days. Her son must keep to the set patterns.[36]

At a little after seven Judy Jones came down-stairs. She wore a blue silk afternoon dress, and he was disappointed at first that she had not put on something more elaborate. This feeling was accentuated when, after a brief greeting, she went to the door of a butler's pantry and pushing it open called: "You can serve dinner, Martha." He had rather expected that a butler would announce dinner, that there would be a cocktail. Then he put these thoughts behind him as they sat down side by side on a lounge and looked at

---

34) peopled ~ with: filled in imagination with~.
35) set off: 돋보이게 하다. 두드러지게 하다.
36) Her son ~ patterns: 아들만은 올바른 모범적인 인간이 되지 않으면 안되었다.

each other.

"Father and mother won't be here," she said thoughtfully.

He remembered the last time he had seen her father, and he was glad the parents were not to be here to-night—they might wonder who he was. He had been born in Keeble, a Minnesota village fifty miles farther north, and he always gave Keeble as his home instead of Black Bear Village. Country towns were well enough to come from if they weren't inconveniently in sight and used as foot-stools by fashionable lakes.

They talked of his university, which she had visited frequently during the past two years, and of the near-by city which supplied Sherry Island with its patrons, and whither Dexter would return next day to his prospering laundries.

During dinner she slipped into a moody depression which gave Dexter a feeling of uneasiness. Whatever petulance she uttered in her throaty voice worried him. Whatever she smiled at—at him, at a chicken liver, at nothing—it disturbed him that her smile could have no root in mirth, or even in amusement. When the scarlet corners of her lips curved down, it was less a smile than an invitation to a kiss.

Then, after dinner, she led him out on the dark sun-porch[37) and deliberately changed the atmosphere.

"Do you mind if I weep a little?" she said.

"I'm afraid I'm boring you," he responded quickly.

"You're not. I like you. But I've just had a terrible afternoon. There was a man I cared about, and this afternoon he told me out of a clear sky that he was poor as a church-mouse. He'd never even hinted it before. Does this sound horribly mundane?"[38)]

"Perhaps he was afraid to tell you."

"Suppose he was," she answered. "He didn't start right. You see, if I'd thought of him as poor—well, I've been mad about loads of

---

37) sun-porch: 유리로 칸막이 한 마루.
38) mundane: 세속적인.

poor men, and fully intended to marry them all. But in this case, I hadn't thought of him that way, and my interest in him wasn't strong enough to survive the shock. As if a girl calmly informed her fiance that she was a widow. He might not object to widows, but—

"Let's start right," she interrupted herself suddenly. "Who are you, anyhow?"

For a moment Dexter hesitated. Then:

"I'm nobody," he announced. "My career is largely a matter of futures."

"Are you poor?"

"No," he said frankly, "I'm probably making more money than any man my age in the Northwest. I know that's an obnoxious remark, but you advised me to start right."

There was a pause. Then she smiled and the corners of her mouth drooped and an almost imperceptible sway brought her closer to him, looking up into his eyes. A lump rose in Dexter's throat,[39] and he waited breathless for the experiment, facing the unpredictable compound that would form mysteriously from the elements of their lips. Then he saw—she communicated her excitement to him, lavishly, deeply, with kisses that were not a promise but a fulfillment. They aroused in him not hunger demanding renewal but surfeit that would demand more surfeit ... kisses that were like charity, creating want by holding back nothing at all.[40]

It did not take him many hours to decide that he had wanted Judy Jones ever since he was a proud, desirous little boy.

IV

It began like that—and continued, with varying shades of intensity, on such a note right up to the denouement. Dexter surren-

---

39) A lump rose in Dexter's throat: 덱스터는 목이 메는 감동을 느꼈다. cf. a lump in one's throat는 (감격해서) 목이 메는 일, 가슴이 벅찬 일.

40) kisses that were ~ at all: 조금도 아낌없이 욕망을 채워주는, 말하자면 자선을 베푸는 것과 같은 키스.

dered a part of himself to the most direct and unprincipled personality with which he had ever come in contact. Whatever Judy wanted, she went after with the full pressure of her charm. There was no divergence of method, no jockeying[41] for position or premeditation of effects—there was a very little mental side to any of her affairs. She simply made men conscious to the highest degree of her physical loveliness. Dexter had no desire to change her. Her deficiencies were knit up with a passionate energy that transcended and justified them. When, as Judy's head lay against his shoulder that first night, she whispered, "I don't know what's the matter with me. Last night I thought I was in love with a man and to-night I think I'm in love with you—"—it seemed to him a beautiful and romantic thing to say. It was the exquisite excitability that for the moment he controlled and owned. But a week later he was compelled to view this same quality in a different light. She took him in her roadster to a picnic supper, and after supper she disappeared, likewise in her roadster, with another man. Dexter became enormously upset and was scarcely able to be decently civil to the other people present. When she assured him that she had not kissed the other man, he knew she was lying—yet he was glad that she had taken the trouble to lie to him.

He was, as he found before the summer ended, one of a varying dozen who circulated about her. Each of them had at one time been favored above all others—about half of them still basked[42] in the solace of occasional sentimental revivals. Whenever one showed signs of dropping out through long neglect, she granted him a brief honeyed hour, which encouraged him to tag along for a year or so longer. Judy made these forays upon the helpless and defeated without malice, indeed half unconscious that there was anything mischievous in what she did.

When a new man came to town every one dropped out—dates

---

41) jockey: 속이다. 비열한 짓을 하다.
42) bask: 햇볕을 쬐다. 은혜를 입다.

were automatically cancelled.

The helpless part of trying to do anything about it was that she did it all herself. She was not a girl who could be "won" in the kinetic sense[43)]—she was proof against cleverness, she was proof against charm; if any of these assailed her too strongly she would immediately resolve the affair to a physical basis, and under the magic of her physical splendor the strong as well as the brilliant played her game and not their own. She was entertained only by the gratification of her desires and by the direct exercise of her own charm. Perhaps from so much youthful love, so many youthful lovers, she had come, in self-defense, to nourish herself wholly from within.

Succeeding Dexter's first exhilaration came restlessness and dissatisfaction. The helpless ecstasy of losing himself in her was opiate rather than tonic. It was fortunate for his work during the winter that those moments of ecstasy came infrequently. Early in their acquaintance it had seemed for a while that there was a deep and spontaneous mutual attraction that first August, for example—three days of long evenings on her dusky veranda, of strange wan kisses through the late afternoon, in shadowy alcoves or behind the protecting trellises of the garden arbors, of mornings when she was fresh as a dream and almost shy at meeting him in the clarity of the rising day. There was all the ecstasy of an engagement about it, sharpened by his realization that there was no engagement. It was during those three days that, for the first time, he had asked her to marry him. She said "maybe some day," she said "kiss me," she said "I'd like to marry you," she said "I love you"—she said—nothing.

The three days were interrupted by the arrival of a New York man who visited at her house for half September. To Dexter's agony, rumor engaged them. The man was the son of the president of a great trust company. But at the end of a month it was reported that Judy was yawning. At a dance one night she sat all evening in a

---

43) in the kinetic sense: 동적인 의미로. 행동적으로 나감으로써.

motor-boat with a local beau, while the New Yorker searched the club for her frantically. She told the local beau that she was bored with her visitor, and two days later he left. She was seen with him at the station, and it was reported that he looked very mournful indeed.

On this note the summer ended. Dexter was twenty-four, and he found himself increasingly in a position to do as he wished. He joined two clubs in the city and lived at one of them. Though he was by no means an integral part of the stag-lines[44)] at these clubs, he managed to be on hand at dances where Judy Jones was likely to appear. He could have gone out socially as much as he liked—he was an eligible young man, now, and popular with down-town fathers. His confessed devotion to Judy Jones had rather solidified his position. But he had no social aspirations and rather despised the dancing men who were always on tap for the Thursday or Saturday parties and who filled in at dinners with the younger married set. Already he was playing with the idea of going East to New York. He wanted to take Judy Jones with him. No disillusion as to the world in which she had grown up could cure his illusion as to her desirability.[45)]

Remember that—for only in the light of it can what he did for her be understood.

Eighteen months after he first met Judy Jones he became engaged to another girl. Her name was Irene Scheerer, and her father was one of the men who had always believed in Dexter. Irene was light-haired and sweet and honorable, and a little stout, and she had two suitors whom she pleasantly relinquished when Dexter formally asked her to marry him.

Summer, fall, winter, spring, another summer, another fall—so much he had given of his active life to the incorrigible[46)] lips of Judy

---

44) stag lines: 여성을 동반하지 않고 댄스파티에 출석하고 있는 남자들.
45) his illusion as to her desirability: 그녀를 요구하는 그의 환상.
46) incorrigible: 고칠 길이 없는, 구제하기 어려운. bad beyond correction or reform.

Jones. She had treated him with interest, with encouragement, with malice, with indifference, with contempt. She had inflicted on him the innumerable little slights and indignities possible in such a case —as if in revenge for having ever cared for him at all. She had beckoned him and yawned at him and beckoned him again and he had responded often with bitterness and narrowed eyes. She had brought him ecstatic happiness and intolerable agony of spirit. She had caused him untold[47] inconvenience and not a little trouble. She had insulted him, and she had ridden over[48] him, and she had played his interest in her against his interest in his work—for fun. She had done everything to him except to criticise him—this she had not done—it seemed to him only because it might have sullied[49] the utter indifference she manifested and sincerely felt toward him.

When autumn had come and gone again it occurred to him that he could not have Judy Jones. He had to beat this into his mind but he convinced himself at last. He lay awake at night for a while and argued it over. He told himself the trouble and the pain she had caused him, he enumerated her glaring deficiencies as a wife. Then he said to himself that he loved her, and after a while he fell asleep. For a week, lest he imagined her husky voice over the telephone or her eyes opposite him at lunch, he worked hard and late, and at night he went to his office and plotted out his years.

At the end of a week he went to a dance and cut in on[50] her once. For almost the first time since they had met he did not ask her to sit out with him or tell her that she was lovely. It hurt him that she did not miss these things—that was all. He was not jealous when he saw that there was a new man to-night. He had been hardened against jealousy long before.

He stayed late at the dance. He sat for an hour with Irene

---

47) untold: 이루 다 말할 수 없는, 헤아릴 수 없는.
48) ride over: 유린하다. 압제하다.
49) sully: stain. blemish.
50) cut in on: 춤추고 있는 여성을 자기 상대로 가로채다.

Scheerer and talked about books and about music. He knew very little about either. But he was beginning to be master of his own time now, and he had a rather priggish notion that he—the young and already fabulously successful Dexter Green—should know more about such things.

That was in October, when he was twenty-five. In January, Dexter and Irene became engaged. It was to be announced in June, and they were to be married three months later.

The Minnesota winter prolonged itself interminably, and it was almost May when the winds came soft and the snow ran down into Black Bear Lake at last. For the first time in over a year Dexter was enjoying a certain tranquility of spirit. Judy Jones had been in Florida, and afterward in Hot Springs, and somewhere she had been engaged, and somewhere she had broken it off. At first, when Dexter had definitely given her up, it had made him sad that people still linked them together and asked for news of her, but when he began to be placed at dinner next to Irene Scheerer people didn't ask him about her any more—they told him about her. He ceased to be an authority on her.

May at last. Dexter walked the streets at night when the darkness was damp as rain, wondering that so soon, with so little done, so much of ecstasy had gone from him. May one year back had been marked by Judy's poignant, unforgivable, yet forgiven turbulence—it had been one of those rare times when he fancied she had grown to care for him. That old penny's worth of happiness he had spent for this bushel of content. He knew that Irene would be no more than a curtain spread behind him, a hand moving among gleaming tea-cups, a voice calling to children... fire and loveliness were gone, the magic of nights and the wonder of the varying hours and seasons...slender lips, down-turning, dropping to his lips and bearing him up into a heaven of eyes... The thing was deep in him. He was too strong and alive for it to die lightly.

In the middle of May when the weather balanced for a few days on the thin bridge that led to deep summer he turned in one night at Irene's house. Their engagement was to be announced in a week now—no one would be surprised at it. And to-night they would sit together on the lounge at the University Club and look on for an hour at the dancers. It gave him a sense of solidity to go with her—she was so sturdily popular, so intensely "great."

He mounted the steps of the brownstone house and stepped inside.

"Irene," he called.

Mrs. Scheerer came out of the living-room to meet him.

"Dexter," she said, "Irene's gone up-stairs with a splitting headache. She wanted to go with you but I made her go to bed."

"Nothing serious, I—"

"Oh, no. She's going to play golf with you in the morning. You can spare her for just one night, can't you, Dexter?"

Her smile was kind. She and Dexter liked each other. In the living-room he talked for a moment before he said good-night.

Returning to the University Club, where he had rooms, he stood in the doorway for a moment and watched the dancers. He leaned against the door-post, nodded at a man or two—yawned.

"Hello, darling."

The familiar voice at his elbow startled him. Judy Jones had left a man and crossed the room to him—Judy Jones, a slender enamelled doll in cloth of gold: gold in a band at her head, gold in two slipper points at her dress's hem. The fragile glow of her face seemed to blossom as she smiled at him. A breeze of warmth and light blew through the room. His hands in the pockets of his dinner-jacket tightened spasmodically. He was filled with a sudden excitement.

"When did you get back?" he asked casually.

"Come here and I'll tell you about it."

She turned and he followed her. She had been away—he could have wept at the wonder of her return. She had passed through enchanted streets, doing things that were like provocative music. All mysterious happenings, all fresh and quickening hopes, had gone away with her, come back with her now.

She turned in the doorway.

"Have you a car here? If you haven't, I have."

"I have a coupe."

In then, with a rustle of golden cloth. He slammed the door. Into so many cars she had stepped—like this—like that—her back against the leather, so—her elbow resting on the door—waiting. She would have been soiled long since had there been anything to soil her—except herself—but this was her own self outpouring.

With an effort he forced himself to start the car and back into the street. This was nothing, he must remember. She had done this before, and he had put her behind him, as he would have crossed a bad account from his books.

He drove slowly down-town and, affecting abstraction, traversed the deserted streets of the business section, peopled here and there where a movie was giving out its crowd or where consumptive or pugilistic youth lounged in front of pool halls.[51] The clink of glasses and the slap of hands on the bars issued from saloons, cloisters of glazed glass and dirty yellow light.

She was watching him closely and the silence was embarrassing, yet in this crisis he could find no casual word with which to profane the hour. At a convenient turning he began to zigzag back toward the University Club.

"Have you missed me?" she asked suddenly.

"Everybody missed you."

He wondered if she knew of Irene Scheerer. She had been back only a day—her absence had been almost contemporaneous with his engagement.

"What a remark!" Judy laughed sadly—without sadness. She looked at him searchingly. He became absorbed in the dashboard.

"You're handsomer than you used to be," she said thoughtfully.

---

51) pool halls: 공개 도박장.

"Dexter, you have the most rememberable eyes."

He could have laughed at this, but he did not laugh. It was the sort of thing that was said to sophomores. Yet it stabbed[52] at him.

"I'm awfully tired of everything, darling." She called every one darling, endowing the endearment with careless, individual comraderie. "I wish you'd marry me."

The directness of this confused him. He should have told her now that he was going to marry another girl, but he could not tell her. He could as easily have sworn that he had never loved her.

"I think we'd get along," she continued, on the same note, "unless probably you've forgotten me and fallen in love with another girl."

Her confidence was obviously enormous. She had said, in effect, that she found such a thing impossible to believe, that if it were true he had merely committed a childish indiscretion—and probably to show off. She would forgive him, because it was not a matter of any moment but rather something to be brushed aside lightly.

"Of course you could never love anybody but me," she continued. "I like the way you love me. Oh, Dexter, have you forgotten last year?"

"No, I haven't forgotten."

"Neither have I!"

Was she sincerely moved—or was she carried along by the wave of her own acting?

"I wish we could be like that again," she said, and he forced himself to answer:

"I don't think we can."

"I suppose not.... I hear you're giving Irene Scheerer a violent rush."

There was not the faintest emphasis on the name, yet Dexter was suddenly ashamed.

"Oh, take me home," cried Judy suddenly; "I don't want to go back to that idiotic dance—with those children."

---

52) stab: 찌르다. 마음이 아프다.

Then, as he turned up the street that led to the residence district, Judy began to cry quietly to herself. He had never seen her cry before.

The dark street lightened, the dwellings of the rich loomed up around them, he stopped his coup in front of the great white bulk of the Mortimer Joneses' house, somnolent, gorgeous, drenched with the splendor of the damp moonlight. Its solidity startled him. The strong walls, the steel of the girders, the breadth and beam and pomp of it were there only to bring out the contrast with the young beauty beside him. It was sturdy to accentuate her slightness—as if to show what a breeze could be generated by a butterfly's wing.

He sat perfectly quiet, his nerves in wild clamor, afraid that if he moved he would find her irresistibly in his arms. Two tears had rolled down her wet face and trembled on her upper lip.

"I'm more beautiful than anybody else," she said brokenly, "why can't I be happy?" Her moist eyes tore at his stability—her mouth turned slowly downward with an exquisite sadness: "I'd like to marry you if you'll have me, Dexter. I suppose you think I'm not worth having, but I'll be so beautiful for you, Dexter."

A million phrases of anger, pride, passion, hatred, tenderness fought on his lips. Then a perfect wave of emotion washed over him, carrying off with it a sediment of wisdom, of convention, of doubt, of honor. This was his girl who was speaking, his own, his beautiful, his pride.

"Won't you come in?" He heard her draw in her breath sharply.

Waiting.

"All right," his voice was trembling, "I'll come in."

V

It was strange that neither when it was over nor a long time afterward did he regret that night. Looking at it from the perspective of ten years, the fact that Judy's flare for him endured just one month seemed of little importance. Nor did it matter that by his yielding he subjected himself to a deeper agony in the end and gave serious hurt to Irene Scheerer and to Irene's parents, who had befriended him. There was nothing sufficiently pictorial about Irene's grief to stamp itself on his mind.

Dexter was at bottom hard-minded. The attitude of the city on his action was of no importance to him, not because he was going to leave the city, but because any outside attitude on the situation seemed superficial. He was completely indifferent to popular opinion. Nor, when he had seen that it was no use, that he did not possess in himself the power to move fundamentally or to hold Judy Jones, did he bear any malice toward her. He loved her, and he would love her until the day he was too old for loving—but he could not have her. So he tasted the deep pain that is reserved only for the strong, just as he had tasted for a little while the deep happiness.

Even the ultimate falsity of the grounds upon which Judy terminated the engagement that she did not want to "take him away" from Irene—Judy, who had wanted nothing else—did not revolt him. He was beyond any revulsion or any amusement.

He went East in February with the intention of selling out his laundries and settling in New York—but the war came to America in March and changed his plans. He returned to the West, handed over the management of the business to his partner, and went into the first officers' training-camp in late April. He was one of those young thousands who greeted the war with a certain amount of relief, welcoming the liberation from webs of tangled emotion.

VI

This story is not his biography, remember, although things creep into it which have nothing to do with those dreams he had when he was young. We are almost done with them and with him now. There is only one more incident to be related here, and it happens seven years farther on.

It took place in New York, where he had done well—so well that there were no barriers too high for him. He was thirty-two years old, and, except for one flying trip immediately after the war, he had not been West in seven years. A man named Devlin from Detroit came into his office to see him in a business way, and then and there this incident occurred, and closed out, so to speak, this particular side of his life.

"So you're from the Middle West," said the man Devlin with careless curiosity. "That's funny—I thought men like you were probably born and raised on Wall Street. You know—wife of one of my best friends in Detroit came from your city. I was an usher[53] at the wedding."

Dexter waited with no apprehension of what was coming.

"Judy Simms," said Devlin with no particular interest; "Judy Jones she was once."

"Yes, I knew her." A dull impatience spread over him. He had heard, of course, that she was married—perhaps deliberately he had heard no more.

"Awfully nice girl," brooded Devlin meaninglessly, "I'm sort of sorry for her."

"Why?" Something in Dexter was alert, receptive, at once.

"Oh, Lud Simms has gone to pieces[54] in a way. I don't mean he ill-uses her, but he drinks and runs around "

"Doesn't she run around?"

"No. Stays at home with her kids."

"Oh."

"She's a little too old for him," said Devlin.

"Too old!" cried Dexter. "Why, man, she's only twenty-seven."

He was possessed with a wild notion of rushing out into the streets and taking a train to Detroit. He rose to his feet spasmodically.

"I guess you're busy," Devlin apologized quickly. "I didn't realize—"

"No, I'm not busy," said Dexter, steadying his voice. "I'm not

53) usher: 안내인. 들러리.
54) go to pieces: become wild.

busy at all. Not busy at all. Did you say she was—twenty-seven? No, I said she was twenty-seven."

"Yes, you did," agreed Devlin dryly.

"Go on, then. Go on."

"What do you mean?"

"About Judy Jones."

Devlin looked at him helplessly.

"Well, that's,—I told you all there is to it. He treats her like the devil. Oh, they're not going to get divorced or anything. When he's particularly outrageous she forgives him. In fact, I'm inclined to think she loves him. She was a pretty girl when she first came to Detroit."

A pretty girl! The phrase struck Dexter as ludicrous.[55)]

"Isn't she—a pretty girl, any more?"

"Oh, she's all right."

"Look here," said Dexter, sitting down suddenly, "I don't understand. You say she was a 'pretty girl' and now you say she's 'all right.' I don't understand what you mean—Judy Jones wasn't a pretty girl, at all. She was a great beauty. Why, I knew her, I knew her. She was—"

Devlin laughed pleasantly.

"I'm not trying to start a row,"[56)] he said. "I think Judy's a nice girl and I like her. I can't understand how a man like Lud Simms could fall madly in love with her, but he did." Then he added: "Most of the women like her."

Dexter looked closely at Devlin, thinking wildly that there must be a reason for this, some insensitivity in the man or some private malice.

"Lots of women fade just like that," Devlin snapped his fingers. "You must have seen it happen. Perhaps I've forgotten how pretty she was at her wedding. I've seen her so much since then, you see.

---

55) ludicrous: ridiculous.

56) row [rau]: 법석. 소동.

She has nice eyes."

A sort of dulness settled down upon Dexter. For the first time in his life he felt like getting very drunk. He knew that he was laughing loudly at something Devlin had said, but he did not know what it was or why it was funny. When, in a few minutes, Devlin went he lay down on his lounge and looked out the window at the New York sky-line into which the sun was sinking in dull lovely shades[57] of pink and gold.

He had thought that having nothing else to lose he was invulnerable at last—but he knew that he had just lost something more, as surely as if he had married Judy Jones and seen her fade away before his eyes.

The dream was gone. Something had been taken from him. In a sort of panic he pushed the palms of his hands into his eyes and tried to bring up a picture of the waters lapping[58] on Sherry Island and the moonlit veranda, and gingham[59] on the golf-links and the dry sun and the gold color of her neck's soft down.[60] And her mouth damp to his kisses and her eyes plaintive[61] with melancholy and her freshness like new fine linen in the morning. Why, these things were no longer in the world! They had existed and they existed no longer.

For the first time in years the tears were streaming down his face. But they were for himself now. He did not care about mouth and eyes and moving hands. He wanted to care, and he could not care. For he had gone away and he could never go back any more. The gates were closed, the sun was gone down, and there was no beauty but the gray beauty of steel that withstands[62] all time. Even the grief he could have borne was left behind in the country of illu-

---

57) lovely shades: lovely colors.
58) lap: 핥다. 찰싹 때리다.
59) gingham: 깅엄(무명, 린네르의 일종).
60) down: 솜털. 잔털.
61) plaintive: 구슬픈, 애처로운.
62) withstand: endure.

sion, of youth, of the richness of life, where his winter dreams had flourished.

"Long ago," he said, "long ago, there was something in me, but now that thing is gone. Now that thing is gone, that thing is gone. I cannot cry. I cannot care. That thing will come back no more."

The First Seven Years

by Bernard Malamud

Introduction to the Author

Bernard Malamud (1914-1986)

American novelist and short story writer who made parables out of Jewish immigrant life. A son of Russian Jews, Malamud was educated at the City College of New York and Columbia University. His first novel, *The Natural*(1952), is a fable about a baseball hero who is gifted with miraculous powers. *The Assistant*(1957) is about a young Gentile hoodlum and an old Jewish grocer. *The Fixer*(1966) won a Pulitzer Prize. His other novels are *A New Life*(1961), *The Tenants*(1971), *Dubin's Lives*(1979), and *God's Grace*(1982). Malamud's genius is most apparent in his short stories. In them, grim city neighborhoods are visited by magical events, and their hard-working residents have glimpses of love and self-sacrifice.

그의 작품의 저변에 흐르는 주요 주제는 "현대를 사는 유태인의 고뇌"이다. "첫 칠 년"이란 단편 제목은 성경의 Genesis 29: 9-20과 관계가 있다.

The First Seven Years

Feld, the shoemaker, was annoyed that his helper, Sobel, was so insensitive to his reverie that he wouldn't for a minute cease his fanatic pounding at the other bench. He gave him a look, but Sobel's bald head was bent over the last[1] as he worked and he didn't notice. The shoemaker shrugged and continued to peer through the partly frosted window at the near-sighted haze of falling February snow. Neither the shifting white blur outside, nor the sudden deep remembrance of the snowy Polish village where he had wasted his youth could turn his thoughts from Max the college boy (a constant visitor in the mind since early that morning when Feld saw him trudging through the snowdrifts on his way to school), whom he so much respected because of the sacrifices he had made throughout the years—in winter or direst heat—to further his education. An old wish returned to haunt the shoemaker: that he had had a son instead of a daughter, but this blew away in the snow, for Feld, if anything, was a practical man. Yet he could not help but contrast the diligence of the boy, who was a peddler's son, with Miriam's unconcern for an education. True, she was always with a book in her hand, yet when the opportunity arose for a college education, she had said no she would rather find a job. He had begged her to go, pointing out how many fathers could not afford to send their children to college, but she said she wanted to be independent. As for education, what was it, she asked, but books, which Sobel, who diligently read the classics, would as usual advise her on.[2] Her answer greatly grieved her father.

A figure emerged from the snow and the door opened. At the counter the man withdrew from a wet paper bag a pair of battered

---

1) last: 구두골.

2) which Sobel, ...would as usual advise her on: on은 앞의 which를 목적어로 함.

shoes for repair. Who he was the shoemaker for a moment had no idea, then his heart trembled as he realized, before he had thoroughly discerned the face, that Max himself was standing there, embarrassedly explaining what he wanted done to his old shoes. Though Feld listened eagerly, he couldn't hear a word, for the opportunity that had burst upon him was deafening.

He couldn't exactly recall when the thought had occurred to him, because it was clear he had more than once considered suggesting to the boy that he go out with Miriam. But he had not dared speak, for if Max said no, how would he face him again? Or suppose Miriam, who harped so often on independence, blew up in anger and shouted at him for his meddling? Still, the chance was too good to let by[3): all it meant was an introduction. They might long ago have become friends had they happened to meet somewhere; therefore was it not his duty—an obligation—to bring them together, nothing more, a harmless connivance to replace an accidental encounter in the subway, let's say, or a mutual friend's introduction in the street? Just let him once see and talk to her and he would for sure be interested. As for Miriam, what possible harm for a working girl in an office, who met only loud-mouthed salesman and illiterate shipping clerks to make the acquaintance of a fine scholarly boy? Maybe he would awaken in her a desire to go to college; if not—the shoemaker's mind at last came to grips with the truth—let her marry an educated man and live a better life.

When Max finished describing what he wanted done to his shoes, Feld marked them, both with enormous holes in the soles which he pretended not to notice, with large white chalk x's, and the rubber heels, thinned to the nails, he marked with o's, though it troubled him he might have mixed up the letters. Max inquired the price, and the shoemaker cleared his throat and asked the boy, above Sobel's insistent hammering, would he please step through the side door there into the hall. Though surprised, Max did as the shoe-

3) to let by: to go let by.

maker requested, and Feld went in after him. For a minute they were both silent, because Sobel had stopped banging, and it seemed they understood neither was to say anything until the noise began again. When it did, loudly, the shoemaker quickly told Max why he had asked to talk to him.

"Ever since you went to high school," he said, in the dimly-lit hallway, "I watched you in the morning go to the subway to school, and I said always to myself, this is a fine boy that he wants so much an education."

"Thanks," Max said, nervously alert. He was tall and grotesquely thin, with sharply cut features, particularly a beaklike nose. He was wearing a loose long slushy overcoat that hung down to his ankles, looking like a rug draped over his bony shoulders, and a soggy, old brown hat, as battered as the shoes he had brought in.

"I am a business man," the shoemaker abruptly said to conceal his embarrassment, "so I will explain you right away why I talk to you. I have a girl, my daughter Miriam—she is nineteen—a very nice girl and also so pretty that everybody looks on her when she passes by in the street. She is smart, always with a book and I thought to myself that a boy like you, an educated boy—I thought maybe you will be interested sometime to meet a girl like this." He laughed a bit when he had finished and was tempted to say more but had the good sense not to.

Max stared down like a hawk. For an uncomfortable second he was silent, then he asked, "Did you say nineteen?"

"Yes."

"Would it be all right to inquire if you have a picture of her?"

"Just a minute." The shoemaker went into the store and hastily returned with a snapshot that Max held up to the light.

"She's all right," he said.

Feld waited.

"And is she sensible—not the flighty kind?"

"She is very sensible."

After another short pause, Max said it was okay with him if he met her.

"Here is my telephone," said the shoemaker, hurriedly handing him a slip of paper. "Call her up. She comes home from work six o'clock."

Max folded the paper and tucked it away into his worn leather wallet.

"About the shoes," he said, "How much did you say they will cost me?"

"Don't worry about the price."

"I just like to have an idea."

"A dollar—dollar fifty. A dollar fifty," the shoemaker said.

At once he felt bad, for he usually charged two twenty-five for this kind of job. Either he should have asked the regular price or done the work for nothing.

Later, as he entered the store, he was startled by a violent clanging and looked up to see Sobel pounding with all his might upon the naked last. It broke, iron striking the floor and jumping with a thump against the wall, but before the enraged shoemaker could cry out, the assistant had torn his hat and coat from the hook and rushed out into the snow.

So Feld, who had looked forward to anticipating how it would go with his daughter and Max, instead had a great worry on his mind. Without his temperamental helper he was a lost man, especially since it was years now that he had carried the store alone. The shoemaker had for an age suffered from a heart condition that threatened collapse if he dared exert himself. Five years ago, after an attack, it had appeared as though he would have either to sacrifice his business upon the auction block[4] and live on a pittance thereafter, or put himself at the mercy of some unscrupulous employee who would in the end probably ruin him. But just at the moment of his darkest despair, this Polish refugee, Sobel, appeared one

4) sacrifice his business upon the auction block: 사업체를 경매 처분하다.

night from the street and begged for work. He was a stocky man, poorly dressed, with a bald head that had once been blond, a severely plain face and soft blue eyes prone to tears over the sad books he read, a young man but old[5)]—no one would have guessed thirty. Though he confessed he knew nothing of shoemaking, he said he was apt and would work for a very little if Feld taught him the trade. Thinking that with after all, a landsman,[6)] he would have less to fear than from a complete stranger, Feld took him on[7)] and within six weeks the refugee rebuilt as good a shoe as he, and not long thereafter expertly ran the business for the thoroughly relieved shoemaker.

Feld could trust him with anything and did, frequently going home after an hour or two at the store, leaving all the money in the till, knowing Sobel would guard every cent of it. The amazing thing was that he demanded so little. His wants were few; in money he wasn't interested—in nothing but books, it seemed—which he one by one lent to Miriam, together with his profuse, queer written comments, manufactured during his lonely rooming house evenings, thick pads of commentary which the shoemaker peered at and twitched his shoulders over as his daughter, from her fourteenth year, read page by sanctified page,[8)] as if the word of God were inscribed on them. To protect Sobel, Feld himself had to see that he received more than he asked for. Yet his conscience bothered him for not insisting that the assistant accept a better wage than he was getting, though Feld had honestly told him he could earn a handsome salary if he worked elsewhere, or maybe opened a place of his own. But the assistant answered, somewhat ungraciously, that he was not interested in going elsewhere, and though Feld frequently asked himself what keeps him here? why does he stay? he finally

---

5) a young man but old: a boy young in age but somewhat old in appearance.

6) a landsman: a fellow country-man.

7) took...on: hired.

8) page by sanctified page: Sobel이 빌려 주는 책을 성경을 읽는 마음가짐으로 읽는 Miriam의 심정과, 그것을 언짢게 여기는 Feld의 심사를 드러내주는 표현이다.

answered it that[9] the man, no doubt because of his terrible experiences as a refugee, was afraid of the world.

After the incident with the broken last, angered by Sobel's behavior, the shoemaker decided to let him stew for a week in the rooming house, although his own strength was taxed dangerously and the business suffered. However, after several sharp nagging warnings from both his wife and daughter, he went finally in search of Sobel, as he had once before, quite recently, when over some fancied slight—Feld had merely asked him not to give Miriam so many books to read because her eyes were strained and red—the assistant had left the place in a huff, an incident which, as usual, came to nothing, for he had returned after the shoemaker had talked to him, and taken his seat at the bench. But this time, after Feld had plodded through the snow to Sobel's house—he had thought of sending Miriam but the idea became repugnant to him—the burly landlady at the door informed him in a nasal voice that Sobel was not at home, and though Feld knew this was a nasty lie, for where had the refugee to go? Still for some reason he was not completely sure of—it may have been the cold and his fatigue—he decided not to insist on seeing him. Instead he went home and hired a new helper.

Having settled the matter, though not entirely to his satisfaction, for he had much more to do than before, and so, for example, could no longer lie late in bed mornings because he had to get up to open the store for the new assistant, a speechless, dark man with an irritating rasp as he worked, whom he would not trust with the key as he had Sobel. Furthermore, this one, though able to do a fair repair job, knew nothing of leather or prices, so Feld had to make his own purchases; and every night at closing time it was necessary to count the money in the till and lock up. However, he was not dissatisfied, for he lived much in his thoughts of Max and Miriam. The college boy had called her, and they had arranged a meeting

---

9) answered it that: that 이하를 가리키는 it는 일반적으로 생략한다. cf. I resent it that you left so soon.

for this coming Friday night. The shoemaker would personally have preferred Saturday, which he felt would make it a date of the first magnitude, but he learned Friday was Miriam's choice, so he said nothing. The day of the week did not matter. What mattered was the aftermath. Would they like each other and want to be friends? He sighed at all the time that would have to go by before he knew for sure. Often he was tempted to talk to Miriam about the boy, to ask whether she thought she would like his type—he had told her only that he considered Max a nice boy and had suggested he call her—but the one time he tried she snapped at him—justly—how should she know?

At last Friday came. Feld was not feeling particularly well so he stayed in bed, and Mrs. Feld thought it better to remain in the bedroom with him when Max called. Miriam received the boy, and her parents could hear their voices, his throaty one, as they talked. Just before leaving, Miriam brought Max to the bedroom door and he stood there a minute, a tall, slightly hunched figure wearing a thick, droopy suit, and apparently at ease as he greeted the shoemaker and his wife, which was surely a good sign. And Miriam, although she had worked all day, looked fresh and pretty. She was a large-framed girl with a well-shaped body, and she had a fine open face[10] and soft hair. They made, Feld thought, a first-class couple.

Miriam returned after 11:30. Her mother was already asleep, but the shoemaker got out of bed and after locating his bathrobe went into the kitchen, where Miriam, to his surprise, sat at the table, reading.

"So where did you go?" Feld asked pleasantly.

"For a walk." she said, not looking up.

"I advised him," Feld said, clearing his throat, "he shouldn't spend so much money."

"I didn't care."

The shoemaker boiled up some water for tea and sat down at

10) open face: frank, honest looking face.

the table with a cupful and a thick slice of lemon.

"So how," he sighed after a sip, "did you enjoy?"

"It was all right."

He was silent. She must have sensed his disappointment, for she added,

"You can't really tell much the first time."

"You will see him again?"

Turning a page, she said that Max had asked for another date.

"For when?"

"Saturday."

"So what did you say?"

"What did I say?" she asked, delaying for a moment—"I said yes."

Afterwards she inquired about Sobel, and Feld, without exactly knowing why, said the assistant had got another job. Miriam said nothing more and began to read. The shoemaker's conscience did not trouble him: he was satisfied with the Saturday date.

During the week, by placing here and there a deft question, he managed to get from Miriam some information about Max. It surprised him to learn that the boy was not studying to be either a doctor or lawyer but was taking a business course leading to a degree in accountancy. Feld was a little disappointed because he thought of accountants as books-keepers and would have preferred "a higher profession." However, it was not long before he had investigated the subject and discovered that Certified Public Accountants[11) were highly respected people, so he was thoroughly content as Saturday approached. But because Saturday was a busy day, he was much in the store and therefore did not see Max when he came to call for Miriam. From his wife he learned there had been nothing especially revealing about their meeting. Max had rung the bell and Miriam had got her coat and left with him—nothing more. Feld did not probe, for his wife was not particularly observant. Instead, he waited up for Miriam with a newspaper on his lap, which he scarcely

11) Certified Public Accountants: 공인회계사.

looked at so lost was he in thinking of the future. He awoke to find her in the room with him, tiredly removing her hat. Greeting her, he was suddenly inexplicably afraid to ask anything about the evening. But since she volunteered nothing he was at last forced to inquire how she had enjoyed herself. Miriam began something non-committal[12] but apparently changed her mind, for she said after a minute, "I was bored."

When Feld sufficiently recovered from his anguished disappointment to ask why, she answered without hesitation, "Because he's nothing more than a materialist."

"What means this word?"

"He has no soul. He's only interested in things."

He considered her statement for a long time but then asked, "Will you see him again?"

"He didn't ask."

"Suppose he will ask you?"

"I won't see him."

He did not argue; however, as the days went by he hoped increasingly she would change her mind. He wished the boy would telephone, because he was sure there was more to him[13] than Miriam, with her inexperienced eye, could discern. But Max didn't call. As a matter of fact he took a different route to school, no longer passing the shoemaker's store and Feld was deeply hurt.

Then one afternoon Max came in and asked for his shoes. The shoemaker took them down from the shelf where he had placed them, apart from the other pairs. He had done the work himself and the soles and heels were built and firm. The shoes had been highly polished and somehow looked better than new. Max's Adam's apple went up once when he saw them, and his eyes had little lights in them.

"How much?" he asked, without directly looking at the shoemaker.

---

12) non-committal: 언질을 안 주는, 애매한.

13) there was more to him: there was something more to him.

"Like I told you before," Feld answered sadly. "One dollar fifty cents."

Max handed him two crumpled bills and received in return a newly-minted silver half dollar.

He left. Miriam had not been mentioned. That night the shoemaker discovered that his new assistant had been all the while stealing from him, and he suffered a heart attack.

Though the attack was very mild, he lay in bed for three weeks. Miriam spoke of going for Sobel, but sick as he was Feld rose in wrath against the idea. Yet in his heart there was no other way, and the first weary day back in the shop thoroughly convinced him, so that night after supper he dragged himself to Sobel's rooming house.

He toiled up the stairs, though he knew it was bad for him, and at the top knocked at the door. Sobel opened it and the shoemaker entered. The room was a small, poor one, with a single window facing the street. It contained a narrow cot, a low table and several stacks of books piled haphazardly around on the floor along the wall, which made him think how queer Sobel was, to be uneducated and read so much. He had once asked him, Sobel, why you read so much? and the assistant could not answer him. Did you ever study in a college someplace? He had asked, but Sobel shook his head. He read, he said, to know. But to know what, the shoemaker demanded, and to know, why? Sobel never explained, which proved he read much because he was queer.

Feld sat down to recover his breath. The assistant was resting on his bed with his heavy back to the wall. His shirt and trousers were clean, and his stubby fingers, away from the shoemaker's bench, were strangely pallid. His face was thin and pale, as if he had shut in this room since the day he had bolted from the store.

"So when you will come back to work?" Feld asked him.

To his surprise, Sobel burst out, "Never,"

Jumping up, he strode over to the window that looked out upon the miserable street. "Why should I come back?" he cried.

"I will raise your wages."

"Who cares for your wages!"

The shoemaker, knowing he didn't care, was at a loss what else to say.

"What do you want from me, Sobel?"

"Nothing."

"I always treated you like you was my son."

Sobel vehemently denied it. "So why you look for strange boys in the street they should go out with Miriam? Why you don't think of me?"

The shoemaker's hands and feet turned freezing cold. His voice became so hoarse he couldn't speak. At last he cleared his throat and croaked. "So what has my daughter got to do with a shoemaker of thirty-five years old who works for me?"

"Why do you think I worked so long for you?" Sobel cried out. "For the stingy wages I sacrificed five years of my life so you could[14] have to eat and drink and where to[15] sleep?"

"Then for what?" shouted the shoemaker.

"For Miriam," he blurted—"for her."

The shoemaker, after a time, managed to say, "I pay wages in cash, Sobel," and lapsed into silence. Though he was seething with excitement, his mind was coldly clear, and he had to admit to himself he had sense all along that Sobel felt this way. He had never so much as thought it consciously, but he had felt it and was afraid.

"Miriam knows?" he muttered hoarsely.

"She knows."

"You told her?"

"No."

"Then how does she know?"

"How does she know?" Sobel said, "because she knows. She knows

---

14) life so you could...: life so that you could...

15) and where to...: and so that you could have the place to...

who I am and what is in my heart."

Feld had a sudden insight. In some devious way, with his books and commentary, Sobel had given Miriam to understand that he loved her. The shoemaker felt a terrible anger at him for his deceit.

"Sobel, you are crazy," he said bitterly. "She will never marry a man so old and ugly like you."

Sobel turned black with rage. He cursed the shoemaker, but then, though he trembled to hold it in, his eyes filled with tears and he broke into deep sobs. With his back to Feld, he stood at the window, fist clenched, and his shoulder shook with his choked sobbing.

Watching him, the shoemaker's anger diminished. His teeth were on edge with pity[16] for the man, and his eyes grew moist. How strange and sad that a refugee, a grown man, bald and old with his miseries, who had by the skin of his teeth escaped Hitler's incinerators[17], should fall in love, when he had got to America, with a girl less than half his age. Day after day, for five years he had sat at his bench, cutting and hammering away, waiting for the girl to become a woman, unable to ease his heart with speech, knowing no protest but desperation.

"Ugly I didn't mean,"[18] he said half aloud.

Then he realized that what he had called ugly was not Sobel but Miriam's life if she married him. He felt for his daughter a strange and gripping sorrow, as if she were already Sobel's bride, the wife, after all, of a shoemaker, and had in her life no more than her mother had had. And all his dreams for her—why he had slaved and destroyed his heart with anxiety and labor—all these dreams of a better life were dead.

The room was quiet. Sobel was standing by the window reading,

---

16) His teeth were on edge with pity: 연민의 정으로 가슴이 메어졌다는 뜻의 비유적 표현.

17) Hitler's incinerators: incinerator는 (쓰레기 따위의) 소각로. 여기서는 히틀러의 유대인 대학살과 연관시켜 쓴 말.

18) Ugly I didn't mean: I didn't mean her to be ugly.

and it was curious that when he read he looked young. "She is only nineteen," Feld said brokenly. "This is too young yet to get married. Don't ask her for two years more, till she is twenty-one, then you can talk to her."

Sobel didn't answer. Feld rose and left. He went slowly down the stairs but once outside, though it was an icy night and the crisp falling snow whitened the street, he walked with a stronger stride.

But the next morning, when the shoemaker arrived, heavy-hearted, to open the store, he saw he needn't have come, for his assistant was already seated at the last, pounding leather for his love.

The Fly

by Katherine Mansfield

Introduction to the Author

Katherine Mansfield (1888-1923)

Short-story writer noted for her distinctive prose style with many overtones of poetry. Her delicate stories, focused upon psychological conflicts, have an obliqueness of narration and a subtlety of observation that reveal the influence of Anton Chekhov. She, in turn, had much influence on the development of the short story as a form of literature. Mansfield left New Zealand at the age of 19 to establish herself in England as a writer. She achieved the height of her powers in *The Garden Party, and Other Stories* (1922), which includes the stories The Garden Party, "At the Bay," "The Voyage," "The Stranger"(with New Zealand settings), and the classic "Daughters of the Late Colonel," a subtle account of genteel frustration.

The Fly

"Y'are very snug in here," piped old Mr. Woodifield, and he peered out of the great, green leather armchair by his friend, the boss's desk, as a baby peers out of its pram. His talk was over; it was time for him to be off. But he did not want to go. Since he had retired, since his...stroke, the wife and the girls kept him boxed up[1] in the house every day of the week except Tuesday. On Tuesday he was dressed up and brushed and allowed to cut back to the City[2] for the day. Though what he did there the wife and girls couldn't imagine. Made a nuisance of himself to his friends, they supposed.... Well, perhaps so. All the same, we cling to our last pleasures as the tree clings to its last leaves. So there sat old Woodifield, smoking a cigar and staring almost greedily at the boss, who rolled in his office chair, stout, rosy, five years older than he, and still going strong, still at the helm.[3] It did one good to see him.[4]

Wistfully, admiringly, the old voice added, "It's snug in here, upon my word!"

"Yes, it's comfortable enough," agreed the boss, and he flipped *The Financial Times* with a paper knife. As a matter of fact he was proud of his room; he liked to have it admired, especially by old Woodifield. It gave him a feeling of deep, solid satisfaction to be planted there[5] in the midst of it in full view of[6] that frail old figure in the muffler.

"I've had it done up[7] lately," he explained, as he had explained

---

1) boxed up: 감금해 두었다. 나가지 못하게 했다.
2) the City: London중심부에 있는 한 구역으로 은행과 회사들이 집중해 있다.
3) at the helm: at the controlling position.
4) It did one good to see him: 그를 보는 것이 사람에게 유익을 주었다.
5) to be planted there: to sit there.
6) in full view of: "that frail old figure in the muffler"의 눈에 자기가 온통 다 보이는 곳이란 뜻이다.

for the past—how many?—weeks. "New carpet," and he pointed to the bright red carpet with a pattern of large white rings. "New furniture," and he nodded towards the massive bookcase and the table with legs like twisted treacle. "Electric heating!" He waved almost exultantly towards the five transparent, pearly sausages glowing so softly in the tilted copper pan.

But he did not draw old Woodifield's attention to the photograph over the table of a grave-looking boy in uniform standing in one of those spectral photographers' parks[8)] with photographers' storm clouds behind him. It was not new. It had been there for over six years.

"There was something I wanted to tell you," said old Woodifield, and his eyes grew dim remembering. "Now what was it? I had it in mind when I started out this morning." His hands began to tremble, and patches of red showed above his beard.

Poor old chap, he's on his last pins,[9)] thought the boss. And, feeling kindly, he winked at the old man, and said jokingly, "I tell you what. I've got a little drop of something here that'll do you good before you go out into the cold again. It's beautiful stuff. It wouldn't hurt a child." He took a key off his watch-chain, unlocked a cupboard below his desk, and drew forth a dark, squat bottle. "That's the medicine," said he. "And the man from whom I got it told me on the strict Q.T.[10)] it came from the cellars at Windsor Castle."

Old Woodifield's mouth fell open at the sight. He couldn't have looked more surprised if the boss had produced a rabbit.

"It's whisky, ain't it?" he piped, feebly.

The boss turned the bottle and lovingly showed him the label. Whisky it was.

"D'you know," said he, peering up at the boss wonderingly, "they

---

7) done up: smartened up; renovated.

8) spectral photographers' parks: 사진관에서 인물 사진의 배경으로 사용하는, 수목을 희미하게 그린 공원 풍경을 말한다.

9) on his last pins: near dying.

10) on the strict Q.T.: (colloq.) 절대비밀로, Q.T.=quiet.

won't let me touch it at home." And he looked as though he was going to cry.

"Ah, that's where we know a bit more than the ladies," cried the boss, swooping across for two tumblers that stood on the table with the water bottle, and pouring a generous finger[11] into each. "Drink it down. It'll do you good. And don't put any water with it. It's sacrilege to tamper with stuff like this. Ah!" He tossed off[12] his, pulled out his handkerchief, hastily wiped his mustaches, and cocked an eye at old Woodifield, who was rolling his in his chaps.[13]

The old man swallowed, was silent a moment, and then said faintly, "It's nutty!"

But it warmed him; it crept into his chill old brain—he remembered.

"That was it," he said, heaving himself out of his chair. "I thought you'd like to know. The girls were in Belgium last week having a look at poor Reggie's grave, and they happened to come across your boy's. They are quite near each other, it seems."

Old Woodifield paused, but the boss made no reply. Only a quiver of his eyelids showed that he heard.

"The girls were delighted with the way the place is kept," piped the old voice. "Beautifully looked after. Couldn't be better if they were at home. You've not been across, have yer?"[14]

"No, no!" For various reasons the boss had not been across.

"There's miles of it," quavered old Woodifield, "and it's all as neat as a garden. Flowers growing on all the graves. Nice broad paths. It was plain from his voice how much he liked a nice broad path.

The pause came again. Then the old man brightened wonderfully.

"D'you know what the hotel made the girls pay for a pot of jam?" he piped. "Ten francs! Robbery, I call it. It was a little pot, so Gertrude

---

11) pouring a generous finger: 술을 손가락 하나 깊이 만큼 넉넉히 따르다.
12) tossed off: 한 숨에 마시다.
13) chaps: chops=jaws=mouth.
14) have yer: have you.

says, no bigger than a half-crown. And she hadn't taken more than a spoonful when they charged her ten francs. Gertrude brought the pot away with her to teach 'em a lesson. Quite right, too; it's trading on[15] our feelings. They think because we're over there having a look around we're ready to pay anything. That's what it is." And he turned towards the door.

"Quite right, quite right!" cried the boss, though what was quite right he hadn't the least idea. He came round by his desk,[16] followed the shuffling footsteps to the door, and saw the old fellow out. Woodifield was gone.

For a long moment the boss stayed, staring at nothing, while the gray-haired office messenger, watching him, dodged in and out of his cubbyhole like a dog that expects to be taken for a run: "I'll see nobody for half an hour. Macey," said the boss. "Understand? Nobody at all."

"Very good, sir."

The door shut, the firm, heavy steps recrossed the bright carpet, the fat body plumped down in the spring chair, and leaning forward, the boss covered his face with his hands. He wanted, he intended, he had arranged to weep....

It had been a terrible shock to him when old Woodifield sprang[17] that remark upon him about the boy's grave. It was exactly as though the earth had opened and he had seen the boy lying there with Woodifield's girls staring down at him. For it was strange. Although over six years had passed away, the boss never thought of the boy except as lying unchanged, unblemished in his uniform, asleep for ever. "My son!" groaned the boss. But no tears came yet. In the past, in the first months and even years after the boy's death, he had only to say those words to be overcome by such grief that

15) trading on: making one's profit out of~. 우리의 기분을 가지고 돈벌이 하다(이익을 남기다).

16) came round by his desk: 책상을 돌아서 나왔다. by는 pass by, go by와 같은 의미.

17) sprang: produced suddenly.

nothing short of a violent fit of weeping could relieve him. Time, he had declared then, he had told everybody, could make no difference. Other men perhaps might recover, might live their loss down,[18] but not he. How was it possible? His boy was an only son. Ever since his birth the boss had worked at building up this business for him; it had no other meaning if it was not for the boy. Life itself had come to have no other meaning. How on earth could he have slaved, denied himself, kept going all these years without the promise for ever before him of the boy's stepping into his shoes[19] and carrying on where he left off?

And that promise had been so near being fulfilled. The boy had been in the office learning the ropes[20] for a year before the war. Every morning they had started off together; they had come back by the same train. And what congratulations he had received as the boy's father! No wonder; he had taken to it[21] marvelously. As to his popularity with the staff, every man jack[22] of them down to old Macey couldn't make enough of the boy. And he wasn't in the least spoiled. No, he was just his bright, natural self, with the right word for everybody, with that boyish look and his habit of saying, "Simply splendid!"

But all that was over and done with as though it never had been. The day had come when Macey had handed him the telegram that brought the whole place crashing about his head. "Deeply regret to inform you..."[23] And he had left the office a broken man, with his life in ruins.

Six years ago, six year... How quickly time passed! It might have happened yesterday. The boss took his hands from his face; he was

---

18) live their loss down: 살아가는 동안에 그들의 죽음에 대한 애닮은 생각이 차차 없어져 간다.
19) stepping into his shoes: succeeding him.
20) the ropes: (사업 운영상의) 요령.
21) take to it: devote himself to it. "it"는 그들의 사업을 가리킨다.
22) every man jack: every man without exception.
23) "Deeply regret to inform you...": 그가 받은 전보의 서두.

puzzled. Something seemed to be wrong with him. He wasn't feeling as he wanted to feel. He decided to get up and have a look at the boy's photograph. But it wasn't a favorite photograph of his; the expression was unnatural. It was cold, even stern-looking. The boy had never looked like that.

At that moment the boss noticed that a fly had fallen into his broad inkpot, and was trying feebly but desperately to clamber out again. Help! help! said those struggling legs. But the sides of the inkpot were wet and slippery; it fell back again and began to swim. The boss took up a pen, picked the fly out of the ink, and shook it on to a piece of blotting paper. For a fraction of a second it lay still on the dark patch that oozed round it. Then the front legs waved, took hold, and, pulling its small sodden body up it began the immense task of cleaning the ink from its wings. Over and under, over and under, went a leg along a wing, as the stone goes over and under the scythe. Then there was a pause, while the fly, seeming to stand on the tips of its toes, tried to expand first one wing and then the other. It succeeded at last, and, sitting down, it began, like a minute cat, to clean its face. Now one could imagine that the little front legs rubbed against each other lightly, joyfully. The horrible danger was over; it had escaped; it was ready for life again.

But just then the boss had an idea. He plunged his pen back into the ink, leaned his thick wrist on the blotting paper, and as the fly tried its wings down came a great heavy blot. What would it make of that?[24] What indeed! The little beggar seemed absolutely cowed, stunned, afraid to move because of what would happen next. But then, as if painfully, it dragged itself forward. The front legs waved, caught hold, and more slowly this time, the task began from the beginning.

"He's a plucky little devil," thought the boss, and he felt a real admiration for the fly's courage. That was the way to tackle things; that was the right spirit. Never say die;[25] it was only a question

---

24) What would it make of that?: 파리가 그것을 어떻게 생각하겠는가?

of...But the fly had again finished its laborious task, and the boss had just time to refill his pen, to shake fair and square on the new-cleaned body yet another dark drop. What about it this time? A painful moment of suspense followed. But behold, the front legs were again waving; the boss felt a rush of relief. He leaned over the fly and said to it tenderly, "You artful little b...."[26] And he actually had the brilliant notion of breathing on it to help the drying process. All the same, there was something timid and weak about its efforts now, and the boss decided that this time should be the last, as he dipped the pen into the inkpot.

It was. The last blot fell on the soaked blotting paper, and the draggled fly lay in it and did not stir. The back legs were stuck to the body; the front legs were not to be seen.

"Come on," said the boss. "Look sharp!" And he stirred it with his pen—in vain. Nothing happened or was likely to happen. The fly was dead.

The boss lifted the corpse on the end of the paper knife and flung it into the wastepaper basket, but such a grinding feeling of wretchedness seized him that he felt positively frightened. He started forward and pressed the bell for Macey.

"Bring me some fresh blotting paper," he said, sternly, "and look sharp about it." And while the old dog padded away he fell to[27] wondering what it was he had been thinking about before. What was it? It was...He took out his handkerchief and passed it inside his collar. For the life of him he could not remember.

---

25) Never say die: Don't despair; Persevere courageous; Keep up courage.

26) little b...: little beggar라 하려다 중단됨. beggar=fellow, chap.

27) fell to: began to.

Red

by William S. Maugham

Introduction to the Author

William S. Maugham (1874-1965)

English novelist, playwright, and short story writer whose work is characterized by a clear, unadorned style, cosmopolitan settings, and a shrewd understanding of human nature. His major novels are *Of Human Bondage* (1915), *The Moon and Six Pence* (1919). Many of his short stories portray the conflict of Europeans in alien surroundings, and Maugham's skill in handling plot is distinguished by economy and suspense.

Red

The skipper thrust his hand into one of his trouser pockets and with difficulty, for they were not at the sides but in front and he was a portly[1] man, pulled out a large silver watch. He looked at it and then looked again at the declining sun. The Kanaka[2] at the wheel gave him a glance, but did not speak. The skipper's eyes rested on the island they were approaching. A white line of foam marked the reef. He knew there was an opening large enough to get his ship through, and when they came a little nearer he counted on seeing it. They had nearly an hour of daylight still before them. In the lagoon the water was deep and they could anchor comfortably. The chief of the village which he could already see among the coconut trees was a friend of the mate's,[3] and it would be pleasant to go ashore for the night. The mate came forward at that minute and the skipper turned to him.

'We'll take a bottle of booze[4] along with us and get some girls in to dance,' he said.

'I don't see the opening,' said the mate.

He was a Kanaka, a handsome, swarthy fellow, with somewhat the look of a later Roman emperor, inclined to stoutness; but his face was fine and clean-cut.

'I'm dead sure there's one right here,' said the captain, looking through his glasses. 'I can't understand why I can't pick it up. Send one of the boys up the mast to have a look.'

The mate called one of the crew and gave him the order. The captain watched the Kanaka climb and waited for him to speak. But the Kanaka shouted down that he could see nothing but the un-

---

1) portly: 뚱뚱한.
2) Kanaka: 남양군도의 원주민(=a native of the South Sea Island).
3) mate: 항해사.
4) booze: 술.

broken line of foam.[5] The captain spoke Samoan like a native, and he cursed him freely.

'Shall he stay up there?' asked the mate.

'What the hell good does that do?' answered the captain.

'The blame fool can't see worth a cent.[6] You bet your sweet life[7] I'd find the opening if I was up there.'

He looked at the slender mast with anger. It was all very well for a native who had been used to climbing up coconut trees all his life. He was fat and heavy.

'Come down,' he shouted. 'You're no more use than a dead dog. We'll just have to go along the reef till we find the opening.'

It was a seventy-ton schooner with paraffin auxiliary,[8] and it ran, when there was no head wind,[9] between four and five knots an hour. It was a bedraggled[10] object; it had been painted white a very long time ago, but it was now dirty, dingy, and mottled. It smelt strongly of paraffin, and of the copra which was its usual cargo. They were within a hundred feet of the reef now and the captain told the steersman[11] to run along it till they came to the opening. But when they had gone a couple of miles he realized that they had missed it. He went about and slowly worked back again. The white foam of the reef continued without interruption and now the sun was setting. With a curse at the stupidity of the crew the skipper resigned himself to waiting[12] till next morning.

'Put her about,' he said, 'I can't anchor here.'

They went out to sea a little and presently it was quite dark. They anchored. When the sail was furled the ship began to roll a

---

5) the unbroken line of foam: 부서지지 않는 파도.
6) The blame fool can't see worth a cent: The blamed fool can't see anything.
7) You bet your sweet life: 틀림없이, 확실히.
8) schooner with paraffin auxiliary: paraffin oil을 때는 보조 엔진을 가진 범선.
9) head wind: 맞바람.
10) bedraggled: 더러운, 진흙투성이의.
11) steersman: 키잡이, 조타수.
12) resigned himself to waiting: 체념하고 기다리기로 했다.

good deal. They said in Apia that one day she would roll right over; and the owner, a German-American who managed one of the largest stores, said that no money was big enough to induce him to go out in her. The cook, a Chinese in white trousers, very dirty and ragged, and a thin white tunic, came to say that supper was ready, and when the skipper went into the cabin he found the engineer[13] already seated at table. The engineer was a long, lean man with a scraggy neck. He was dressed in blue overalls[14] and a sleeveless jersey which showed his thin arms tattooed from elbow to wrist.

'Hell, having to spend the night outside,' said the skipper.

The engineer did not answer, and they ate their supper in silence. The cabin was lit by a dim oil-lamp. When they had eaten the canned apricots with which the meal finished the Chink brought them a cup of tea. The skipper lit a cigar and went on the upper deck. The island now was only a darker mass against the night. The stars were very bright. The only sound was the ceaseless breaking of the surf.[15] The skipper sank into a deck-chair and smoked idly. Presently three or four members of the crew came up and sat down. One of them had a banjo and another a concertina.[16] They began to play, and one of them sang. The native song sounded strange on these instruments. Then to the singing a couple began to dance. It was a barbaric dance, savage and primeval, rapid, with quick movements of the hands and feet and contortions[17] of the body; it was sensual, sexual even, but sexual without passion. It was very animal, direct, weird without mystery, natural in short, and one might almost say childlike. At last they grew tired. They stretched themselves on the deck and slept, and all was silent. The skipper lifted himself heavily out of his chair and clambered down

---

13) engineer: 기관사.
14) overalls: 작업복. 작업바지(가슴까지 올라오는, 어깨에서 멜빵으로 맨 헐렁헐렁한 작업바지).
15) surf: 파도, 물결.
16) concertina: 콘체르티나. 손풍금의 일종.
17) contortions: 비틀기. 비꼬기.

the companion.[18] He went into his cabin and got out of his clothes. He climbed into his bunk[19] and lay there. He panted a little in the heat of the night.

But next morning, when the dawn crept over the tranquil sea, the opening in the reef which had eluded them the night before was seen a little to the east of where they lay. The schooner entered the lagoon. There was not a ripple on the surface of the water. Deep down among the coral rocks you saw little coloured fish swim. When he had anchored his ship the skipper ate his breakfast and went on deck. The sun shone from an unclouded sky, but in the early morning the air was grateful and cool. It was Sunday, and there was a feeling of quietness, a silence as though nature were at rest, which gave him a peculiar sense of comfort. He sat, looking at the wooded coast, and felt lazy and well at ease. Presently a slow smile moved his lips and he threw the stump of his cigar[20] into the water.

'I guess I'll go ashore,' he said. 'Get the boat out.'

He climbed stiffly down the ladder and was rowed to a little cove.[21] The coconut trees came down to the water's edge, not in rows, but spaced out with an ordered formality.[22] They were like a ballet of spinsters,[23] elderly but flippant,[24] standing in affected attitudes with the simpering graces of a bygone age. He sauntered idly through them, along a path that could be just seen winding its tortuous way, and it led him presently to a broad creek. There was a bridge across it, but a bridge constructed of single trunks of coconut trees, a dozen of them, placed end to end and supported where they met by forked branch driven[25] into the bed[26] of the creek. You

---

18) companion: 갑판 승강구 계단.
19) bunk: 침대.
20) stump of his cigar: 담배꽁초.
21) cove: small bay.
22) spaced out with ~ formality: 규칙적으로 일정한 간격을 두고 서 있었다.
23) spinster: 노처녀.
24) flippant: 경솔한, 경박한.
25) forked branch: 포크 모양으로 가지가 벌어진 나무.

walked on a smooth, round surface, narrow and slippery, and there was no support for the hand. To cross such a bridge required sure feet and a stout heart.[27] The skipper hesitated. But he saw on the other side, nestling[28] among the trees, a white man's house; he made up his mind and, rather gingerly, began to walk. He watched his feet carefully, and where one trunk joined on to the next and there was a difference of level, he tottered a little. It was with a gasp of relief[29] that he reached the last tree and finally set his feet on the firm ground of the other side. He had been so intent on the difficult crossing that he never noticed anyone was watching him, and it was with surprise that he heard himself spoken to.

'It takes a bit of nerve[30] to cross these bridges when you're not used to them.'

He looked up and saw a man standing in front of him. He had evidently come out of the house which he had seen.

'I saw you hesitate,' the man continued, with a smile on his lips, 'and I was watching to see you fall in.'

'Not on your life.' said the captain, who had now recovered his confidence.

'I've fallen in myself before now. I remember, one evening I came back from shooting, and I fell in, gun and all. Now I get a boy to carry my gun for me.'

He was a man no longer young, with a small beard, now somewhat grey, and a thin face. He was dressed in a singlet without arms,[31] and a pair of duck trousers. He wore neither shoes nor socks. He spoke English with a slight accent.

'Are you Neilson?' asked the skipper.

'I am.'

---

26) bed: 개울 바닥. 하상(河床).
27) a stout heart: 강심장.
28) nestle: 깃들이다. 자리 잡고 있다.
29) a gasp of relief: 안도의 한숨.
30) nerve: 용기.
31) a singlet without arms: 소매가 없는 내의.

'I've heard about you. I thought you lived somewheres round here.

The skipper followed his host into the little bungalow and sat down heavily in the chair which the other motioned him to take. While Neilson went out to fetch whisky and glasses he took a look round the room. It filled him with amazement. He had never seen so many books. The shelves reached from floor to ceiling on all four walls, and they were closely packed. There was a grand piano littered with music,[32] and a large table on which books and magazines lay in disorder. The room made him feel embarrassed. He remembered that Neilson was a queer fellow. No one knew very much about him, although he had been in the islands for so many years, but those who knew him agreed that he was queer. He was a Swede.

'You've got one big heap of books here,' he said, when Neilson returned.

'They do no harm,' answered Neilson with a smile.

'Have you read them all?' asked the skipper.

'Most of them.'

'I'm a bit of a reader myself. I have the *Saturday Evening Post* sent me regler.'

Neilson poured his visitor a good stiff[33] glass of whisky and gave him a cigar. The skipper volunteered a little information.

'I got in last night, but I couldn't find the opening, so I had to anchor outside. I never been this run before, but my people had some stuff they wanted to bring over here. Gray, d'you know him?'[34]

'Yes, he's got a store a little way along.'

'Well, there was a lot of canned stuff that he wanted over, an' he's got some copra. They thought I might just as well come over as lie idle at Apia. I run between Apia and Pago-Pago mostly, but

32) a grand piano littered with music: 악보가 널려 있는 그랜드 피아노.
33) stiff: (술 등이) 독한.
34) 그레이란 사람을 아세요?

they've got smallpox there just now, and there's nothing stirring.'

He took a drink of his whisky and lit a cigar. He was a taciturn[35] man but there was something in Neilson that made him nervous, and his nervousness made him talk. The Swede was looking at him with large dark eyes in which there was an expression of faint amusement.

'This is a tidy little place you've got here.'

'I've done my best with it.'

'You must do pretty well with your trees. They look fine. With copra at a price it is now.[36] I had a bit of a plantation myself once, in Upolu it was, but I had to sell it.'

He looked round the room again, where all those books gave him a feeling of something incomprehensible and hostile.

'I guess you must find it a bit lonesome here though,' he said.

'I've got used to it. I've been here for twenty-five years.'

Now the captain could think of nothing more to say, and he smoked in silence. Neilson had apparently no wish to break it. He looked at his guest with meditative eye. He was a tall man, more than six feet high, and very stout. His face was red and blotchy,[37] with a network of little purple veins on the cheeks, and his features were sunk into its fatness. His eye were bloodshot. His neck was buried in rolls of fat. But for a fringe of long curly hair,[38] nearly white, at the back of his head, he was quite bald; and that immense, shiny surface of forehead, which might have given him a false look of intelligence, on the contrary gave him one of peculiar imbecility. He wore a blue flannel shirt, open at the neck and showing his fat chest covered with a mat of reddish hair, and a very old pair of blue serge trousers. He sat in his chair in a heavy ungainly[39] attitude, his great belly thrust forward and his fat legs uncrossed. All elasticity

---

35) taciturn: 말이 적은, 과묵한.

36) With copra~it is now: 요즘 코프라 값이 꽤 나간다.

37) blotchy: 부스럼[얼룩]투성이의.

38) fringe of long curly hair: 머리 주위에 드리워진 긴 곱슬머리

39) ungainly: 꼴사나운, 볼품없는.

had gone from his limbs. Neilson wondered idly what sort of man he had been in his youth. It was almost impossible to imagine that this creature of vast bulk had ever been a boy who ran about. The skipper finished his whisky, and Neilson pushed the bottle towards him.

'Help yourself.'

The skipper leaned forward and with his great hand seized it.

'And how come you in these parts anyways?' he said.

'Oh, I came out to the islands for my health. My lungs were bad and they said I hadn't a year to live. You see they were wrong.'

'I meant, how come you to settle down right here?'

'I am a sentimentalist.'

'Oh!'

Neilson knew that the skipper had not an idea what he meant, and he looked at him with an ironical twinkle in his dark eyes. Perhaps just because the skipper was so gross and dull a man the whim seized him to talk further.[40)]

'You were too busy keeping your balance to notice, when you crossed the bridge, but this spot is generally considered rather pretty.'

'It's a cute little house you've got here.'

'Ah, that wasn't here when I first came. There was a native hut, with its beehive roof and its pillars, overshadowed by a great tree with red flowers; and the croton bushes, their leaves yellow and red and golden, made a pied fence around it. And then all about were the coconut trees, as fanciful as women, and as vain. They stood at the water's edge and spent all day looking at their reflections. I was a young man then—good heavens, it's a quarter of a century ago—and I wanted to enjoy all the loveliness of the world in the short time allotted to me before I passed into the darkness.[41)] I thought it was the most beautiful spot I had ever seen. The first

---

40) the whim ~ further: 말을 더하고 싶은 기분(변덕)이 생겼다.
41) before I ~ darkness: 내가 죽기 전에.

time I saw it I had a catch at my heart,[42] and I was afraid I was going to cry. I wasn't more than twenty-five, and though I put the best face I could on it, I didn't want to die. And somehow it seemed to me that the very beauty of this place made it easier for me to accept my fate. I felt when I came here that all my past life had fallen away, Stockholm and its University, and then Bonn: it all seemed the life of somebody else, as though now at last I had achieved the reality which our doctors of philosophy—I am one myself, you know—had discussed so much. "A year," I cried to myself. "I have a year. I will spend it here and then I am content to die."

'We are foolish and sentimental and melodramatic at twenty-five, but if we weren't perhaps we should be less wise at fifty.'[43]

'Now drink, my friend. Don't let the nonsense I talk interfere with you.'

He waved his thin hand towards the bottle, and the skipper finished what remained in his glass.

'You ain't drinking nothin',[44] he said, reaching for the whisky.

'I am of sober habit,'[45] smiled the Swede. 'I intoxicate myself in ways which I fancy are more subtle. But perhaps that is only vanity. Anyhow, the effects are more lasting and the results less deleterious.'[46]

'They say there's a deal of cocaine taken in the States now,' said the captain.

Neilson chuckled.

'But I do not see a white man often,' he continued, 'and for once I don't think a drop of whisky can do me any harm.'

He poured himself out a little, added some soda, and took a sip.

'And presently I found out why the spot had such an unearthly loveliness. Here love had tarried[47] for a moment like a migrant bird

---

42) I had a catch at my heart: 완전히 매료되었다. 홀딱 반했다.
43) 바보같이 감정에 빠져 멜로 드라마 같은 사랑을 하지 않는다면 50세가 되어도 지혜롭지 못할 것이다.
44) nothin': nothing.
45) of sober habit: 술을 안 마신다.
46) deleterious: 해로운, 유독한.

that happens on a ship in mid-ocean and for a little while folds its tired wings. The fragrance of a beautiful passion hovered over it like the fragrance of hawthorn in May in the meadows of my home. It seems to me that the places where men have loved or suffered keep about them always some faint aroma of something that has not wholly died. It is as though they had acquired a spiritual significance which mysteriously affects those who pass. I wish I could make myself clear.' He smiled a little. 'Though I cannot imagine that if I did[48] you would understand.'

He paused.

'I think this place was beautiful because here for a period the ecstasy of love had invested it with beauty.' And now he shrugged his shoulders. 'But perhaps it is only that my aesthetic sense is gratified by the happy conjunction of young love and a suitable setting.

Even a man less thick-witted than the skipper might have been forgiven if he were bewildered by Neilson's words. For he seemed faintly to laugh at what he said. It was as though he spoke from emotion which his intellect found ridiculous. He had said himself that he was a sentimentalist, and when sentimentality is joined with scepticism there is often the devil to pay.

He was silent for an instant and looked at the captain with eyes in which there was a sudden perplexity.

'You know, I can't help thinking that I've seen you before somewhere or other,' he said.

'I couldn't say as I remember you,' returned the skipper.

'I have a curious feeling as though your face were familiar to me. It's been puzzling me for some time. But I can't situate my recollection in any place or at any time.'

The skipper massively shrugged his heavy shoulders.

'It's thirty years since I first come to the islands. A man can't figure on remembering all the folk he meets in a while like that.'

---

47) tarry: 머물다. 체제하다.

48) if I did: even if I made myself clear.

The Swede shook his head.

'You know how one sometimes has the feeling that a place one has never been to before is strangely familiar. That's how I seem to see you.' He gave a whimsical smile. 'Perhaps I knew you in some past existence. Perhaps, perhaps you were the master of a galley in ancient Rome and I was a slave at the oar. Thirty years have you been here?'

'Every bit of thirty years.'

'I wonder if you knew a man called Red?'

'Red?'

'That is the only name I've ever known him by. I never knew him personally. I never even set eyes on him. And yet I seem to see him more clearly than many men, my brothers, for instance, with whom I passed my daily life for many years. He lives in my imagination with the distinctness of a Paolo Malatesta[49] or a Romeo. But I dare say you have never read Dante or Shakespeare?'

'I can't say as I have,' said the captain.

Neilson, smoking a cigar, leaned back in his chair and looked vacantly at the ring of smoke which floated in the still air. A smile played on his lips, but his eyes were grave. Then he looked at the captain. There was in his gross obesity[50] something extraordinarily repellent. He had the plethoric[51] self-satisfaction of the very fat. It was an outrage. It set Neilson's nerves on edge. But the contrast between the man before him and the man he had in mind was pleasant.

'It appears that Red was the most comely thing you ever saw. I've talked to quite a number of people who knew him in those days, white men, and they all agree that the first time you saw him his beauty just took your breath away.[52] They called him Red on ac-

---

49) Paolo Malatesta: 단테의 『신곡』 지옥편에 나오는 인물. 형수 Francesca가 그를 사랑하다가 남편에게 살해된다.

50) obesity: 뚱뚱함, 비만.

51) plethoric: 다혈질의, 과다한.

52) 사람들이 이구동성으로 레드가 너무 잘 생겨서 보는 순간 숨이 막힐 정도라고 했다.

count of his flaming hair. It had a natural wave and he wore it long. It must have been of that wonderful colour that the pre-Raphaelites raved over. I don't think he was vain of it, he was much too ingenuous for that, but no one could have blamed him if he had been. He was tall, six feet and an inch or two—in the native house that used to stand here was the mark of his height cut with a knife on the central trunk that supported the roof—and he was made like a Greek god, broad in the shoulders and thin in the flanks; he was like Apollo, with just that soft roundness which Praxiteles[53] gave him, and that suave, feminine grace which has in it something troubling and mysterious. His skin was dazzling white, milky, like satin; his skin was like a woman's.'

'I had kind of a white skin myself when I was a kiddie,' said the skipper, with a twinkle in his bloodshot eyes.

But Neilson paid no attention to him. He was telling his story now and interruption made him impatient.

'And his face was just as beautiful as his body. He had large blue eyes, very dark, so that some say they were black, and unlike most red-haired people he had dark eyebrows and long dark lashes. His features were perfectly regular and his mouth was like a scarlet wound. He was twenty.'

On these words the Swede stopped with a certain sense of the dramatic. He took a sip of whisky.

'He was unique. There never was anyone more beautiful. There was no more reason for him than for a wonderful blossom to flower on a wild plant.[54] He was a happy accident of nature.

'One day he landed at that cove into which you must have put this morning. He was an American sailor, and he had deserted from a man-of-war in Apia. He had induced some good-humoured native to give him a passage on a cutter[55] that happened to be sailing

---

53) Praxiteles: 기원전 350년 경의 아테네의 조각가.
54) 잡초에 아름다운 꽃이 피는 데에 이유가 없는 것처럼 그가 잘 생긴 외모를 가진 데에는 이유가 없다.

from Apia to Safoto, and he had been put ashore here in a dug-ou t.[56] I do not know why he deserted. Perhaps life on a man-of-war with its restrictions irked him, perhaps he was in trouble, and perhaps it was the South Seas and these romantic islands that got into his bones. Every now and then they[57] take a man strangely, and he finds himself like a fly in a spider's web. It may be that there was a softness of fibre in him, and these green hills with their soft airs, this blue sea, took the northern strength from him as Delilah took the Nazarite's.[58] Anyhow, he wanted to hide himself, and he thought he would be safe in this secluded nook till his ship had sailed from Samoa.

'There was a native hut at the cove and as he stood there, wondering where exactly he should turn his steps, a young girl came out and invited him to enter. He knew scarcely two words of the native tongue and she as little English. But he understood well enough what her smiles meant, and her pretty gestures, and he followed her. He sat down on a mat and she gave him slices of pineapple to eat. I can speak of Red only from hearsay,[59] but I saw the girl three years after he first met her, and she was scarcely nineteen then. You cannot imagine how exquisite she was. She had the passionate grace of the hibiscus and the rich colour. She was rather tall, slim, with the delicate features of her race, and large eyes like pools of still water under palm trees; her hair, black and curling, fell down her back, and she wore a wreath of scented flower. Her hands were lovely. They were so small, so exquisitely formed, they gave your heart-strings a wrench.[60] And in those days she laughed easily. Her smile was so delightful that it made your knees

55) cutter: 소형 범선. 돛단배.
56) dug-out: 카누.
57) they: the South Seas and these romantic islands를 지칭함.
58) Delilah took the Nazarite's: 들릴라가 나사렛 사람 삼손의 힘을 뺀 것처럼. 구약 성경 사사기 16장 참조.
59) hearsay: 소문, 풍문.
60) gave your heart-strings a wrench: 사람의 심금을 흔들어놓았다.

shake. Her skin was like a field of ripe corn on a summer day. Good heavens, how can I describe her? She was too beautiful to be real.

'And these two young things, she was sixteen and he was twenty, fell in love with one another at first sight. That is the real love, not the love that comes from sympathy, common interests, of intellectual community, but love pure and simple. That is the love that Adam felt for Eve when he awoke and found her in the garden gazing at him with dewy eyes. That is the love that draws the beasts to one another, and the Gods. That is the love that makes the world a miracle. That is the love which gives life its pregnant meaning. You have never heard of the wise, cynical French duke who said that with two lovers there is always one who loves and one who lets himself be loved; it is bitter truth to which most of us have to resign ourselves; but now and then there are two who love and two who let themselves be loved. Then one might fancy that the sun stands still as it stood when Joshua prayed to the God of Israel.

'And even now after all these years, when I think of these two, so young, so fair, so simple, and of their love, I feel a pang. It tears my heart just as my heart is torn when on certain nights I watch the full moon shining on the lagoon[61] from an unclouded sky. There is always pain in the contemplation of perfect beauty.

'They were children. She was good and sweet and kind. I know nothing of him, and I like to think that then at all events he was ingenuous[62] and frank. I like to think that his soul was as comely[63] as his body. But I dare say he had no more soul than the creatures of the woods and forests[64] who made pipes from reeds and bathed in the mountain streams when the world was young, and you might catch sight of little fawns galloping through the glade on the back

---

61) lagoon: 석호(潟湖).
62) ingenuous: 솔직한, 꾸밈없는.
63) comely: 잘 생긴, 아름다운.
64) he had no more soul than the creatures of the woods and forests...: 숲속의 생물들과 같이 영혼을 가지고 있지 않았다.

of a bearded centaur. A soul is a troublesome possession and when man developed it he lost the Garden of Eden.

'Well, when Red came to the island it had recently been visited by one of those epidemics which the white man brought to the South Seas, and one third of the inhabitants had died. It seems that the girl had lost all her near kin and she lived now in the house of distant cousins. The household consisted of two ancient crones, bowed and wrinkled, two younger women, and a man and a boy. For a few days he stayed there. But perhaps he felt himself too near the shore, with the possibility that he might fall in with[65] white men who would reveal his hiding-place; perhaps the lovers could not bear that the company of others should rob them for an instant of the delight of being together. One morning they set out, the pair of them, with the few things that belonged to the girl, and walked along a grassy path under the coconuts, till they came to the creek you see. They had to cross the bridge you crossed, and the girl laughed gleefully because he was afraid. She held his hand till they came to the end of the first tree, and then his courage failed him and he had to go back. He was obliged to take off all his clothes before he could risk it, and she carried them over for him on her head. They settled down in the empty hut that stood there. Whether she had any rights over it (land tenure is a complicated business in the islands), or whether the owner had died during the epidemic, I do not know, but anyhow no one questioned them, and they took possession. Their furniture consisted of a couple of grass mats on which they slept, a fragment of looking-glass, and a bowl or two. In this pleasant land that is enough to start housekeeping on.

'They say that happy people have no history, and certainly a happy love had none. They did nothing all day long and yet the days seemed all too short. The girl had a native name, but Red called her Sally. He picked up the easy language very quickly, and he used to lie on the mat for hours while she chattered gaily to him. He

65) fall in with: 우연히 마주치다.

was a silent fellow, and perhaps his mind was lethargic. He smoked incessantly the cigarettes which she made him out of the native tobacco and pandanus leaf, and he watched her while with deft fingers she made grass mats. Often natives would come in and tell long stories of the old days when the island was disturbed by tribal wars. Sometimes he would go fishing on the reef, and bring home a basket full of coloured fish. Sometimes at night he would go out with a lantern to catch lobster. There were plantains round the hut and Sally would roast them for their frugal meal. She knew how to make delicious messes from coconuts, and the breadfruit tree by the side of the creek gave them its fruit. On feast-days they killed a little pig and cooked it on hot stones. They bathed together in the creek; and in the evening they went down to the lagoon and paddled about in a dug-out, with its great outrigger. The sea was deep blue, wine-coloured at sundown, like the sea of Homeric Greece; but in the lagoon the colour had an infinite variety, aquamarine[66] and amethyst and emerald; and the setting sun turned it for a short moment to liquid gold. Then there was the colour of the coral, brown, white, pink, red, purple; and the shapes it took were marvellous. It was like a magic garden, and the hurrying fish were like butterflies. It strangely lacked reality. Among the coral were pools with a floor of white sand and here, where the water was dazzling clear, it was very good to bathe. Then, cool and happy, they wandered back in the gloaming[67] over the soft grass road to the creek, walking hand in hand, and now the mynah[68] birds filled the coconut trees with their clamour. And then the night, with that great sky shining with gold, that seemed to stretch more widely than the skies of Europe, and the soft airs that blew gently through the open hut, the long night again was all too short. She was sixteen and he was barely twenty. The dawn crept in among the wooden pillars of the hut and

---

66) aqumarine: 청록색.
67) in the gloaming: 황혼, 해질 무렵.
68) mynah: 구관조.

looked at those lovely children sleeping in one another's arms. The sun hid behind the great tattered leaves of the plantains so that it might not disturb them, and then, with playful malice, shot a golden ray, like the outstretched paw of a Persian cat, on their faces. They opened their sleepy eyes and they smiled to welcome another day. The weeks lengthened into months, and a year passed. They seemed to love one another as—I hesitate to say passionately, for passion has in it always a shade of sadness, a touch of bitterness or anguish, but as wholeheartedly, as simply and naturally as on that first day on which, meeting, they had recognized that a god was in them.

'If you had asked them I have no doubt that they would have thought it impossible to suppose their love could ever cease. Do we not know that the essential element of love is a belief in its own eternity? And yet perhaps in Red there was already a very little seed, unknown to himself and unsuspected by the girl, which would in time have grown to weariness.[69] For one day one of the natives for the cove told them that some way down the coast at the anchorage was a British whaling-ship.

"Gee," he said, "I wonder if I could make a trade of some nuts and plantains for a pound or two of tobacco."

'The pandanus cigarettes that Sally made him with untiring hands were strong and pleasant enough to smoke, but they left him unsatisfied; and he yearned on a sudden for real tobacco, hard, rank, and pungent. He had not smoked a pipe for many months. His mouth watered at the thought of it. One would have thought some premonition of harm would have made Sally seek to dissuade him, but love possessed her so completely that it never occurred to her any power on earth could take him from her. They went up into the hills together and gathered a great basket of wild oranges, green, but sweet and juicy; and they picked plantains from around the hut, and coconuts from their trees, and breadfruit and mangoes

---

69) weariness: 권태. 피로.

and they carried them down to the cove. They loaded the unstable canoe with them, and Red and the native boy who had brought them the news of the ship paddled along outside the reef.

'It was the last time she ever saw him.'

'Next day the boy came back alone. He was all in tears. This is the story he told. When after their long paddle they reached the ship and Red hailed it, a white man looked over the side and told them to come on board. They took the fruit they had brought with them and Red piled it up on the deck. The white man and he began to talk, and they seemed to come to some agreement. One of them went below and brought up tobacco. Red took some at once and lit a pipe. The boy imitated the zest with which he blew a great cloud of smoke from his mouth. Then they said something to him and he went into the cabin. Through the open door the boy, watching curiously, saw a bottle brought out and glasses. Red drank and smoked. They seemed to ask him something, for he shook his head and laughed. The man, the first man who had spoken to them, laughed too, and he filled Red's glass once more. They went on talking and drinking, and presently, growing tired of watching a sight that meant nothing to him, the boy curled himself up on the deck and slept. He was awakened by a kick; and jumping to his feet, he saw that the ship was slowly sailing out of the lagoon. He caught sight of Red seated at the table, with his head resting heavily on his arms, fast asleep. He made a movement towards him, intending to wake him, but a rough hand seized his arm, and a man, with a scowl and words which he did not understand, pointed to the side. He shouted to Red, but in a moment he was seized and flung overboard. Helpless, he swam round to his canoe, which was drifting a little way off, and pushed it on to the reef. He climbed in and, sobbing all the way, paddled back to shore.

'What had happened was obvious enough. The whaler, by desertion or sickness, was short of hands, and the captain when Red came aboard had asked him to sign on; on his refusal he had made him drunk and kidnapped him.

'Sally was beside herself with grief. For three days she screamed and cried. The natives did what they could to comfort her, but she would not be comforted. She would not eat. And then, exhausted, she sank into a sullen apathy. She spent long days at the cove, watching the lagoon, in the vain hope that Red somehow or other would manage to escape. She sat on the white sand, hour after hour, with the tears running down her cheeks, and at night dragged herself wearily back across the creek to the little hut where she had been happy. The people with whom she had lived before Red came to the island wished her to return to them, but she would not; she was convinced that Red would come back, and she wanted him to find her where he had left her. Four months later she was delivered of a still-born child, and the old woman who had come to help her through her confinement[70] remained with her in the hut. All joy was taken from her life. If her anguish with time became less intolerable it was replaced by a settled melancholy.[71] You would not have thought that among these people, whose emotions, though so violent, are very transient, a woman could be found capable of so enduring a passion. She never lost the profound conviction that sooner or later Red would come back. She watched for him, and every time someone crossed this slender little bridge of coconut trees she looked. It might at last be he.'

Neilson stopped talking and gave a faint sigh.

'And what happened to her in the end?' asked the skipper. Neilson smiled bitterly.

'Oh, three years afterwards she took up with[72] another white man.'

The skipper gave a fat, cynical chuckle.

'That's generally what happens to them,' he said.

---

70) through her confinement: 해산 기간 동안.

71) settled melancholy: 만성 우울증.

72) take up with: 사귀다. 친하게 되다.

The Swede shot him a look of hatred. He did not know why that gross, obese man excited in him so violent a repulsion. But his thoughts wandered and he found his mind filled with memories of the past. He went back five-and-twenty years. It was when he first came to the island, weary of Apia, with its heavy drinking, its gambling and coarse sensuality, a sick man, trying to resign himself to the loss of the career which had fired his imagination with ambitious thought. He set behind him resolutely all his hopes of making a great name for himself and strove to content himself with the few poor months of careful life which was all that he could count on. He was boarding with a half-caste trader who had a store a couple of miles along the coast at the edge of a native village; and one day, wandering aimlessly along the grassy paths of the coconut groves, he had come upon the hut in which Sally lived. The beauty of the spot had filled him with a rapture so great that it was almost painful, and then he had seen Sally. She was the loveliest creature he had ever seen, and the sadness in those dark, magnificent eyes of hers affected him strangely. The Kanakas were a handsome race, and beauty was not rare among them, but it was the beauty of shapely animals. It was empty. But those tragic eyes were dark with mystery, and you felt in them the bitter complexity of the groping, human soul. The trader told him the story and it moved him.

'Do you think he'll ever come back?' asked Neilson.

'No fear.[73] Why, it'll be a couple of years before the ship is paid off,[74] and by then he'll have forgotten all about her. I bet he was pretty mad when he woke up and found he'd been shanghaied,[75] and I shouldn't wonder but he wanted to fight somebody. But he'd got to grin and bear it, and I guess in a month he was thinking it the best thing that had ever happened to him that he got away from the island.'

---

73) fear: hope.
74) pay off: 계약이 만료되다.
75) shanghaied: 유괴되다, 납치되다.

But Neilson could not get the story out of his head. Perhaps because he was sick and weakly, the radiant health of Red appealed to his imagination. Himself an ugly man, insignificant of appearance, he prized very highly comeliness in others. He had never been passionately in love, and certainly he had never been passionately loved. The mutual attraction of those two young things gave him a singular delight. It had the ineffable beauty[76] of the Absolute. He went again to the little hut by the creek. He had a gift for languages and an energetic mind, accustomed to work, and he had already given much time to the study of the local tongue. Old habit was strong in him and he was gathering together material for a paper on the Samoan speech. The old crone who shared the hut with Sally invited him to come in and sit down. She gave him kava[77] to drink and cigarettes to smoke. She was glad to have someone to chat with and while she talked he looked at Sally. She reminded him of the Psyche in the museum at Naples. Her features had the same clear purity of line, and though she had borne a child she had still a virginal aspect.

It was not till he had seen her two or three times that he induced her to speak. Then it was only to ask him if he had seen in Apia a man called Red. Two years had passed since his disappearance, but it was plain that she still thought of him incessantly.[78]

It did not take Neilson long to discover that he was in love with her. It was only by an effort of will[79] now that he prevented himself from going every day to the creek, and when he was not with Sally his thoughts were.[80] At first, looking upon himself as a dying man, he asked only to look at her, and occasionally hear her speak, and his love gave him a wonderful happiness. He exulted in its purity.[81]

---

76) ineffable: 말로 표현할 수 없는.
77) kava: 술의 종류.
78) incessantly: 여전히, 끊임없이.
79) effort of will: 의지적 노력.
80) his thoughts were: 그의 마음은 샐리에게 가 있었다.(his thoughts were with Sally.)

He wanted nothing from her but the opportunity to weave around her graceful person a web of beautiful fancies. But the open air, the equable temperature,[82] the rest,[83] the simple fare,[84] began to have an unexpected effect on his health. His temperature did not soar at night to such alarming heights, he coughed less and began to put on weight; six months passed without his having a haemorrhage;[85] and on a sudden he saw the possibility that he might live. He had studied his disease carefully, and the hope dawned upon[86] him that with great care he might arrest its course.[87] It exhilarated him to look forward once more to the future. He made plans. It was evident that any active life was out of the question,[88] but he could live on the islands, and the small income he had, insufficient elsewhere, would be ample to keep him. He could grow coconuts; that would give him an occupation; and he would send for his books and a piano; but his quick mind saw that in all this he was merely trying to conceal from himself the desire which obsessed him.

He wanted Sally. He loved not only her beauty, but that dim soul which he divined behind her suffering eyes. He would intoxicate[89] her with his passion. In the end he would make her forget. And in an ecstasy of surrender he fancied himself giving her too the happiness which he had thought never to know[90] again, but had now so miraculously achieved.

He asked her to live with him. She refused. He had expected that and did not let it depress him, for he was sure that sooner or later she would yield. His love was irresistible.[91] He told the old

---

81) exulted in its purity: 사랑의 순수성을 무척 기뻐하였다.
82) equable temperature: 한결같은 기온.
83) rest: 휴식, 쉼.
84) fare: food.
85) haemorrhage: 출혈.
86) dawn upon: 떠오르다, 어렴풋이 생각이 나다.
87) arrest its course: 병의 진행을 막다. 멈추게 하다.
88) out of the question: 불가능한(impossible).
89) intoxicate: 취하게 하다.
90) know: experience.

woman of his wishes, and found somewhat to his surprise that she and the neighbours, long aware of them, were strongly urging Sally to accept his offer. After all, every native was glad to keep house[92] for a white man, and Neilson according to the standards of the island was a rich one. The trader with whom he boarded went to her and told her not to be fool; such an opportunity would not come again, and after so long she could not still believe that Red would ever return. The girl's resistance only increased Neilson's desire, and what had been a very pure love now became an agonizing passion. He was determined that nothing should stand in his way.[93] He gave Sally no peace. At last, worn out[94] by his persistence and the persuasions, by turns pleading and angry, of everyone around her, she consented. But the day after, when exultant he went to see her he found that in the night she had burnt down the hut in which she and Red had lived together. The old crone ran towards him full of angry abuse of Sally, but he waved her aside; it did not matter; they would build a bungalow on the place where the hut had stood. A European house would really be more convenient if he wanted to bring out a piano and a vast number of books.

And so the little wooden house was built in which he had now lived for many years, and Sally became his wife. But after the first few weeks of rapture,[95] during which he was satisfied with what she gave him, he had known little happiness. She had yielded to him, through weariness,[96] but she had only yielded what she set no store on.[97] The soul which he had dimly glimpsed escaped him. He knew that she cared nothing for him. She still loved Red, and

---

91) irresistible: 저항할 수 없는, 막무가내의.
92) keep house: 살림을 차리다.
93) stand in one's way: 방해가 되다.
94) worn out: 지쳐서.
95) rapture: 큰 기쁨.
96) through weariness: 치쳐서.
97) she had only yielded what she set no store on: 그녀가 중요하다고 생각하지 않은 것만 양보했다.

all the time she was waiting for his return. At a sign from him, Neilson knew that, notwithstanding his love, his tenderness, his sympathy, his generosity, she would leave him without a moment's hesitation. She would never give a thought to his distress. Anguish seized him and he battered at that impenetrable self of hers which sullenly resisted him. His love became bitter. He tried to melt her heart with kindness, but it remained as hard as before; he feigned[98] indifference, but she did not notice it. Sometimes he lost his temper and abused[99] her, and then she wept silently. Sometimes he thought she was nothing but a fraud, and that soul simply an invention of his own, and that he could not get into the sanctuary[100] of her heart because there was no sanctuary there. His love became a prison from which he longed to escape, but he had not the strength merely to open the door—that was all it needed[101]—and walk out into the open air. It was torture and at last he became numb and hopeless. In the end the fire burnt itself out and, when he saw her eyes rest for an instant on the slender bridge, it was no longer rage that filled his heart but impatience. For many years now they had lived together bound by the ties of habit and convenience, and it was with a smile that he looked back on his old passion. She was an old woman, for the women on the islands age[102] quickly, and if he had no love for her any more he had tolerance. She left him alone. He was contented with his piano and his books.

His thoughts led him to a desire for words.

'When I look back now and reflect on that brief passionate love of Red and Sally, I think that perhaps they should thank the ruthless fate[103] that separated them when their love seemed still to be at its height. They suffered, but they suffered in beauty. They were

98) feign: ~인체하다.
99) abuse: 학대하다. 욕보이다.
100) sanctuary: 신성한 장소, 보호구역. 성역.
101) that was all it needed: 열기만 하면 되는데.
102) age: (동사) 나이가 들다. 늙어가다.
103) ruthless fate: 무자비한 운명.

spared[104] the real tragedy of love.'

'I don't know exactly as I get you,' said the skipper.

'The tragedy of love is not death or separation. How long do you think it would have been before one or other of them ceased to care? Oh, it is dreadfully bitter to look at a woman whom you have loved with all your heart and soul, so that you felt you could not bear to let her out of your sight, and realize that you would not mind if you never saw her again. The tragedy of love is indifference.'

But while he was speaking a very extraordinary thing happened. Though he had been addressing the skipper he had not been talking to him, he had been putting his thoughts into words for himself, and with his eyes fixed on the man in front of him he had not seen him. But now an image presented itself to them,[105] an image not of the man he was, but of another man. It was as though he were looking into one of those distorting mirrors[106] that make you extraordinarily squat or outrageously elongate,[107] but here exactly the opposite took place, and in the obese, ugly old man he caught the shadowy glimpse of a stripling.[108] He gave him now a quick, searching scrutiny. Why had a haphazard stroll[109] brought him just to this place? A sudden tremor of his heart made him slightly breathless. An absurd suspicion[110] seized him. What had occurred to him was impossible, and yet it might be a fact.

'What is your name?' he asked a abruptly.

The skipper's face puckered[111] and he gave a cunning chuckle. He looked then malicious and horribly vulgar.

'It's such a damned long time since I heard it that I almost forget

---

104) were spared: 겪지 않았다. 면제 받았다.
105) them: his eyes.
106) distorting mirror: 곡 유리거울.
107) squat or outrageously elongate: 땅딸막하거나, 엄청나게 길어진.
108) stripling: 풋내기, 애송이, 젊은이.
109) a haphazard stroll: 우연한 산책.
110) an absurd suspicion: 터무니없는 의심.
111) pucker: 주름 잡히다.

it myself.[112] But for thirty years now in the islands they've always called me Red.'

His huge form shook as he gave a low, almost silent laugh. It was obscene.[113] Neilson shuddered. Red was hugely amused, and from his bloodshot eyes tears ran down his cheeks.

Neilson gave a gasp, for at that moment a woman came in. She was a native, a woman if somewhat commanding presence, stout without being corpulent, dark, for the natives grow darker with age, with very grey hair. She wore a black Mother Hubbard,[114] and its thinness showed her heavy breasts. The moment had come.

She made an observation to Neilson about some household matter and he answered. He wondered if his voice sounded as unnatural to her as it did to himself. She gave the man who was sitting in the chair by the window an indifferent glance, and went out of the room. The moment had come and gone.

Neilson for a moment could not speak. He was strangely shaken. Then he said;

'I'd be very glad if you'd stay and have a bit of dinner with me. Pot luck.'

'I don't think I will.' said Red. 'I must go after this fellow Gray. I'll give him his stuff and then I'll get away. I want to be back in Apia tomorrow.'

'I'll send a boy along with you to show you the way.'

'That'll be fine.'

Red heaved himself out of his chair,[115] while the Swede called one of the boys who worked on the plantation. He told him where the skipper wanted to go, and the boy stepped along the bridge. Red prepared to follow him.

'Don't fall in,'[116] said Neilson.

---

112) such ~ that 구문: 들어본지 너무 오래 되어서 그 이름을 거의 잊어버렸다.
113) obscene: 못생긴, 외설스러운.
114) Mother Hubbard: 원주민 여성이 입는 헐렁하고 느슨한 옷.
115) heaved himself out of his chair: 의자에서 일어서다.
116) don't fall in: 다리 아래로 떨어지지 말아라.

'Not on your life.'

Neilson watched him make his way across and when he had disappeared among the coconuts he looked still. Then he sank heavily in his chair. Was that the man who had prevented him from being happy? Was that the man whom Sally had loved all these years and for whom she had waited so desperately? It was grotesque.[117] A sudden fury seized him so that he had an instinct to spring up and smash everything around him. He had been cheated. They had seen each other at last and had not known it. He began to laugh, mirthlessly, and his laughter grew till it became hysterical. The Gods had played him a cruel trick. And he was old now.

At last Sally came in to tell him dinner was ready. He sat down in front of her and tried to eat. He wondered what she would say if he told her now that the fat old man sitting in the chair was the lover whom she remembered still with the passionate abandonment of her youth. Years ago, when he hated her because she made him so unhappy, he would have been glad to tell her. He wanted to hurt her then as she hurt him, because his hatred was only love. But now he did not care. He shrugged his shoulders listlessly.[118]

'What did that man want?' she asked presently.

He did not answer at once. She was too old, a fat old native woman. He wondered why he had ever loved her so madly. He had laid at her feet all the treasures of his soul, and she had cared nothing for them. Waste, what waste! And now, when he looked at her, he felt only contempt. His patience was at last exhausted. He answered her question.

'He's the captain of a schooner. He's come from Apia.'

'Yes.'

'He brought me news from home. My eldest brother is very ill and I must go back.'

---

117) grotesque: 우스꽝스러운.

118) shrugged his shoulders listlessly: 무관심한 듯 어깨를 으쓱했다.

'Will you be gone long?'

He shrugged his shoulders.

Shooting an Elephant

by George Orwell

Introduction to the Author

George Orwell (1903-1950)

English novelist, essayist, and critic famous for his novels *Animal Farm* (1945) and *Nineteen Eighty Four*(1949). Orwell attended Eton. In 1922, he went to Burma (now Myanmar) to serve in the Indian Imperial Police. Later he was to recount his experiences and his reactions to imperial rule in two brilliant autobiographical sketches, “Shooting an Elephant” and “A Hanging,” classics of expository prose. 인도의 뱅갈 지방에서 영국식민지 관리의 아들로 태어난 오웰이 영국의 식민 통치를 받던 미얀마에서 경찰관으로 근무할 때의 경험을 이 글에 적었다.

Shooting an Elephant

In Moulmein, in Lower Burma, I was hated by large numbers of people—the only time in my life that I have been important enough for this to happen to me. I was subdivisional police[1)] officer of the town, and in an aimless, petty kind of way anti-European feeling was very bitter. No one had the guts[2)] to raise a riot, but if a European woman went through the bazaars alone somebody would probably spit betel[3)] juice over her dress. As a police officer I was an obvious target and was baited[4)] whenever it seemed safe to do so. When a nimble Burman tripped me up[5)] on the football field and the referee (another Burman) looked the other way, the crowd yelled with hideous laughter. This happened more than once. In the end the sneering yellow faces of young men that met me everywhere, the insults hooted[6)] after me when I was at a safe distance, got badly on my nerves. The young Buddhist priests were the worst of all. There were several thousands of them in the town and none of them seemed to have anything to do except stand on street corners and jeer at Europeans.

All this was perplexing and upsetting. For at that time I had already made up my mind that imperialism was an evil thing and the sooner I chucked up[7)] my job and got out of it the better. Theoretically—and secretly, of course—I was all for the Burmese and all against their oppressors, the British. As for the job I was doing, I hated it more bitterly than I can perhaps make clear. In a job

---

1) subdivisional police: 파출소.
2) guts: 용기. 배짱.
3) betel: 인도 후추.
4) baited: 미끼로 유혹을 받다. 유인 당하다. 조롱당하다. 괴롭힘을 당하다.
5) trip me up: 나를 걸려서 넘어지게 하다.
6) hoot: 조롱하다. 야유하다.
7) chuck up: 그만 두다. 집어 치우다. give up.

like that you see the dirty work of Empire at close quarters.[8] The wretched prisoners huddling in the stinking cages of the lock-ups,[9] the grey, cowed faces of the long-term convicts,[10] the scarred buttocks of the men who had been flogged with bamboos—all these oppressed me with an intolerable sense of guilt. But I could get nothing into perspective. I was young and ill-educated and I had had to think out my problems in the utter silence that is imposed on every Englishman in the East. I did not even know that the British Empire is dying, still less did I know that it is a great deal better than the younger empires that are going to supplant[11] it. All I knew was that I was stuck between my hatred of the empire I served and my rage against the evil-spirited little beasts who tried to make my job impossible. With one part of my mind I thought of the British Raj[12] as an unbreakable tyranny, as something clamped down, in saecula saeculorum,[13] upon the will of prostrate peoples; with another part I thought that the greatest joy in the world would be to drive a bayonet[14] into a Buddhist priest's guts. Feelings like these are the normal by-products of imperialism; ask any Anglo-Indian official, if you can catch him off duty.

One day something happened which in a roundabout way was enlightening.[15] It was a tiny incident in itself, but it gave me a better glimpse than I had had before of the real nature of imperialism—the real motives for which despotic governments act. Early one morning the sub-inspector at a police station the other end of the town rang me up on the phone and said that an elephant was ravaging the bazaar. Would I please come and do something about it? I did not

8) at close quarters: 아주 가까이서.
9) lock-ups: 구치소. 교도소.
10) convict: 기결 죄수.
11) supplant: 찬탈하다. 대신하다.
12) Raj: 라쥐. 지배. 통치.
13) saecula saeculorum: generation after generation. for ages and ages. 수 세대 동안.
14) bayonet: 대검. 총검.
15) enlightening: 시사성 있는. 깨닫게 해주는.

know what I could do, but I wanted to see what was happening and I got on to a pony and started out. I took my rifle, an old .44 Winchester and much too small to kill an elephant, but I thought the noise might be useful *in terrorem.*[16] Various Burmans stopped me on the way and told me about the elephant's doings. It was not, of course, a wild elephant, but a tame one which had gone 'must'.[17] It had been chained up, as tame elephants always are when their attack of 'must' is due, but on the previous night it had broken its chain and escaped. Its mahout,[18] the only person who could manage it when it was in that state, had set out in pursuit, but had taken the wrong direction and was now twelve hours' journey away, and in the morning the elephant had suddenly reappeared in the town. The Burmese population had no weapons and were quite helpless against it. It had already destroyed somebody's bamboo hut, killed a cow and raided some fruit stalls[19] and devoured the stock; also it had met the municipal rubbish van and, when the driver jumped out and took to his heels, had turned the van over and inflicted violences upon[20] it.

The Burmese sub-inspector and some Indian constables[21] were waiting for me in the quarter where the elephant had been seen. It was a very poor quarter, a labyrinth of squalid[22] bamboo huts, thatched with palm leaf, winding all over a steep hillside. I remember that it was a cloudy, stuffy morning at the beginning of the rains. We began questioning the people as to where the elephant had gone and, as usual, failed to get any definite information. That is invariably the case in the East; a story always sounds clear enough at a distance, but the nearer you get to the scene of events the vaguer it

---

16) in terrorem: (라틴어) as a warning in order to terrify others. 겁내게 하기에.
17) must: 발정. go must: 발정하여 난폭해지다.
18) mahout: elephant driver. 코끼리 부리는 사람.
19) stall: 가게. 매점.
20) inflict violences upon: 해치다. 손상시키다.
21) constable: 순경.
22) squalid: 누추한.

becomes. Some of the people said that the elephant had gone in one direction, some said that he had gone in another, some professed not even to have heard of any elephant. I had almost made up my mind that the whole story was a pack of lies, when we heard yells a little distance away. There was a loud, scandalized[23] cry of 'Go away, child! Go away this instant!' and an old woman with a switch[24] in her hand came round the corner of a hut, violently shooing[25] away a crowd of naked children. Some more women followed, clicking their tongues and exclaiming; evidently there was something that the children ought not to have seen. I rounded the hut and saw a man's dead body sprawling in the mud. He was an Indian, a black Dravidian[26] coolie,[27] almost naked, and he could not have been dead many minutes. The people said that the elephant had come suddenly upon him round the corner of the hut, caught him with its trunk, put its foot on his back and ground him into the earth. This was the rainy season and the ground was soft, and his face had scored[28] a trench a foot deep and a couple of yards long. He was lying on his belly with arms crucified and head sharply twisted to one side. His face was coated with mud, the eyes wide open, the teeth bared and grinning with an expression of unendurable agony. (Never tell me, by the way, that the dead look peaceful. Most of the corpses I have seen looked devilish.) The friction of the great beast's foot had stripped the skin from his back as neatly as one skins a rabbit. As soon as I saw the dead man I sent an orderly[29] to a friend's house nearby to borrow an elephant rifle. I had already sent back the pony, not wanting it to go mad with fright and throw me if it smelt the elephant.

---

23) scandalized: shocked. 아연실색한.
24) switch: 회초리.
25) shoo: (쉬잇 소리로) 쫓아버리다. 내쫓다.
26) Dravidian: ancient Indian race.
27) coolie: 품팔이 일군.
28) score: 파다. 새기다.
29) orderly: 연락병. 전령.

The orderly came back in a few minutes with a rifle and five cartridges, and meanwhile some Burmans had arrived and told us that the elephant was in the paddy fields[30] below, only a few hundred yards away. As I started forward practically the whole population of the quarter flocked out of the houses and followed me. They had seen the rifle and were all shouting excitedly that I was going to shoot the elephant. They had not shown much interest in the elephant when he was merely ravaging their homes, but it was different now that he was going to be shot. It was a bit of fun to them, as it would be to an English crowd; besides they wanted the meat. It made me vaguely uneasy. I had no intention of shooting the elephant—I had merely sent for the rifle to defend myself if necessary—and it is always unnerving to have a crowd following you. I marched down the hill, looking and feeling a fool, with the rifle over my shoulder and an ever-growing army of people jostling at my heels. At the bottom, when you got away from the huts, there was a metalled[31] road and beyond that a miry waste of paddy fields a thousand yards across, not yet ploughed but soggy from the first rains and dotted with coarse grass. The elephant was standing eight yards from the road, his left side towards us. He took not the slightest notice of the crowd's approach. He was tearing up bunches of grass, beating them against his knees to clean them and stuffing them into his mouth.

I had halted on the road. As soon as I saw the elephant I knew with perfect certainty that I ought not to shoot him. It is a serious matter to shoot a working elephant—it is comparable to destroying a huge and costly piece of machinery—and obviously one ought not to do it if it can possibly be avoided. And at that distance, peacefully eating, the elephant looked no more dangerous than a cow. I thought then and I think now that his attack of 'must' was already passing off; in which case he would merely wander harmlessly about

---

30) paddy fields: 논. rice field.
31) metalled: (도로가) 포장된.

until the mahout came back and caught him. Moreover, I did not in the least want to shoot him. I decided that I would watch him for a little while to make sure that he did not turn savage again, and then go home.

But at that moment I glanced round at the crowd that had followed me. It was an immense crowd, two thousand at the least and growing every minute. It blocked the road for a long distance on either side. I looked at the sea of yellow faces above the garish[32] clothes—faces all happy and excited over this bit of fun, all certain that the elephant was going to be shot. They were watching me as they would watch a conjurer about to perform a trick. They did not like me, but with the magical rifle in my hands I was momentarily worth watching. And suddenly I realized that I should have to shoot the elephant after all. The people expected it of me and I had got to do it; I could feel their two thousand wills pressing me forward, irresistibly. And it was at this moment, as I stood there with the rifle in my hands, that I first grasped the hollowness, the futility of the white man's dominion in the East. Here was I, the white man with his gun, standing in front of the unarmed native crowd—seemingly the leading actor of the piece; but in reality I was only an absurd puppet pushed to and fro by the will of those yellow faces behind. I perceived in this moment that when the white man turns tyrant it is his own freedom that he destroys. He becomes a sort of hollow, posing dummy,[33] the conventionalized figure of a sahib.[34] For it is the condition of his rule that he shall spend his life in trying to impress the 'natives', and so in every crisis he has got to do what the 'natives' expect of him. He wears a mask, and his face grows to fit it. I had got to shoot the elephant. I had committed myself to doing it when I sent for the rifle. A sahib has got to act like a sahib; he has got to appear resolute, to know his own mind

32) garish: 반짝거리는.
33) dummy: 바보. 얼간이.
34) sahib: 나으리. 각하. 선생. native expression for European gentleman.

and do definite things. To come all that way, rifle in hand, with two thousand people marching at my heels, and then to trail feebly away, having done nothing—no, that was impossible. The crowd would laugh at me. And my whole life, every white man's life in the East, was one long struggle not to be laughed at.

But I did not want to shoot the elephant. I watched him beating his bunch of grass against his knees, with that preoccupied grand-motherly air that elephants have. It seemed to me that it would be murder to shoot him. At that age I was not squeamish[35] about killing animals, but I had never shot an elephant and never wanted to. (Somehow it always seems worse to kill a large animal.) Besides, there was the beast's owner to be considered. Alive, the elephant was worth at least a hundred pounds; dead, he would only be worth the value of his tusks, five pounds, possibly. But I had got to act quickly. I turned to some experienced-looking Burmans who had been there when we arrived, and asked them how the elephant had been behaving. They all said the same thing: he took no notice of you if you left him alone, but he might charge if you went too close to him.

It was perfectly clear to me what I ought to do. I ought to walk up to within, say, twenty-five yards of the elephant and test his behavior. If he charged, I could shoot; if he took no notice of me, it would be safe to leave him until the mahout came back. But also I knew that I was going to do no such thing. I was a poor shot with a rifle and the ground was soft mud into which one would sink at every step. If the elephant charged and I missed him, I should have about as much chance as a toad under a steam-roller.[36] But even then I was not thinking particularly of my own skin, only of the watchful yellow faces behind. For at that moment, with the crowd watching me, I was not afraid in the ordinary sense, as I would have been if I had been alone. A white man mustn't be frightened

---

35) squeamish: 까다로운, 소심한.

36) toad under a steam-roller: 증기 롤러 밑에 깔린 두꺼비

in front of 'natives'; and so, in general, he isn't frightened. The sole thought in my mind was that if anything went wrong those two thousand Burmans would see me pursued, caught, trampled on and reduced to a grinning corpse like that Indian up the hill. And if that happened it was quite probable that some of them would laugh. That would never do.[37)] There was only one alternative. I shoved the cartridges into the magazine and lay down on the road to get a better aim.

The crowd grew very still, and a deep, low, happy sigh, as of people who see the theatre curtain go up at last, breathed from innumerable throats. They were going to have their bit of fun after all. The rifle was a beautiful German thing with cross-hair sights.[38)] I did not then know that in shooting an elephant one would shoot to cut an imaginary bar running from ear-hole to ear-hole. I ought, therefore, as the elephant was sideways on, to have aimed straight at his ear-hole, actually I aimed several inches in front of this, thinking the brain would be further forward.

When I pulled the trigger I did not hear the bang or feel the kick[39)]—one never does when a shot goes home[40)]—but I heard the devilish roar of glee that went up from the crowd. In that instant, in too short a time, one would have thought, even for the bullet to get there, a mysterious, terrible change had come over the elephant. He neither stirred nor fell, but every line of his body had altered. He looked suddenly stricken, shrunken, immensely old, as though the frightful impact of the bullet had paralysed him without knocking him down. At last, after what seemed a long time—it might have been five seconds, I dare say—he sagged[41)] flabbily to his knees. His mouth slobbered.[42)] An enormous senility[43)] seemed to have settled

---

37) That would never do: 그것은 절대 안 될 일이다.
38) cross-hair sights: 십자선이 그려진 조준경.
39) kick: 발사 순간의 총의 반동.
40) go home: 적중하다.
41) sag: 꺼지다. 가라앉다.
42) slobber: 침을 흘리다. 우는 소리를 내다.

upon him. One could have imagined him thousands of years old. I fired again into the same spot. At the second shot he did not collapse but climbed with desperate slowness to his feet and stood weakly upright, with legs sagging and head drooping. I fired a third time. That was the shot that did for[44] him. You could see the agony of it jolt his whole body and knock the last remnant of strength from his legs. But in falling he seemed for a moment to rise, for as his hind legs collapsed beneath him he seemed to tower upward like a huge rock toppling, his trunk reaching skyward like a tree. He trumpeted, for the first and only time. And then down he came, his belly towards me, with a crash that seemed to shake the ground even where I lay.

I got up. The Burmans were already racing past me across the mud. It was obvious that the elephant would never rise again, but he was not dead. He was breathing very rhythmically with long rattling gasps,[45] his great mound of a side painfully rising and falling. His mouth was wide open—I could see far down into caverns of pale pink throat. I waited a long time for him to die, but his breathing did not weaken. Finally I fired my two remaining shots into the spot where I thought his heart must be. The thick blood welled out of him like red velvet, but still he did not die. His body did not even jerk when the shots hit him, the tortured breathing continued without a pause. He was dying, very slowly and in great agony, but in some world remote from me where not even a bullet could damage him further. I felt that I had got to put an end to that dreadful noise. It seemed dreadful to see the great beast lying there, powerless to move and yet powerless to die, and not even to be able to finish him. I sent back for my small rifle and poured shot after shot into his heart and down his throat. They seemed to make no impression. The tortured gasps continued as steadily as the ticking of a clock.

---

43) senility: 노쇠. 노령.
44) do for: finish off. kill.
45) gasp: 헐떡임. 숨참.

In the end I could not stand it any longer and went away. I heard later that it took him half an hour to die. Burmans were bringing dahs[46] and baskets even before I left, and I was told they had stripped his body almost to the bones by the afternoon.

Afterwards, of course, there were endless discussions about the shooting of the elephant. The owner was furious, but he was only an Indian and could do nothing. Besides, legally I had done the right thing, for a mad elephant has to be killed, like a mad dog, if its owner fails to control it. Among the Europeans opinion was divided. The older men said I was right, the younger men said it was a damn shame to shoot an elephant for killing a coolie, because an elephant was worth more than any damn Coringhee coolie. And afterwards I was very glad that the coolie had been killed; it put me legally in the right and it gave me a sufficient pretext[47] for shooting the elephant. I often wondered whether any of the others grasped that I had done it solely to avoid looking a fool.

---

46) dahs: (미얀마 사람들이 나무를 자르는) 큰 칼.
47) pretext: 구실. 변명. 핑계.

The Horse Dealer's Daughter

by D. H Lawrence

Introduction to the Author

D. H. Lawrence (1885-1930)

Born at Eastwood, Nottinghamshire, England. Short-story writer, poet, and one of the most important and controversial 20th century English novelists. His works are notable for their passionate intensity and for a sensuality that centers on, but is not limited to, the erotic. His major novels are *Sons and Lovers*(1913), *The Rainbow*(1915), *Kangaroo*(1923), *Women in Love*(1923), and *Lady Chatterley's Lover*(1928).

The Horse Dealer's Daughter

'Well, Mabel, and what are you going to do with yourself?' asked Joe, with foolish flippancy.[1] He felt quite safe himself. Without listening for an answer, he turned aside, worked a grain of tobacco to the tip of his tongue, and spat it out. He did not care about anything, since he felt safe himself.[2]

The three brothers and the sister sat round the desolate breakfast table, attempting some sort of desultory consultation.[3] The morning's post had given the final tap to the family fortunes, and all was over. The dreary dining-room itself, with its heavy mahogany furniture, looked as if it were waiting to be done away with.

But the consultation amounted to nothing.[4] There was a strange air of ineffectuality about the three men, as they sprawled at table, smoking and reflecting vaguely on their own condition. The girl was alone, a rather short, sullen-looking young woman of twenty-seven. She did not share the same life as her brothers. She would have been good-looking, save for the impassive fixity of her face,[5] 'bull-dog', as her brothers called it.

There was a confused tramping of horses' feet outside. The three men all sprawled round in their chairs to watch. Beyond the dark holly bushes that separated the strip of lawn from the high-road, they could see a cavalcade of shire horses[6] swinging out of their own yard, being taken for exercise. This was the last time. These were the last horses that would go through their hands. The young

---

1) flippancy: 경솔. 경박.
2) since he felt safe himself: 자기 자신은 안전하다고 생각하기 때문에. since는 because의 뜻이다.
3) desultory consultation: 두서없이 산만한 협의.
4) amount to nothing: 아무 소용이 없다. 효과가 없다.
5) impassive fixity of her face: 늘 똑같은 굳은 얼굴.
6) shire horse: 영국 중부 지방산의 마차 끄는 말.

men watched with critical, callous look. They were all frightened at the collapse of their lives, and the sense of disaster in which they were involved left them no inner freedom.

Yet they were three fine, well-set fellows enough. Joe, the eldest, was a man of thirty-five, broad and handsome in a hot flushed way. His face was red, he twisted his black moustache over a thick finger, his eyes were shallow and restless. He had a sensual way of uncovering his teeth when he laughed, and his bearing was stupid. Now he watched the horses with a glazed[7)] look of helplessness in his eyes, a certain stupor of downfall.

The great draught-horses[8)] swung past. They were tied head to tail, four of them, and they heaved along to[9)] where a lane branched off from the high-road, planting their great hoofs floutingly in the fine black mud, swinging their great rounded haunches sumptuously, and trotting a few sudden steps as they were led into the lane, round the corner. Every movement showed a massive, slumbrous strength, and a stupidity which held them in subjection. The groom at the head looked back, jerking the leading rope. And the cavalcade moved out of sight up the lane, the tail of the last horse, bobbed up tight and stiff, held out taut from the swinging great haunches as they rocked behind the hedges in a motion-like sleep.

Joe watched with glazed hopeless eyes. The horses were almost like his own body to him. He felt he was done for[10)] now. Luckily he was engaged to a woman as old as himself, and therefore her father, who was steward of a neighbouring estate, would provide him with a job. He would marry and go into harness. His life was over, he would be a subject animal now.

He turned uneasily aside, the retreating steps of the horses echoing in his ears. Then, with foolish restlessness, he reached for the

---

7) glazed: (눈이) 흐리멍덩한. 흐릿한.
8) draught-horse: (=draft-horse). 짐 끄는 말. 마차용 말.
9) heave to: 전진을 멈추다. 멎다.
10) do for: 망하다. 망치다. 끝장이 나다.

scraps of bacon-rind from the plates, and making a faint whistling sound, flung them to the terrier that lay against the fender. He watched the dog swallow them, and waited till the creature looked into his eyes. Then a faint grin came on his face, and in a high, foolish voice he said:

'You won't get much more bacon, shall you, you little bitch?'

The dog faintly and dismally wagged its tail, then lowered its haunches, circled round, and lay down again.

There was another hopeless silence at the table. Joe sprawled uneasily in his seat, not willing to go till the family conclave was dissolved. Fred Henry, the second brother, was erect, clean-limbed, alert. He had watched the passing of the horses with more sang-froid.[11] If he was an animal, like Joe, he was an animal which controls, not one which is controlled. He was master of any horse, and he carried himself with a well-tempered air of mastery. But he was not master of the situation of life. He pushed his coarse brown moustache upwards, off his lip, and glanced irritably at his sister, who sat impassive and inscrutable.

'You'll go and stop with Lucy[12] for a bit, shan't you?' he asked. The girl did not answer.

'I don't see what else you can do,' persisted Fred Henry.

'Go as a skivvy,'[13] Joe interpolated laconically.

The girl did not move a muscle.

'If I was her, I should go in for training for a nurse,' said Malcolm, the youngest of them all. He was the baby of the family, a young man of twenty-two, with a fresh, jaunty *museau.*[14]

But Mabel did not take any notice of him. They had talked at her and round her for so many years, that she hardly heard them at all.

---

11) sang-froid: 태연자약. 침착. 냉정.
12) Lucy: 결혼한 장녀의 이름.
13) skivvy: 하녀. servant girl.
14) jaunty *museau*: 미끈한 콧마루.

The marble clock on the mantel piece softly chimed the half-hour, the dog rose uneasily from the hearth-rug and looked at the party at the breakfast-table. But still they sat on in ineffectual conclave.

'Oh, all right,' said Joe suddenly, apropos of nothing.[15] 'Ill get a move on.'

He pushed back his chair, straddled his knees with a downward jerk, to get them free, in horsey fashion, and went to the fire. Still, he did not go out of the room; he was curious to know what the others would do or say. He began to charge his pipe, looking down at the dog and saying in a high affected voice:

'Going wi' me? Going wi' me are ter? Tha'rt goin' further than that counts on just now, dost hear?'[16]

The dog faintly wagged its tail, the man stuck out his jaw and covered his pipe with his hands, and puffed intently, losing himself in the tobacco, looking down all the while at the dog with an absent brown eye. The dog looked up at him in mournful distrust. Joe stood with his knees stuck out, in real horsey fashion.

'Have you had a letter from Lucy?' Fred Henry asked of his sister.

'Last week,' came the neutral reply.

'And what does she say?'

There was no answer.

'Does she ask you to go and stop there?' persisted Fred Henry.

'She says I can if I like.'

'Well, then, you'd better. Tell her you'll come on Monday.'

This was received in silence.

'That's what you'll do then, is it ?' said Fred Henry, in some exasperation.[17]

But she made no answer. There was a silence of futility and irritation in the room. Malcolm grinned fatuously.[18]

---

15) apropos of nothing: 별안간. 갑자기.
16) 넌 네가 생각하는 것보다 더 멀리 가게 될 거다. 알겠니?
17) exasperation: 분개. 격노. 격분.

'You'll have to make up your mind between now and next Wednesday,' said Joe loudly, 'or else find your lodgings on the kerbstone.'

The face of the young woman darkened, but she sat on immutable.

'Here's Jack Fergusson!' exclaimed Malcolm, who was looking aimlessly out of the window.

'Where?' exclaimed Joe loudly.

'Just gone past.'

'Coming in?'

Malcolm craned his neck to see the gate.

'Yes,' he said.

There was a silence. Mabel sat on like one condemned, at the head of the table. Then a whistle was heard from the kitchen. The dog got up and barked sharply. Joe opened the door and shouted:

'Come on.'

After a moment a young man entered. He was muffled in overcoat and a purple woollen scarf, and his tweed[19] cap, which he did not remove, was pulled down on his head. He was of medium height, his face was rather long and pale, his eyes looked tired.

'Hello, Jack! Well, Jack!' exclaimed Malcolm and Joe. Fred Henry merely said: 'Jack.'

'What's doing?' asked the newcomer, evidently addressing Fred Henry.

'Same. We've got to be out by Wednesday. Got a cold?'

'I have—got it bad, too.'

'Why don't you stop in?'

'Me stop in? When I can't stand on my legs, perhaps I shall have a chance.' The young man spoke huskily. He had a slight Scotch accent.

'It's a knock-out, isn't it,' said Joe, boisterously, 'if a doctor goes round croaking with a cold. Looks bad for the patients, doesn't it?'

The young doctor looked at him slowly.

---

18) fatuously: 멍청하게. 얼빠진듯이.
19) tweed: 트위드 천.

'Anything the matter with you then ?' he asked sarcastically.

'Not as I know of. Damn your eyes, I hope not. Why?'

'I thought you were very concerned about the patients, wondered if you might be one yourself.'

'Damn it, no, I've never been a patient to no flaming doctor, and hope I never shall be,' returned Joe.

At this point Mabel rose from the table, and they all seemed to become aware of her existence. She began putting the dishes together. The young doctor looked at her, but did not address her. He had not greeted her. She went out of the room with the tray, her face impassive and unchanged.

'When are you off then, all of you?' asked the doctor.

'I'm catching the eleven-forty,' replied Malcolm. 'Are you goin' down wi' th' trap, Joe?'

'Yes, I've told you I'm going down wi' th' trap, haven't I?'

'We'd better be getting her in then.[20] So long, Jack, if I don't see you before I go,' said Malcolm, shaking hands.

He went out, followed by Joe, who seemed to have his tail between his legs.[21]

'Well, this is the devil's own,' exclaimed the doctor, when he was left alone with Fred Henry. 'Going before Wednesday, are you?'

'That's the orders,' replied the other.

'Where, to Northampton?'

'That's it.'

'The devil!' exclaimed Fergusson, with quiet chagrin.

And there was silence between the two.

All settled up, are you?' asked Fergusson.

'About.'

There was another pause.

'Well, I shall miss yer, Freddy, boy,' said the young doctor.

'And I shall miss thee, Jack,' returned the other.

---

20) We'd better be getting her in then: 그러면 누이를 태우는 게 낫겠다.
21) tail between his legs: 겁이 나서. 꽁무니를 빼고.

'Miss you like hell,' mused the doctor.

Fred Henry turned aside. There was nothing to say. Mabel came in again, to finish clearing the table.

'What are you going to do, then, Miss Pervin ?' asked Fergusson. 'Going to your sister's, are you?'

Mabel looked at him with her steady, dangerous eyes, that always made him uncomfortable, unsettling his superficial ease.

'No,' she said.

'Well, what in the name of fortune are you going to do? Say what you mean to do,' cried Fred Henry, with futile intensity.

But she only averted her head, and continued her work. She folded the white table-cloth, and put on the chenille cloth.

'The sulkiest bitch that ever trod' muttered her brother.

But she finished her task with perfectly impassive face, the young doctor watching her interestedly[22] all the while. Then she went out.

Fred Henry stared after her, clenching his lips, his blue eyes fixing in sharp antagonism,[23] as he made a grimace of sour exasperation.

'You could bray[24] her into bits, and that's all you'd get out of her,' he said, in a small, narrowed tone.

The doctor smiled faintly.

'What's she going to do, then?' he asked.

'Strike me if I know!' returned the other.

There was a pause. Then the doctor stirred.

'I'll be seeing you to-night, shall I ?' he said to his friend.

'Ay—where's it to be? Are we going over to Jessdale?'

'I don't know. I've got such a cold on me. I'll come round to the "Moon and Stars", anyway.'

'Let Lizzie and May miss their night for once, eh?'

'That's it—if I feel as I do now.'

---

22) interestedly: 흥미롭게.

23) antagonism: 적대감. 적의. 반목.

24) bray: 부수다. 빻다. 찧다. 갈아 바수다.

'All's one—'

The two young men went through the passage and down to the back door together. The house was large, but it was servantless now, and desolate. At the back was a small bricked house-yard and beyond that a big square, gravelled fine and red, and having stables on two sides. Sloping, dank, winter-dark fields stretched away on the open sides.

But the stables were empty. Joseph Pervin, the father of the family, had been a man of no education, who had become a fairly large horse-dealer. The stables had been full of horses, there was a great turmoil and come-and-go of horses and of dealers and grooms. Then the kitchen was full of servants. But of late[25)] things had declined. The old man had married a second time, to retrieve his fortunes. Now he was dead and everything was gone to the dogs,[26)] there was nothing but debt and threatening.

For months, Mabel had been servantless in the big house, keeping the home together in penury[27)] for her ineffectual brothers. She had kept house for ten years. But previously it was with unstinted[28)] means. Then, however brutal and coarse everything was, the sense of money had kept her proud, confident. The men might be foul-mouthed, the women in the kitchen might have bad reputations, her brothers might have illegitimate children. But so long as there was money, the girl felt herself established, and brutally proud, reserved.[29)]

No company came to the house, save dealers and coarse men. Mabel had no associates of her own sex, after her sister went away. But she did not mind. She went regularly to church, she attended to her father. And she lived in the memory of her mother, who had died when she was fourteen, and whom she had loved. She had loved her father, too, in a different way, depending upon him, and

---

25) of late: 최근에.
26) go to the dogs: 영락하다. 타락하다. 파멸하다.
27) penury: poverty.
28) unstinted: 제한받지 않는. 인색하지 않은.
29) reserved: 조심성 있는. 과묵한. 신중한.

feeling secure in him, until at the age of fifty-four he married again. And then she had set hard against him. Now he had died and left them all hopelessly in debt.

She had suffered badly during the period of poverty. Nothing, however, could shake the curious, sullen, animal pride that dominated each member of the family. Now, for Mabel, the end had come. Still she would not cast about her. She would follow her own way just the same. She would always hold the keys of her own situation. Mindless and persistent, she endured from day to day. Why should she think? Why should she answer anybody? It was enough that this was the end, and there was no way out. She need not pass any more darkly along the main street of the small town, avoiding every eye. She need not demean herself any more, going into the shops and buying the cheapest food. This was at an end. She thought of nobody, not even herself. Mindless and persistent, she seemed in a sort of ecstasy to be coming nearer to her fulfilment, her own glorification, approaching her dead mother, who was glorified.

In the afternoon she took a little bag, with shears[30) and sponge and a small scrubbing-brush, and went out. It was a grey, wintry day, with saddened, dark green fields and an atmosphere blackened by the smoke of foundries[31) not far off. She went quickly, darkly along the causeway,[32) heeding nobody, through the town to the churchyard.

There she always felt secure, as if no one could see her, although as a matter of fact she was exposed to the stare of everyone who passed along the churchyard wall. Nevertheless, once under the shadow of the great looming church, among the graves, she felt immune from the world, reserved within the thick churchyard wall as in another country.

Carefully she clipped the grass from the grave, and arranged the

---

30) shears: 큰 가위.
31) foundry: 주물 공장.
32) causeway: 뚝길. 인도.

pinky white, small chrysanthemums in the tin cross. When this was done, she took an empty jar from a neighbouring grave, brought water, and carefully, most scrupulously sponged the marble headstone[33] and the coping-stone.[34]

It gave her sincere satisfaction to do this. She felt in immediate contact with the world of her mother. She took minute pains, went through the park in a state bordering on pure happiness, as if in performing this task she came into a subtle, intimate connection with her mother. For the life she followed here in the world was far less real than the world of death she inherited from her mother.

The doctor's house was just by the church. Fergusson, being a mere hired assistant, was slave to the country-side. As he hurried now to attend to the outpatients in the surgery, glancing across the graveyard with his quick eye, he saw the girl at task at the grave. She seemed so intent and remote, it was like looking into another world. Some mystical element was touched in him. He slowed down as he walked, watching her as if spellbound.

She lifted her eyes, feeling him looking. Their eyes met. And each looked again at once, each feeling, in some way, found out by the other. He lifted his cap and passed on down the road. There remained distinct in consciousness, like a vision, the memory of her face, lifted from the tombstone in the churchyard, and looking at him with slow, large, portentous[35] eyes. It was portentous, her face. It seemed to mesmerise him. There was a heavy power in her eyes which laid hold of his whole being, as if he had drunk some powerful drug. He had been feeling weak and done[36] before. Now the life came back into him, he felt delivered from his own fretted, daily self.

He finished his duties at the surgery as quickly as might be,

---

33) headstone: (묘의 頭部에 세운) 묘표. 묘석.
34) coping-stone: (=copestone) 관석(冠石). 갓돌.
35) portentous: 불길한, 이상스런, 무서운.
36) done: worn out. exhausted.

hastily filling up the bottles of the waiting people with cheap drugs. Then, in perpetual haste, he set off again to visit several cases in another part of his round, before teatime. At all times he preferred to walk if he could, but particularly, when he was not well. He fancied the motion restored him.

The afternoon was falling. It was grey, deadened, and wintry, with a slow, moist, heavy coldness sinking in and deadening all the faculties. But why should he think or notice? He hastily climbed the hill and turned across the dark green fields, following the black cinder-track. In the distance, across a shallow dip in the country, the small town was clustered like smouldering ash, a tower, a spire, a heap of low, raw, extinct houses. And on the nearest fringe of the town, sloping into the dip, was Oldmeadow, the Pervins' house. He could see the stables and the outbuildings distinctly, as they lay towards him on the slope. Well, he would not go there many more times! Another resource would be lost to him, another place gone: the only company he cared for in the alien, ugly little town he was losing. Nothing but work, drudgery, constant hastening from dwelling to dwelling among the colliers and the iron-workers. It wore him out, but at the same time he had a craving for it. It was a stimulant to him to be in the homes of the working people, moving, as it were, through the innermost body of their life. His nerves were excited and gratified. He could come so near, into the very lives of the rough, inarticulate, powerfully emotional men and women. He grumbled, he said he hated the hellish hole.[37] But as a matter of fact it excited him, the contact with the rough, strongly-feeling people was a stimulant applied direct to his nerves.

Below Old meadow, in the green, shallow, soddened hollow of fields, lay a square, deep pond. Roving across the landscape, the doctor's quick eye detected a figure in black passing through the gate of the field, down towards the pond. He looked again. It would be Mabel Pervin. His mind suddenly became alive and attentive.

---

37) hole: 광구.

Why was she going down there? He pulled up on the path on the slope above, and stood staring. He could just make sure of the small black figure moving in the hollow of the failing day. He seemed to see her in the midst of such obscurity, that he was like a clairvoyant, seeing rather with the mind's eye than with ordinary sight. Yet he could see her positively enough, whilst he kept his eye attentive. He felt, if he looked away from her, in the thick, ugly falling dusk, he would lose her altogether.

He followed her minutely as she moved, direct and intent, like something transmitted rather than stirring in voluntary activity,[38] straight down the field towards the pond. There she stood on the bank for a moment. She never raised her head. Then she waded slowly into the water.

He stood motionless as the small black figure walked slowly and deliberately towards the centre of the pond, very slowly, gradually moving deeper into the motionless water, and still moving forward as the water got up to her breast. Then he could see her no more in the dusk of the dead afternoon.

'There!' he exclaimed. 'Would you believe it?'[39]

And he hastened straight down, running over the wet, soddened fields, pushing through the hedges, down into the depression of callous wintry obscurity. It took him several minutes to come to the pond. He stood on the bank, breathing heavily. He could see nothing. His eyes seemed to penetrate the dead water. Yes, perhaps that was the dark shadow of her black clothing beneath the surface of water.

He slowly ventured into the pond. The bottom was deep, soft clay, he sank in, and the water clasped dead cold round his legs. As he stirred he could smell the cold, rotten clay that fouled up into the water. It was objectionable in his lungs. Still, repelled and yet

---

38) like something transmitted rather than stirring in voluntary activity: 자발적인 활동에서 움직이고 있다기보다 무엇에 홀린 것처럼.

39) Would you believe it?: 저럴수가?

not heeding, he moved deeper into the pond. The cold water rose over his thighs, over his loins, upon his abdomen The lower part of body was all sunk in the hideous cold element. And the bottom was so deeply soft and uncertain, he was afraid of pitching with his mouth underneath. He could not swim, and was afraid.

He crouched a little, spreading his hands under the water and moving them round, trying to feel for her. The dead cold pond swayed upon his chest. He moved again, a little deeper, and again, with his hands underneath, he felt all around under the water. And he touched her clothing. But it evaded his fingers. He made a desperate effort to grasp it.

And so doing he lost his balance and went under, horribly, suffocating in the foul earthy water, struggling madly for a few moments. At last, after what seemed an eternity, he got his footing, rose again into the air and looked around. He gasped, and knew he was in the world. Then he looked at the water. She had risen near him. He grasped her clothing, and drawing her nearer, turned to take his way to land again.

He went very slowly, carefully, absorbed in the slow process. He rose higher, climbing out of the pond. The water was now only about his legs; he was thankful, full of relief to be out of the clutches of the pond. He lifted her and staggered on to the bank, out of the horror of wet, grey clay.

He laid her down on the bank. She was quite unconscious and running with water. He made the water come from her mouth, he worked to restore her. He did not have to work very long before he could feel the breathing begin again in her; she was breathing heavily naturally. He worked a little longer. He could feel her live beneath his hands; she was coming back. He wiped her face, wrapped her in his overcoat, looked round into the dim, dark grey world, then lifted her and staggered down the bank and across the fields.

It seemed an unthinkably long way, and his burden so heavy he felt he would never get to the house. But at last he was in the stable-yard, and then in the house-yard. He opened the door and went into the house. In the kitchen he laid her down on the hearth-rug and called. The house was empty. But the fire was burning in the grate.

Then again he kneeled to attend to her. She was breathing regularly, her eyes wide open and as if conscious, but there seemed something missing in her look. She was conscious in herself, but unconscious of her surroundings.

He ran upstairs, took blankets from a bed and put them before the fire to warm. Then he removed her saturated, earthy-smelling clothing, rubbed her dry with a towel, and wrapped her naked in the blankets. Then he went into the dining-room, to look for spirits.[40) There was a little whisky. He drank a gulp himself, and put some into her mouth.

The effect was instantaneous. She looked full into his face, as if she had been seeing him for some time, and yet had only just become conscious of him.

'Dr. Fergusson?' she said.

'What?' he answered.

He was divesting himself of his coat, intending to find some dry clothing upstairs. He could not bear the smell of the dead, clayey water, and he was mortally afraid for his own health.

'What did I do?' she asked.

'Walked into the pond,' he replied. He had begun to shudder like one sick, and could hardly attend to her. Her eyes remained full on him, he seemed to be going dark in his mind, looking back at her helplessly. The shuddering became quieter in him, his life came back to him, dark and unknowing, but strong again.

'Was I out of my mind?' she asked, while her eyes were fixed on him all the time.

'Maybe, for the moment,' he replied. He felt quiet, because his strength had come back. The strange fretful strain had left him.

---

40) spirits: 술.

'Am I out of my mind now?' she asked.

'Are you?' he reflected a moment. 'No,' he answered truthfully, 'I don't see that you are.' He turned his face aside. He was afraid now, because he felt dazed, and felt dimly that her power was stronger than his, in this issue. And she continued to look at him fixedly all the time. 'Can you tell me where I shall find some dry things to put on?' he asked.

'Did you dive into the pond for me?' she asked.

'No,' he answered. 'I walked in. But I went in overhead as well.'

There was silence for a moment. He hesitated. He very much wanted to go upstairs to get into dry clothing. But there was another desire in him. And she seemed to hold him. His will seemed to have gone to sleep, and left him, standing there slack before her. But he felt warm inside himself. He did not shudder at all, though his clothes were sodden on him.

'Why did you?' she asked.

'Because I didn't want you to do such a foolish thing,' he said.

'It wasn't foolish,' she said, still gazing at him as she lay on the floor, with a sofa cushion under her head. 'It was the right thing to do. I knew best, then.'

'I'll go and shift these wet things,' he said. But still he had not the power to move out of her presence, until she sent him. It was as if she had the life of his body in her hands, and he could not extricate himself. Or perhaps he did not want to.

Suddenly she sat up. Then she became aware of her own immediate condition. She felt the blankets about her, she knew her own limbs. For a moment it seemed as if her reason were going. She looked round, with wild eye, as if seeking something. He stood still with fear. She saw her clothing lying scattered.

'Who undressed me?' she asked, her eyes resting full and inevitable on his face.

'I did,' he replied, 'to bring you round.'

For some moments she sat and gazed at him awfully, her lips

parted.

'Do you love me, then?' she asked.

He only stood and stared at her, fascinated. His soul seemed to melt.

She shuffled forward on her knees, and put her arms round him, round his legs, as he stood there, pressing her breasts against his knees and thighs, clutching him with strange, convulsive certainty, pressing his thighs against her, drawing him to her face, her throat, as she looked up at him with flaring, humble eyes and transfiguration, triumphant in first possession.

'You love me,' she murmured, in strange transport,[41] yearning and triumphant and confident. 'You love me. I know you love me, I know.'

And she was passionately kissing his knees, through the wet clothing, passionately and indiscriminately kissing his knees, his legs, as if unaware of everything.

He looked down at the tangled wet hair, the wild, bare, animal shoulders. He was amazed, bewildered and afraid. He had never thought of loving her. He had never wanted to love her. When he rescued her and restored her, he was a doctor, and she was a patient. He had had no single personal thought of her. Nay, this introduction of the personal element was very distasteful to him, a violation of his professional honour. It was horrible to have her there embracing his knees. It was horrible. He revolted from it, violently. And yet—and yet—he had not the power to break away.

She looked at him again, with the same supplication of powerful love, and that same transcendent, frightening light of triumph. In view of the delicate flame which seemed to come from her face like a light, he was powerless. And yet he had never intended to love her. He had never intended. And something stubborn in him could not give way.

'You love me,' she repeated, in a murmur of deep, rhapsodic

---

41) transport: 황홀. 기쁨.

assurance. 'You love me.'

Her hands were drawing him, drawing him down to her. He was afraid, even a little horrified. For he had, really, no intention of loving her. Yet her hands were drawing him towards her. He put out his hand quickly to steady himself, and grasped her bare shoulder. He had no intention of loving her: his whole will was against his yielding. It was horrible. And yet wonderful was the touch of her shoulders, beautiful the shining of her face. Was she perhaps mad? He had a horror of yielding to her. Yet something in him ached also.

He had been staring away at the door, away from her. But his hand remained on her shoulder. She had gone suddenly very still. He looked down at her. Her eyes were now wide with fear, with doubt, the light was dying from her face, a shadow of terrible greyness was returning. He could not bear the touch of her eyes' question upon him, and the look of death behind the question.

With an inward groan he gave way, and let his heart yield towards her. A sudden gentle smile came on his face. And her eyes, which never left his face, slowly, slowly filled with tears. He watched the strange water rise in her eyes, like some slow fountain coming up. And his heart seemed to burn and melt away in his breast.

He could not bear to look at her any more. He dropped on his knees and caught her head with his arms and pressed her face against his throat. She was very still. His heart, which seemed to have broken, was burning with a kind of agony in his breast. And he felt her slow, hot tears wetting his throat. But he could not move.

He felt the hot tears wet his neck and the hollows of his neck, and he remained motionless, suspended through one of man's eternities. Only now it had become indispensable to him to have her face pressed close to him; he could never let her go again. He could never let her head go away from the close clutch of his arm. He wanted to remain like that for ever, with his heart hurting him in a pain that was also life to him. Without knowing, he was looking down on her damp, soft brown hair.

Then, as it were suddenly, he smelt the horrid stagnant smell of that water. And at the same moment she drew away from him and looked at him. Her eyes were wistful and unfathomable. He was afraid of them, and he fell to kissing her, not knowing what he was doing. He wanted her eyes not to have that terrible, wistful, unfathomable look.

When she turned her face to him again, a faint delicate flush was glowing, and there was again dawning that terrible shining of joy in her eyes, which really terrified him, and yet which he now wanted to see, because he feared the look of doubt still more.

'You love me?' she said, rather faltering.

'Yes.' The word cost him a painful effort. Not because it wasn't true. But because it was too newly true, the saying seemed to tear open again his newly-torn heart. And he hardly wanted it to be true, even now.

She lifted her face to him, and he bent forward and kissed her on the mouth, gently, with the one kiss that is an eternal pledge. And as he kissed her his heart strained again in his breast. He never intended to love her. But now it was over. He had crossed over the gulf to her, and all that he had left behind had shrivelled and become void.

After the kiss, her eyes again slowly filled with tears. She sat still, away from him, with her face drooped aside, and her hands folded in her lap. The tears fell very slowly. There was complete silence. He too sat there motionless and silent on the hearth-rug. The strange pain of his heart that was broken seemed to consume him. That he should love her? That this was love! That he should be ripped open in this way! Him, a doctor! How they would all jeer if they knew! It was agony to him to think they might know.

In the curious naked pain of the thought he looked again to her. She was sitting there drooped into a muse. He saw a tear fall, and his heart flared hot. He saw for the first time that one of her shoulders was quite uncovered, one arm bare, he could see one of her small breasts; dimly, because it had become almost dark in the room.

'Why are you crying?' he asked, in an altered voice.

She looked up at him, and behind her tears the consciousness of her situation for the first time brought a dark look of shame to her eyes.

'I'm not crying, really,' she said, watching him, half-frightened.

He reached his hand, and softly closed it on her bare arm.

'I love you! I love you!' he said in a soft, low vibrating voice, unlike himself.

She shrank, and dropped her head. The soft, penetrating grip of his hand on her arm distressed her. She looked up at him.

'I want to go,' she said. 'I want to go and get you some dry things.'

'Why?' he said. 'I'm all right.'

'But I want to go,' she said. 'And I want you to change your things.'

He released her arm, and she wrapped herself in the blanket, looking at him rather frightened. And still she did not rise.

'Kiss me,' she said wistfully.

He kissed her, but briefly, half in anger.

Then, after a second, she rose nervously, all mixed up in the blanket. He watched her in her confusion as she tried to extricate herself and wrap herself up so that she could walk. He watched her relentlessly, as she knew. And as she went, the blanket trailing, and he saw a glimpse of her feet and her white leg, he tried to remember her as she was when he had wrapped her up in the blanket. But then he didn't want to remember, because she had been nothing to him then, and his nature revolted from remembering her as she was when she was nothing to him.

A tumbling, muffled noise from within the dark house startled him. Then he heard her voice: 'There are clothes.' He rose and went to the foot of the stairs, and gathered up the garments she had thrown down. Then he came back to the fire, to rub himself down and dress. He grinned at his own appearance when he had finished.

The fire was sinking, so he put on coal. The house was now quite dark, save for the light of a street-lamp that shone in faintly from beyond the holly trees. He lit the gas with matches he found on the mantelpiece. Then he emptied the pockets of his own clothes, and threw all his wet things in a heap into the scullery. After which he gathered up her sodden clothes, gently, and put them in a separate heap on the copper-top[42] in the scullery.

It was six o'clock on the clock. His own watch had stopped. He ought to go back to the surgery. He waited, and still she did not come down. So he went to the foot of the stairs and called:

'I shall have to go.'

Almost immediately he heard her coming down. She had on her best dress of black voile, and her hair was tidy, but still damp. She looked at him—and in spite of herself, smiled.

'I don't like you in those clothes,' she said.

'Do I look a sight?' he answered.

They were shy of one another.

'I'll make you some tea,' she said.

'No, I must go.'

'Must you?' And she looked at him again with the wide, strained, doubtful eyes. And again, from the pain of his breast, he knew how he loved her. He went and bent to kiss her, gently, passionately, with his heart's painful kiss.

'And my hair smells so horrible,' she murmured in distraction. 'And I'm so awful, I'm so awful! Oh no, I'm too awful.' And she broke into bitter, heart-broken sobbing. 'You can't want to love me, I'm horrible.'

'Don't be silly, don't be silly,' he said, trying to comfort her, kissing her, holding her in his arms. 'I want you, I want to marry you, we're going to be married, quickly, quickly—tomorrow if I can.'

But she only sobbed terribly, and cried:

---

42) copper-top: 구리 솥.

'I feel awful. I feel awful. I feel I'm horrible to you.'

'No, I want you, I want you,' was all he answered, blindly, with that terrible intonation which frightened her almost more than her horror lest he should not want her.

The Mark on the Wall

by Virginia Woolf

Introduction to the Author

Virginia Woolf (1882-1941)

Born in London, daughter of Leslie Stephen, the late Victorian critic, biographer, and scholar. She grew up as a member of a large and talented family, educating herself in her father's library. Woolf was a skilled exponent of the "stream of consciousness" technique in her novels, exploring problems of personal identity and personal relationships as well as the significance of time, change, and memory for human personality. Woof was much concerned with the position of women, especially professional women, and the constrictions they suffered under. Her major novels are *Mrs. Dalloway* (1925), *To the Lighthouse*(1927), *The Waves*(1931), and *Between the Acts*(1941).

The Mark on the Wall

Perhaps it was the middle of January in the present year that I first looked up and saw the mark on the wall. In order to fix a date it is necessary to remember what one saw. So now I think of the fire; the steady film of yellow light upon the page of my book; the three chrysanthemums in the round glass bowl on the mantelpiece. Yes, it must have been the winter time, and we had just finished our tea, for I remember that I was smoking a cigarette when I looked up and saw the mark on the wall for the first time. I looked up through the smoke of my cigarette and my eye lodged[1)] for a moment upon the burning coals, and that old fancy of the crimson flag flapping from the castle tower came into my mind, and I thought of the cavalcade[2)] of red knights riding up the side of the black rock. Rather to my relief the sight of the mark interrupted the fancy, for it is an old fancy, an automatic fancy, made as a child perhaps.[3)] The mark was a small round mark, black upon the white wall, about six or seven inches above the mantelpiece.

How readily our thoughts swarm[4)] upon a new object, lifting it a little way, as ants carry a blade of straw so feverishly, and then leave it.... If that mark was made by a nail, it can't have been for a picture, it must have been for a miniature[5)]—the miniature of a lady with white powdered curls, powder-dusted cheeks, and lips like red carnations. A fraud[6)] of course, for the people who had this house before us would have chosen pictures in that way—an old picture

---

1) lodge: 머물다; 숙식하다.
2) cavalcade: 기마 행렬. 마차 행렬.
3) an automatic fancy, made as a child perhaps: 어쩌면 어릴 때 만들어졌을 습관성의 공상.
4) swarm: 떼지어 몰리다.
5) miniature: 축소화. 세밀 초상화.
6) fraud: 기만. 속임. 가짜. 엉터리.

for an old room. That is the sort of people they were—very interesting people, and I think of them so often, in such queer places, because one will never see them again, never know what happened next. They wanted to leave this house because they wanted to change their style of furniture, so he said, and he was in process of saying that in his opinion art should have ideas behind it when we were torn asunder,[7)] as one is torn from the old lady about to pour out tea and the young man about to hit the tennis ball in the back garden of the suburban villa as one rushes past in the train. But as for that mark, I'm not sure about it; I don't believe it was made by a nail after all; it's too big, too round, for that. I might get up, but if I got up and looked at it, ten to one I shouldn't be able to say for certain; because once a thing's done, no one ever knows how it happened. Oh! dear me, the mystery of life! The inaccuracy of thought! The ignorance of humanity! To show how very little control of our possessions we have—what an accidental affair this living is after all our civilization—let me just count over a few of the things lost in our lifetime, beginning, for that seems always the most mysterious of losses—what cat would gnaw, what rat would nibble—three pale blue canisters of book-binding tools?[8)] Then there were the bird cages, the iron hoops,[9)] the steel skates, the Queen Anne coal-scuttle,[10)] the bagatelle[11)] board, the hand organ—all gone, and jewels, too. Opals and emeralds, they lie about the roots of turnips. What a scraping paring affair it[12)] is to be sure! The wonder is that I've any clothes on my back, that I sit surrounded by solid furniture

---

7) he was in process of saying ~ when we were torn asunder: 그가 ~라고 말하려는 순간에 우리는 헤어졌다.

8) three pale blue canisters of book-binding tools: 책을 제본하는 도구들이 든 세 개의 푸른 색 깡통.

9) iron hoop: 굴렁쇠.

10) Queen Anne coal-scuttle: 앤 여왕 시대식 석탄통.

11) bagatelle: 바가텔. 큐로 공을 쳐서 반대쪽 끝에 있는 구멍에 넣는 선상(船上)에서 하는 공놀이.

12) it: life.

at this moment. Why, if one wants to compare life to anything, one must liken it to being blown through the Tube[13] at fifty miles an hour—landing at the other end without a single hairpin in one's hair! Shot out at the feet of God entirely naked! Tumbling head over heels in the asphodel meadows[14] like brown paper parcels pitched down a shoot[15] in the post office! With one's hair flying back like the tail of a race-horse. Yes, that seems to express the rapidity of life, the perpetual waste and repair; all so casual, all so haphazard....

But after life. The slow pulling down of thick green stalks so that the cup of the flower, as it turns over, deluges one with purple and red light. Why, after all, should one not be born there as one is born here, helpless, speechless, unable to focus one's eyesight, groping at the roots of the grass, at the toes of the Giants? As for saying which are trees, and which are men and women, or whether there are such things, that one won't be in a condition to do for fifty years or so. There will be nothing but spaces of light and dark, intersected by thick stalks, and rather higher up perhaps, rose-shaped blots of an indistinct colour—dim pinks and blues—which will, as time goes on, become more definite, become—I don't know what....

And yet that mark on the wall is not a hole at all. It may even be caused by some round black substance, such as a small rose leaf, left over from the summer, and I, not being a very vigilant housekeeper—look at the dust on the mantelpiece, for example, the dust which, so they say, buried Troy three times over, only fragments of pots utterly refusing annihilation, as one can believe.[16]

The tree outside the window taps very gently on the pane....I want to think quietly, calmly, spaciously, never to be interrupted,

---

13) Tube: London underground railway.

14) asphodel meadows: heaven, the next world (in Greek mythology, asphodel flowers grow in the Elysian fields).

15) shoot: 활송 운반 장치.

16) look at the dust on the mantelpiece ~ as one can believe: 예를 들면 벽난로 위에 있는 먼지를 보아라. 오로지 항아리 조각들만 완전히 파멸되는 것을 거부했지만, 트로이를 세 번은 덮을 먼지라고 그들은 말하고, 누구라도 믿을 수 있다.

never to have to rise from my chair, to slip easily from one thing to another, without any sense of hostility, or obstacle. I want to sink deeper and deeper, away from the surface, with its hard separate facts. To steady myself, let me catch hold of the first idea that passes.... Shakespeare....Well, he will do as well as another. A man who sat himself solidly in an arm-chair, and looked into the fire, so—A shower of ideas fell perpetually from some very high Heaven down through his mind. He leant his forehead on his hand, and people, looking in through the open door,—for this scene is supposed to take place on a summer's evening—But how dull this is, this historical fiction! It doesn't interest me at all. I wish I could hit upon a pleasant track of thought, a track indirectly reflecting credit upon myself, for those are the pleasantest thoughts, and very frequent even in the minds of modest mouse-coloured people, who believe genuinely that they dislike to hear their own praises. They are not thoughts directly praising oneself; that is the beauty of them; they are thoughts like this:

"And then I came into the room. They were discussing botany. I said how I'd seen a flower growing on a dust heap on the site of an old house in Kingsway.[17] The seed, I said, must have been sown in the reign of Charles the First.[18] What flowers grew in the reign of Charles the First?" I asked—(but, I don't remember the answer). Tall flowers with purple tassels to them perhaps. And so it goes on. All the time I'm dressing up the figure of myself in my own mind, lovingly, stealthily, not openly adoring it, for if I did that, I should catch myself out,[19] and stretch my hand at once for a book in self-protection. Indeed, it is curious how instinctively one protects the image of oneself from idolatry or any other handling that could make it ridiculous, or too unlike the original to be believed in any longer.[20] Or is it not so very curious after all? It is a matter of

---

17) Kingsway: street in London.

18) Charles the First: 찰스 1세(1600-1649년). 재임 기간은 1625년~1649년.

19) catch out: (부정 따위를) 간파하다. 잘못을 발견하다.

great importance. Suppose the looking glass smashes, the image disappears, and the romantic figure with the green of forest depths all about it is there no longer, but only that shell of a person which is seen by other people—what an airless, shallow, bald, prominent world it becomes! A world not to be lived in. As we face each other in omnibuses and underground railways we are looking into the mirror that accounts for[21] the vagueness, the gleam of glassiness, in our eyes. And the novelists in future will realize more and more the importance of these reflections, for of course there is not one reflection but an almost infinite number; those are the depths they will explore, those the phantoms they will pursue, leaving the description of reality more and more out of their stories,[22] taking a knowledge of it for granted, as the Greeks did and Shakespeare perhaps—but these generalizations are very worthless. The military sound of the word is enough. It recalls leading articles, cabinet ministers—a whole class of things indeed which as a child one thought the thing itself, the standard thing, the real thing, from which one could not depart save at the risk of nameless damnation. Generalizations bring back somehow Sunday in London, Sunday afternoon walks, Sunday luncheons, and also ways of speaking of the dead, clothes, and habits —like the habit of sitting all together in one room until a certain hour, although nobody liked it. There was a rule for everything. The rule for tablecloths at that particular period was that they should be made of tapestry with little yellow compartments marked upon them, such as you may see in photographs of the carpets in the corridors of the royal palaces. Tablecloths of a different kind were not real tablecloths. How shocking, and yet how wonderful it was to discover that these real things, Sunday luncheons, Sunday walks,

---

20) Indeed, it is curious ~ to be believed in any longer: 사실, 사람이 자신을 우상처럼 숭배하거나, 우스꽝스럽게 만들거나, 너무 원형과 달라서 더 이상 믿을 수 없게 취급하려 하면, 본능적으로 보호하는 것이 신기했다.

21) account for: 설명하다. 책임을 지다. 원인이 되다.

22) leaving the description of reality more and more out of their stories: 점점 더 현실 묘사는 그들의 이야기에서 사라지게 하면서.

country houses, and tablecloths were not entirely real, were indeed half phantoms, and the damnation which visited the disbeliever in them was only a sense of illegitimate freedom. What now takes the place of those things I wonder, those real standard things? Men perhaps, should you be a woman; the masculine point of view which governs our lives, which sets the standard, which establishes Whitaker's Table of Precedency,[23] which has become, I suppose, since the war half a phantom to many men and women, which soon—one may hope, will be laughed into the dustbin where the phantoms go, the mahogany sideboards and the Landseer[24] prints, Gods and Devils, Hell and so forth, leaving us all with an intoxicating sense of illegitimate freedom—if freedom exists....

In certain lights that mark on the wall seems actually to project from the wall. Nor is it entirely circular. I cannot be sure, but it seems to cast a perceptible shadow, suggesting that if I ran my finger down that strip of the wall it would, at a certain point, mount and descend a small tumulus,[25] a smooth tumulus like those barrows on the South Downs[26] which are, they say, either tombs or camps.[27] Of the two I should prefer them to be tombs, desiring melancholy like most English people, and finding it natural at the end of a walk to think of the bones stretched beneath the turf....There must be some book about it. Some antiquary must have dug up those bones and given them a name....What sort of a man is an antiquary, I wonder? Retired Colonels for the most part, I daresay, leading parties of aged labourers to the top here, examining clods of earth and stone, and getting into correspondence with the neighbouring clergy, which, being opened at breakfast time, gives them a feeling of importance, and the comparison of arrow-heads neces-

---

23) Whitaker's Table of Precedency: 휘터커의 연감에 포함된 서열표.
24) Sir Edwin Henry Landseer(1802-1873): 그의 유명한 그림 대부분이 형인 Thomas에 의해 강철 인화 방식으로 복사 재생되었다.
25) tumulus: 무덤. 분묘. 둔덕. barrow.
26) the South Downs: 사우스 다운즈. 영국 잉글랜드 남부의 낮은 구릉 지대.
27) camp: 야영지.

sitates cross-country journeys to the county towns, an agreeable necessity both to them and to their elderly wives, who wish to make plum jam or to clean out the study, and have every reason for keeping that great question of the camp or the tomb in perpetual suspension, while the Colonel himself feels agreeably philosophic in accumulating evidence on both sides of the question. It is true that he does finally incline to believe in the camp; and, being opposed, indites[28)] a pamphlet which he is about to read at the quarterly meeting of the local society when a stroke lays him low,[29)] and his last conscious thoughts are not of wife or child, but of the camp and that arrowhead there, which is now in the case at the local museum, together with the foot of a Chinese murderess, a handful of Elizabethan nails, a great many Tudor clay pipes, a piece of Roman pottery, and the wine-glass that Nelson drank out of—proving I really don't know what.

No, no, nothing is proved, nothing is known. And if I were to get up at this very moment and ascertain that the mark on the wall is really—what shall we say?—the head of a gigantic old nail, driven in two hundred years ago, which has now, owing to the patient attrition[30)] of many generations of housemaids, revealed its head above the coat of paint, and is taking its first view of modern life in the sight of a white-walled fire-lit room, what should I gain?—Knowledge? Matter for further speculation? I can think sitting still as well as standing up. And what is knowledge? What are our learned men save the descendants of witches and hermits who crouched in caves and in woods brewing herbs, interrogating shrew-mice[31)] and writing down the language of the stars? And the less we honour them as our superstitions dwindle and our respect for beauty and health of mind increases.... Yes, one could imagine a very pleasant world. A quiet, spacious world, with the flowers so red and blue in

---

28) indite: 쓰다. 작성하다.

29) when a stroke lays him low: 그때 그는 뇌졸중으로 쓰러졌다.

30) attrition: 마멸. 마손.

31) shrew-mice: 뒤쥐.

the open fields. A world without professors or specialists or house-keepers with the profiles of policemen, a world which one could slice with one's thought as a fish slices the water with his fin, grazing the stems of the water-lilies, hanging suspended over nests of white sea eggs.... How peaceful it is down here, rooted in the centre of the world and gazing up through the grey waters, with their sudden gleams of light, and their reflections—if it were not for Whitaker's Almanack—if it were not for the Table of Precedency!

I must jump up and see for myself what that mark on the wall really is—a nail, a rose-leaf, a crack in the wood?

Here is nature once more at her old game of self-preservation. This train of thought, she perceives, is threatening mere waste of energy, even some collision with reality, for who will ever be able to lift a finger against Whitaker's Table of Precedency? The Archbishop of Canterbury is followed by the Lord High Chancellor;[32] the Lord High Chancellor is followed by the Archbishop of York. Everybody follows somebody, such is the philosophy of Whitaker; and the great thing is to know who follows whom. Whitaker knows, and let that, so Nature counsels, comfort you, instead of enraging you; and if you can't be comforted, if you must shatter this hour of peace, think of the mark on the wall.

I understand Nature's game—her prompting to take action as a way of ending any thought that threatens to excite or to pain. Hence, I suppose, comes our slight contempt for men of action—men, we assume, who don't think. Still, there's no harm in putting a full stop to one's disagreeable thoughts by looking at a mark on the wall.

Indeed, now that I have fixed my eyes upon it, I feel that I have grasped a plank[33] in the sea; I feel a satisfying sense of reality which at once turns the two Archbishops and the Lord High Chancellor to the shadows of shades. Here is something definite, something real. Thus, waking from a midnight dream of horror, one hastily turns

---

32) Lord High Chancellor: 대법관.
33) plank: 널빤지.

on the light and lies quiescent,[34] worshipping the chest of drawers, worshipping solidity, worshipping reality, worshipping the impersonal world which is a proof of some existence other than ours. That is what one wants to be sure of.... Wood is a pleasant thing to think about. It comes from a tree; and trees grow, and we don't know how they grow. For years and years they grow, without paying any attention to us, in meadows, in forests, and by the side of rivers—all things one likes to think about. The cows swish their tails beneath them on hot afternoons; they paint rivers so green that when a moorhen[35] dives one expects to see its feathers all green when it comes up again. I like to think of the fish balanced against the stream like flags blown out; and of water-beetles[36] slowly raising domes of mud upon the bed of the river. I like to think of the tree itself:—first the close dry sensation of being wood; then the grinding of the storm; then the slow, delicious ooze of sap. I like to think of it, too, on winter's nights standing in the empty field with all leaves close-furled, nothing tender exposed to the iron bullets of the moon, a naked mast upon an earth that goes tumbling, tumbling, all night long. The song of birds must sound very loud and strange in June; and how cold the feet of insects must feel upon it, as they make laborious progresses up the creases of the bark, or sun themselves upon the thin green awning of the leaves, and look straight in front of them with diamond-cut red eyes.... One by one the fibres snap beneath the immense cold pressure of the earth, then the last storm comes and, falling, the highest branches drive deep into the ground again. Even so, life isn't done with; there are a million patient, watchful lives still for a tree, all over the world, in bedrooms, in ships, on the pavement, living rooms, where men and women sit after tea, smoking cigarettes. It is full of peaceful thoughts, happy thoughts, this tree. I should like to take each one separately—but

34) quiescent: 조용한, 활발하지 않은.
35) moorhen: 붉은 뇌조.
36) water-beetles: 수생 갑충. 물방개.

something is getting in the way....Where was I? What has it all been about? A tree? A river? The Downs? Whitaker's Almanack? The fields of asphodel? I can't remember a thing. Everything's moving, falling, slipping, vanishing.... There is a vast upheaval of matter. Someone is standing over me and saying—

"I'm going out to buy a newspaper."

"Yes?"

"Though it's no good buying newspapers.... Nothing ever happens. Curse this war; God damn this war!... All the same, I don't see why we should have a snail on our wall."

Ah, the mark on the wall! It was a snail.

The Dead

by James Joyce

Introduction to the Author

James Joyce (1882-1941)

He carried the "stream of consciousness" method farther than any other novelist. He was born in Dublin, Ireland, of a talented but loose-ended father who had been a typical Irishman, a composite of all the best-known features of Irishmen, and perhaps, Ireland itself. The younger Joyce was surrounded by poverty, religion, and many brothers and sisters. From the age of six to the age of sixteen, Joyce was educated in Jesuit institutions. Later, he studied modern languages at University College, Dublin. By 1902, when he received his B.A. degree, he was a confirmed anti-Catholic, exile, and writer. After graduation, Joyce went to Paris, returned briefly to Dublin to see his dying mother, served briefly as a schoolteacher, and then returned to the Continent in 1904 to teach English at Trieste and Zurich. His chief companion (and officially his wife in 1931) was Nora Barnacle, a simple Galway girl. From 1920 to 1940, they lived in Paris (with their two children), and early in 1941 Joyce died in Zurich. His works are *Dubliners*(1914), *A Portrait of the Artist as a Young Man*(1916), *Ulysses* (1922) and *Finnegans Wake*(1939).

The Dead

Lily, the caretaker's daughter, was literally run off her feet.[1)] Hardly had she brought one gentleman into the little pantry behind the office on the ground floor and helped him off with his overcoat, than the wheezy hall-door bell clanged again and she had to scamper along the bare hallway to let in another guest.[2)] It was well for her she had not to attend[3)] to the ladies also. But Miss Kate and Miss Julia had thought of that and had converted the bathroom upstairs into a ladies' dressing-room. Miss Kate and Miss Julia were there, gossiping and laughing and fussing, walking after each other to the stairs, peering down over the banisters and calling down to Lily to ask her who had come.

It was always a great affair, the Misses Morkan's annual dance.[4)] Everybody who knew them came to it, members of the family, old friends of the family, the members of the Julia's choir, any of Kate's pupils that were grown up enough, and even some of Mary Jane's pupils too. Never once had it fallen flat.[5)] For years and years it had gone off in splendid style, as long as anyone could remember: ever since Kate and Julia, after the death of their brother Pat, had left the house in Stoney Batter and taken Mary Jane, their only niece, to live with them in the dark, gaunt house on Usher's Island, the upper part of which they had rented from Mr. Fulham, the corn-factor on the ground floor. That was a good thirty years ago if it was a day.[6)] Mary Jane, who was then a little girl in short clothes, was now the main prop[7)] of the household, for she had the

---

1) was literally run off her feet: 그녀는 말 그대로 발붙일 틈도 없이 바빴다.
2) harly~than~: ~하자마자 곧.
3) attend to: 돌보다, 시중들다, 모시다.
4) the Misses Morkan's annual dance: 모칸 여사 자매의 연례 무도회.
5) flat: dull, uninteresting.
6) That was a good thirty years ago if it was a day: 그 일은 족히 30년 전의 일이다.

organ in Haddington Road. She had been through the Academy[8] and gave a pupil's concert every year in the upper room of the Antient Concert Rooms.[9] Many of her pupils belonged to the better-class families on the Kingstown and Dalkey line. Old as they were, her aunts[10] also did their share. Julia, though she was quite grey, was still the leading soprano in Adam and Eve's, and Kate, being too feeble to go about much, gave music lessons to beginners on the old square piano in the back room. Lily, the caretaker's daughter, did housemaid's work for them. Though their life was modest, they believed in eating well; the best of everything: diamond-bone sirloins, three-shilling tea and the best bottled stout. But Lily seldom made a mistake in the orders, so that she got on well with her three mistresses. They were fussy, that was all. But the only thing they would not stand was back answers.[11]

Of course, they had good reason to be fussy on such a night. And then it was long after ten o'clock and yet there was no sign of Gabriel[12] and his wife. Besides they were dreadfully afraid that Freddy Malins might turn up screwed. They would not wish for worlds[13] that any of Mary Jane's pupils should see him under the influence; and when he was like that it was sometimes very hard to manage him. Freddy Malins always came late, but they wondered what could be keeping Gabriel[14]: and that was what brought them every two minutes to the banisters to ask Lily had Gabriel or Freddy come.[15]

---

7) prop: 지주, 기둥(=person who gives support).
8) the Academy: 여기서는 음악학원을 지칭한다.
9) Antient Concert Rooms: 더블린 시내에 있는 음악회관.
10) her aunts: Mary Jane의 고모들.
11) back answers: 말대꾸.
12) Gabriel: 남자 주인공 이름. 원래 Gabriel은 천사의 이름이다. "하나님의 사람" 또는 "하나님은 능력이 많으시다"라는 뜻을 갖고 있다. 성모 마리아에게 예수의 잉태를 알려주었음. 일곱 대천사 중의 하나로 인간에게 위안과 동정을 베푼다고 함.
13) for worlds: 절대로, 어떤 일이 있더라도(=for all the world).
14) what could be keeping Gabriel: 가브리엘이 왜 늦을까.

'O, Mr Conroy,' said Lily to Gabriel when she opened the door for him, 'Miss Kate and Julia thought you were never coming. Good night, Mrs Conroy.'

'I'll engage they did,' said Gabriel, 'but they forget that my wife here takes three mortal[16] hours to dress herself.'

He stood on the mat, scraping the snow from his goloshes,[17] while Lily led his wife to the foot of the stairs and called out:

'Miss Kate, here's Mrs Conroy.'

Kate and Julia came toddling down the dark stairs at once. Both of them kissed Gabriel's wife, said she must be perished alive[18], and asked was Gabriel with her.[19]

'Here I am as right as the mail, Aunt Kate! Go on up. I'll follow,' called out Gabriel from the dark.

He continued scraping his feet vigorously while the three women went upstairs, laughing, to the ladies' dressing-room. A light fringe of snow lay like a cape on the shoulders of his overcoat and like toecaps on the toes of his goloshes; and, as the buttons of his overcoat slipped with a squeaking noise through the snow-stiffened frieze, a cold, fragrant air from out-of-doors escaped from crevices and folds.

'Is it snowing again, Mr Conroy?' asked Lily.

She had preceded him into the pantry to help him off with his overcoat. Gabriel smiled at the three syllables she had given his surname and glanced her. She was a slim, growing girl, pale in complexion and with hay-coloured hair. The gas in the pantry made her look still paler. Gabriel had known her when she was a child and used to sit in the lowest step nursing a rag doll.

'Yes, Lily,' he answered, 'and I think we're in for[20] a night of it.'

---

15) had Gabriel or Freddy come: whether Gabriel or Freddy had come.
16) mortal: 지긋지긋한, 지겨운(tediously long).
17) goloshes: 갈로시, 고무로 만든 장화(덧신)(=galoshes).
18) must be perished alive: 추워서 얼어 죽을 뻔 했겠다.
19) was Gabriel with her: whether Gabriel was with her.
20) be in for: likely to have or experience.

He looked up at the pantry ceiling, which was shaking with the stamping and shuffling of feet on the floor above, listened for a moment to the piano and then glanced at the girl, who was folding his overcoat carefully at the end of a shelf.

'Tell me, Lily,' he said in a friendly tone, 'do you still go to school?'

'O no, sir,' she answered. 'I'm done schooling this year and more.'[21)]

'O, then,' said Gabriel gaily, 'I suppose we'll be going to your wedding one of these fine days with your young man, eh?'

The girl glanced back at him over her shoulder and said with great bitterness:

'The men that is now is only all palaver and what they can get out of you.'[22)]

Gabriel coloured, as if he felt he had made a mistake, and, without looking at her, kicked off his goloshes and flicked actively with his muffler at his patent-leather-shoes.

He was a stout, tallish young man. The high colour of his cheeks pushed upwards even to his forehead, where it scattered itself in a few formless patches of pale red; and on his hairless face there scintillated restlessly the polished lenses and the bright gilt rims of the glasses which screened his delicate and restless eyes. His glossy black hair was parted in the middle and brushed in a long curve behind his ears where it curled slightly beneath the groove left by his hat.

When he had flicked lustre into his shoes he stood up and pulled his waistcoat down more tightly on his plump body. Then he took a coin rapidly from his pocket.

'O Lily,' he said, thrusting it into her hands, 'it's Christmas-time, isn't it? Just... here's a little....'

He walked rapidly towards the door.

'O no, sir!' cried the girl, following him. 'Really, sir, I wouldn't

---

21) I'm done schooling this year and more: I finished schooling more than a year ago.

22) The men~out of you: 요사이 남자들은 모두 감언이설로 여자에게서 무엇이든 빼앗아가려고 해요.

take it.'

'Christmas-time! Christmas-time!' said Gabriel, almost trotting to the stairs and waving his hand to her in deprecation.[23)]

The girl, seeing that he had gained[24)] the stairs, called out after him:

'Well, thank you, sir.'

He waited outside the drawing-room until the waltz should finish, listening to the skirts that swept against it and to the shuffling of feet. He was still discomposed by the girl's bitter and sudden retort. It had cast a gloom over him which he tried to dispel by arranging his cuffs and the bows of his tie. He then took from his waistcoat pocket a little paper and glanced at the headings he had made for his speech. He was undecided about the lines from Robert Browning, for he feared they would be above the heads of his hearers.[25)] Some quotation that they would recognize from Shakespeare or from the Melodies would be better. The indelicate clacking of the men's heels and the shuffling of their soles reminded him that their grade of culture differed from his.[26)] He would only make himself ridiculous by quoting poetry to them which they could not understand. They would think that he was airing[27)] his superior education. He would fail with them just as he had failed with the girl in the pantry. He had taken up a wrong tone. His whole speech was a mistake from first to last, an utter failure.

Just then his aunts and his wife came out of the ladies' dressing-room. His aunts[28)] were two small, plainly dressed old women. Aunt Julia was an inch or so the taller. Her hair, drawn low over the tops of her ears, was grey; and grey also, with darker shadows,

---

23) in deprecation: 애원하듯이, 호소하듯이.
24) gain: reach, arrive at.
25) above the heads of his hearers: 청중들이 이해 못하는.
26) their grade of culture differed from his: 그들의 교양 수준이 자기와 다르다고 생각하는 가브리엘의 우월감 혹은 교만이 드러난다.
27) air: 뽐내다, 자랑하다.
28) his aunts: 가브리엘의 이모들.

was her large flaccid face. Though she was stout in build and stood erect, her slow eyes and parted lips gave her the appearance of a woman who did not know where she was or where she was going. Aunt Kate was more vivacious. Her face, healthier than her sister's, was all puckers and creases, like a shrivelled red apple, and her hair, braided in the same old-fashioned way, had not lost its ripe nut colour.

They both kissed Gabriel frankly. He was their favourite nephew, the son of their dead elder sister, Ellen, who had married T. J. Conroy of the Port and Docks.[29)]

'Gretta tells me you're not going to take a cab back to Monkstown tonight, Gabriel!' said Aunt Kate.

'No,' said Gabriel, turning to his wife, 'we had quite enough of that last year,[30)] hadn't we? Don't you remember, Aunt Kate, what a cold Gretta got out of it? Cab windows rattling all the way, and the east wind blowing in after we passed Merrion. Very jolly it was. Gretta caught a dreadful cold.'

Aunt Kate frowned severely and nodded her head at every word.

'Quite right, Gabriel, quite right,' she said. 'You can't be too careful.'[31)]

'But as for Gretta there,' said Gabriel, 'she'd walk home in the snow if she were let.'

Mrs Conroy laughed.

'Don't mind him, Aunt Kate,' she said. 'He's really an awful bother, what with green shades for Tom's eyes at night and making him do the dumb-bells, and forcing Eva[32)] to eat the stirabout. The poor child! And she simply hates the sight of it!...O, but you'll never guess what he makes me wear now!'

She broke out into a peal of laughter and glanced at her hus-

---

29) the Port and Docks: 항만청.
30) we had quite enough of that: 우리는 아주 혼이 났었다.
31) You can't be too careful: 아무리 조심해도 지나치지 않다.
32) Tom, Eva: Conroy 부부의 아들과 딸.

band, whose admiring and happy eyes had been wandering from her dress to her face and hair. The two aunts laughed heartily, too, for Gabriel's solicitude was a standing joke[33] with them.

'Goloshes!' said Mrs Conroy. 'That's the latest.[34] Whenever it's wet underfoot I must put on my goloshes. Tonight even, he wanted me to put them on, but I wouldn't. The next thing he'll buy me will be a diving suit.'

Gabriel laughed nervously and patted his tie reassuringly, while Aunt Kate nearly doubled herself, so heartily did she enjoy the joke. The smile soon faded from Aunt Julia's face and her mirthless eyes were directed towards her nephew's face. After a pause she asked:

'And what are goloshes, Gabriel?'

'Golishes, Julia!' exclaimed her sister. 'Goodness me,[35] don't you know what goloshes are? You wear them over your... over your boots, Gretta, isn't it?'

'Yes,' said Mrs Conroy. 'Gutta-percha thing. We both have a pair now. Gabriel says everyone wears them on the Continent.'

'O, on the Continent,' murmured Aunt Julia, nodding her head slowly.

Gabriel knitted his brows and said, as if he were slightly angered:

'It's nothing very wonderful, but Gretta thinks it very funny, because she says the word reminds her of Christy Minstrels.'

'But tell me, Gabriel,' said Aunt Kate, with brisk tact. 'Of course, you've seen about the room. Gretta was saying ...'[36]

'O, the room is all right,' replied Gabriel. I've taken one in the Gresham.'

'To be sure,' said Aunt Kate, by far the best thing to do. And the children, Gretta, you're not anxious about them?'

---

33) a standing joke: 여전한 웃음거리.

34) the latest: the latest joke.

35) Goodness me: 맙소사, 어머나.

36) Of course~saying~: 물론 숙박할 방은 알아보았겠지. 그레타가 그러든데..."

'O, for one night,' said Mrs Conroy. 'Besides, Bessie will look after them.'

'To be sure,' said Aunt Kate again. What a comfort it is to have a girl like that, one you can depend on! There's that Lily, I'm sure I don't know what has come over her lately. She's not the girl she was[37] at all.'

Gabriel was about to ask his aunt some questions on this points, but she broke off suddenly to gaze after her sister, who had wandered down the stairs and was craning her neck over the banisters.

'Now, I ask you,' she said almost testily, 'where is Julia going? Julia! Julia! Where are you going?'

Julia, who had gone half-way down one flight, came back and announced blandly:

'Here's Freddy.'

At the same moment a clapping of hands and a final flourish[38] of the pianist told that the waltz had ended. The drawing-room door was opened from within and some couples came out. Aunt Kate drew Gabriel aside hurriedly and whispered into his ear:

'Slip down, Gabriel, like a good fellow[39] and see if he's all right, and don't let him up if he's screwed. I'm sure he's screwed.[40] I'm sure he is.'

Gabriel went to the stairs and listened over the banisters. He could hear two persons talking in the pantry. Then he recognized Freddy Malins' laugh. He went down the stairs noisily.

'It's such a relief,' said Aunt Kate to Mrs Conroy, 'that Gabriel is here. I always feel easier in my mind when he's here.... Julia, there's Miss Daly and Miss Power will take some refreshment. Thanks for your beautiful waltz, Miss Daly. It made lively time.'

A tall wizen-faced[41] man, with a stiff grizzled moustache and

---

37) the girl she was: 옛날의 릴리.

38) flourish: 장식악구, 화려한 연주(=a decorative addition introduced by player or singer).

39) like a good fellow: 착한 사람답게, 제발 바라건대.

40) screwed: drunken.

swarthy skin, who was passing out with his partner, said:

'And may we have some refreshment, too, Miss Morkan?'

'Julia,' said Aunt Kate summarily, 'and here's Mr Browne and Miss Furlong. Take them in, Julia, with Miss Daly and Miss Power.'

'I'm the man for the ladies,' said Mr Browne, pursing his lips until his moustaches bristled, and smiling in all his wrinkles. 'You know, Miss Morkan, the reason they are so fond of me is—'

He did not finish his sentence, but, seeing that Aunt Kate was out of earshot, at once led the three young ladies into the back room. The middle of the room was occupied by two square tables placed end to end,[42] and on these Aunt Julia and the caretaker were straightening and smoothing a large cloth. On the sideboard were arrayed dishes and plates, and glasses and bundles of knives and forks and spoons. The top of the closed square piano served also as a sideboard for viands and sweets. At a smaller sideboard in one corner two young men were standing, drinking hop-bitters.

Mr Browne led his charges[43] thither and invited them all, in jest, to some ladies' punch, hot, strong, and sweet. As they said they never took anything strong, he opened three bottles of lemonade for them. Then he asked one of the young men to move aside, and taking hold of the decanter, filled out for himself a goodly measure of whisky. The young men eyed him respectfully while he took a trial sip.

'God help me,' he said, smiling, 'it's the doctor's orders.'

His wizened face broke into a broader smile, and the three young ladies laughed in musical echo to his pleasantry,[44] swaying their bodies to and fro, with nervous jerks of their shoulders. The boldest said:

'O, now, Mr Browne, I'm sure the doctor never ordered anything

---

41) wizen-faced: 얼굴이 쭈굴쭈굴한.
42) tables placed end to end: 끝과 끝을 서로 맞대어 놓은 식탁들.
43) his charges: 그가 담당한 사람들.
44) pleasantry: 농담, 재담.

of the kind.'

Mr Browne took another sip of his whisky and said, with sidling mimicry.[45)]

'Well, you see, I'm like the famous Mrs Cassidy, who is reported to have said: "Now, Mary Grimes, if I don't take it, make me take it, for I feel I want it." '

His hot face had leaned forward a little too confidentially and he had assumed a very low Dublin accent, so that the young ladies, with one instinct, received his speech in silence. Miss Furlong, who was one of Mary Jane's pupils, asked Miss Daly what was the name of the pretty waltz she had played; and Mr Browne, seeing that he was ignored, turned promptly to the two young men, who were more appreciative.[46)]

A red-faced young woman, dressed in pansy, came into the room, excitedly clapping her hands and crying:

'Quadrilles! Quadrilles!'[47)]

Close on her heels came Aunt Kate, crying:

'Two gentlemen and three ladies, Mary Jane!'

'O, here's Mr Bergin and Mr Kerrigan,' said Mary Jane. 'Mr Kerrigan, will you take Miss Power? Miss Furlong, may I get you a partner, Mr Bergin. O, that'll just do now.'

'Three ladies, Mary Jane,' said Aunt Kate.

The two young gentlemen asked the ladies if they might have the pleasure, and Mary Jane turned to Miss Daly.

'O, Miss Daly, you're really awful good, after playing for the last two dances, but really we're so short of ladies to-night.'

'I don't mind in the least, Miss Morkan.'

'But I've a nice partner for you, Mr Bartell D'Arcy, the tenor. I'll get him to sing later on. All Dublin is raving[48)] about him.'

---

45) with sidling mimicry: 은근한 흉내조로.
46) more appreciative: 좀 더 알아주는.
47) Quadrilles: 카드리유 춤. 2명 또는 4명이 짝지어 추는 춤.
48) rave: 지껄이다, 고함치다, 미친 듯이 기뻐하다.

'Lovely voice, lovely voice!' said Aunt Kate.

As the piano had twice begun the prelude to the first figure Mary Jane led her recruits quickly from the room. They had hardly gone when Aunt Julia wandered slowly into the room, looking behind her at something.

'What is the matter, Julia?' asked Aunt Kate anxiously. 'Who is it?'

Julia, who was carrying in a column of table-napkins, turned to her sister and said, simply, as if the question had surprised her:

'It's only Freddy, Kate, and Gabriel with him.'

In fact, right behind her Gabriel could be seen piloting[49] Freddy Malins across the landing. The latter, a young man of about forty, was of Gabriel's size and build, with very round shoulders. His face was fleshy and pallid, touched with colour only at the thick hanging lobes of his ears and at the wide wings of his nose. He had coarse features, a blunt nose, a convex and receding brow, tumid and protruded lips. His heavy-lidded eyes and the disorder of his scanty hair made him look sleepy. He was laughing heartily in a high key at a story which he had been telling Gabriel on the stairs and at the same time rubbing the knuckles of his left fist backwards into his left eye.

'Good evening, Freddy,' said Aunt Julia.

Freddy Malins bade the Misses Morkan good evening in what seemed an off-hand fashion by reason of the habitual catch in his voice and then, seeing that Mr Browne was grinning at him from the sideboard, crossed the room on rather shaky legs and began to repeat in an undertone the story he had just told to Gabriel.

'He's not so bad, is he?' said Aunt Kate to Gabriel.

Gabriel's brows were dark, but he raised them quickly and answered:

'O, no, hardly noticeable.'

'Now, isn't he a terrible fellow!' she said. 'And his poor mother

---

49) pilot: 조종하다, 안내하다.

made him take the pledge on New Year's Eve. But come on, Gabriel, into the drawing-room.'

Before leaving the room with Gabriel she signalled to Mr Browne by frowning and shaking her forefinger in warning to and fro. Mr Browne nodded in answer and, when she had gone, said to Freddy Malins:

'Now, then, Teddy, I'm going to fill you out a good glass of lemonade just to buck you up.'[50)]

Freddy Malins, who was nearing the climax of his story, waved the offer aside impatiently, but Mr Browne, having first called Freddy Malins' attention to a disarray in his dress, filled out and handed him a full glass of lemonade. Freddy Malins' left hand accepted the glass mechanically, his right hand being engaged in the mechanical readjustment of his dress. Mr Browne, whose face was once more wrinkling with mirth, poured out for himself a glass of whisky while Freddy Malins exploded, before he had well reached the climax of his story, in a kink of high-pitched bronchitic laughter[51)] and, setting down his untasted and overflowing glass, began to run the knuckles of his left fist backwards and forwards into his left eye, repeating words of his last phrase as well as his fit of laughter would allow him.

*

Gabriel could not listen while Mary Jane was playing her Academy piece, full of runs[52)] and difficult passages, to the hushed drawing-room. He liked music, but the piece she was playing had no melody for him and he doubted whether it had any melody for the other listeners, though they had begged Mary Jane to play something.[53)] Four young men, who had come from the refreshment-room to

---

50) buck up: 기운 차리게 하다(=make vigorous or cheerful).

51) high-pitched bronchitic laughter: 기관지염에 걸린 듯한 높은 웃음소리.

52) runs: (음악)빨리 연주해야 하는 장식 부분.

53) 메리 제인에게 음악을 연주해달라고 간청했던 사람들이 피아노 연주를 듣고 있지 않는 우스꽝스러운 상황이다. 마치 『더블린 사람들』 작품에 나타난 마비된 모습의 한 예이다.

stand in the doorway at the sound of the piano, had gone away quietly in couples after a few minutes. The only persons who seemed to follow the music were Mary Jane herself, her hands racing along the keyboard or lifted from it at the pauses like those of a priestess in momentary imprecation, and Aunt Kate standing at her elbow to turn the page.

Gabriel's eyes, irritated by the floor, which glittered with beeswax under the heavy chandelier, wandered to the wall above the piano. A picture of the balcony scene in *Romeo and Juliet* hung there and beside it was a picture of two murdered princes in the Tower which Aunt Julia had worked[54] in red, blue, and brown wools when she was a girl. Probably in the school they had gone to as girls that kind of work had been taught for one year.[55] His mother had worked for him as a birthday present a waistcoat of purple tabinet,[56] with little foxes' heads upon it, lined with brown satin and having round mulberry buttons. It was strange that his mother had no musical talent, though Aunt Kate used to call her the brains carrier of the Morkan family. Both she and Julia had always seemed a little proud of their serious and matronly sister. Her photograph stood before the pier-glass. She had an open book on her knees and was pointing out something in it to Constantine who, dressed in a man-o'-war suit, lay at her feet. It was she who had chosen the name of her sons, for she was very sensible of the dignity of family life. Thanks to her, Constantine was now senior curate in Balbriggan and, thanks to her, Gabriel himself had taken his degree in the Royal University. A shadow passed over his face as he remembered her sullen opposition to his marriage. Some slighting phrases she had used still rankled[57] in his memory; once she had spoken of Gretta as being country cute and that was not

54) work: 수놓다(=embroider).

55) 아마 그들이 소녀시절에 다녔던 학교에서는 1년 동안 이런 수놓기(자수)를 가르쳤던 모양이다.

56) tabinet: 물결 무늬가 든 견모직물(실내장식용).

57) rankle: continue to be remembered with bitterness and anger.

true of Gretta at all. It was Gretta who had nursed her during all her last long illness in their house at Monkstown.

He knew that Mary Jane must be near the end of her piece, for she was playing again the opening melody with runs of scales after every bar,[58] and while he waited for the end the resentment died down in his heart. The piece ended with a trill of octaves in the treble and a final deep octave in the bass. Great applause greeted Mary Jane as, blushing and rolling up her music nervously, she escaped from the room. The most vigorous clapping came from the four young men in the doorway who had gone away to the refreshment-room at the beginning of the piece but had come back when the piano had stopped.[59]

Lancers were arranged. Gabriel found himself partnered with Miss Ivors. She was a frank-mannered, talkative young lady, with a freckled face and prominent brown eyes. She did not wear a low-cut bodice, and the large brooch which was fixed in the front of her collar bore on it an Irish device and motto.[60]

When they had taken their places she said abruptly:

'I have a crow to pluck with you.'

'With me?' said Gabriel.

She nodded her head gravely.

'What is it?' asked Gabriel, smiling at her solemn manner.

'Who is G. C.?' answered Miss Ivors, turning her eyes upon him.

Gabriel coloured and was about to knit his brows, as if he did not understand, when she said bluntly:

'O, innocent Amy! I have found out that you write for *The Daily Express*. Now, aren't you ashamed of yourself?'

'Why should I be ashamed of myself?' asked Gabriel, blinking

---

58) she was playing~every bar: 제인이 매소절 끝마다 음계를 화려하게 재빨리 연주하며 처음 멜로디를 반복하고 있었다.

59) 네 젊은 남자들이 연주가 시작될 무렵에 자리를 떴다가 마칠 무렵에 다시 나타나 제일 큰 박수로 환호하는 것도 부조리한 상황의 한 예이다.

60) 칼라 전면에 달고 있는 큰 브로우치에 아일랜드의 문양과 표어가 새겨져 있다. 이 사실은 아이버스 양이 아일랜드의 민족주의자임을 예증한다.

his eyes and trying to smile.

'Well, I'm ashamed of you,' said Miss Ivors frankly. 'To say you'd write for a paper like that. I didn't think you were a West Briton.'[61)]

A look of perplexity appeared on Gabriel's face. It was true that he wrote a literary column every Wednesday in *The Daily Express*, for which he was paid fifteen shillings. But that did not make him a West Briton surely. The books he received for review were almost more welcome than the paltry cheque. He loved to feel the covers and turn over the pages of newly printed books. Nearly every day when his teaching in the college was ended he used to wander down the quays to the second-hand booksellers, to Hickey's on Bachelor's Walk, to Webb's or Massey's on Aston's Quay, or to O'Clohissey's in the by-street. He did not know how to meet her charge. He wanted to say that literature was above politics.[62)] But they were friends of many years' standing and their careers had been parallel, first at the University and then as teachers: he could not risk a grandiose phrase with her. He continued blinking his eyes and trying to smile and murmured lamely that he saw nothing political in writing reviews of books.

When their turn to cross had come he was still perplexed and inattentive. Miss Ivors promptly took his hand in a warm grasp and said in a soft friendly tone:

'Of course, I was only joking. Come, we cross now.'

When they were together again she spoke of the University question and Gabriel felt more at ease. A friend of hers had shown her his review of Browning's poems. That was how she had found out the secret: but she liked the review immensely. Then she said suddenly:

'O, Mr Conroy, will you come for an excursion to the Aran Isles[63)]

---

61) West Briton: 친영파 아일랜드인.

62) literature was above politics: 문학은 정치를 초월하는 것이다. 문학은 정치와 상관이 없다.

63) Aran Isles: 애란 섬. Gallway에서 떨어진 섬들. 아일랜드의 언어와 고유한 풍습이 유지되는 곳으로 민족주의자들이 가고 싶어 하는 곳이다.

this summer? We're going to stay there a whole month. It will be splendid out in the Atlantic. You ought to come. Mr Clancy is coming, and Mr Kilkelly and Kathleen Kearney. It would be splendid for Gretta too if she'd come. She's from Connacht, isn't she?'

'Her people are,' said Gabriel shortly.

'But you will come, won't you?' said Miss Ivors, laying her warm hand eagerly on his arm.

'The fact is' said Gabriel, 'I have just arranged to go—'

'Go where?' asked Miss Ivors.

'Well, you know, every year I go for a cycling tour with some fellows and so—'

'But where?' asked Miss Ivors.

'Well, we usually go to France or Belgium or perhaps Germany,' said Gabriel awkwardly.

'And why do you go to France and Belgium,' said Miss Ivors, 'instead of visiting your own land?'

'Well,' said Gabriel, 'it's partly to keep in touch with the languages and partly for a change.'

'And haven't you your own language to keep in touch with—Irish?' asked Miss Ivors.

'Well,' said Gabriel, 'if it comes to that, you know, Irish is not my language.'

Their neighbours had turned to listen to the cross-examination. Gabriel glanced right and left nervously and tried to keep his good humour under the ordeal,[64] which was making a blush invade his forehead.

'And haven't you your own land to visit,' continued Miss Ivors, 'that you know nothing of, your own people, and your own country?'

'O, to tell you the truth,' retorted Gabriel suddenly, 'I'm sick of my own country, sick of it!'

'Why?' asked Miss Ivors.

Gabriel did not answer, for his retort had heated him.

---

64) under the ordeal: 그 시련 속에서도.

'Why?' repeated Miss Ivors.

They had to go visiting together and, as he had not answered her, Miss Ivors said warmly:

'Of course, you've no answer.'

Gabriel tried to cover his agitation by taking part in the dance with great energy. He avoided her eyes, for he had seen a sour expression on her face. But when they met in the long chain he was surprised to feel his hand firmly pressed. She looked at him from under her brows for a moment quizzically until he smiled. Then, just as the chain was about to start again, she stood on tiptoe and whispered into his ear:

'West Briton!'

When the lancers were over Gabriel went away to a remote corner of the room where Freddy Malins' mother was sitting. She was a stout, feeble old woman with white hair. Her voice had a catch in it like her son's and she stuttered slightly. She had been told that Freddy had come and that he was nearly all right. Gabriel asked her whether she had had a good crossing. She lived with her married daughter in Glasgow and came to Dublin on a visit once a year. She answered placidly that she had had a beautiful crossing and that the captain had been most attentive to her. She spoke also of the beautiful house her daughter kept in Glasgow, and of all the friends they had there. While her tongue rambled on Gabriel tried to banish from his mind all memory of the unpleasant incident with Miss Ivors. Of course the girl, or woman, or whatever she was, was enthusiast, but there was a time for all things. Perhaps he ought not to have answered her like that. But she had no right to call him a West Briton before people, even in joke. She had tried to make him ridiculous before people, heckling him and staring at him with her rabbit's eyes.

He saw his wife making her way towards him through the waltzing couples. When she reached him she said into his ear:

'Gabriel, Aunt Kate wants to know won't you carve the goose as usual. Miss Daly will carve the ham and I'll do the pudding.'

'All right,' said Gabriel.

'She's sending in the younger ones first as soon as this waltz is over so that we'll have the table to ourselves.'

'Were you dancing?' asked Gabriel.

'Of course I was. Didn't you see me? What row[65] had you with Molly Ivors?'

'No row. Why? Did she say so?'

'Something like that. I'm trying to get that Mr D'Arcy to sing. He's full of conceit, I think.'

'There was no row,' said Gabriel moodily, 'only she wanted me to go for a trip to the west of Ireland and I said I wouldn't.'

His wife clasped her hands excitedly and gave a little jump.

'O, do go, Gabriel,' she cried. 'I'd love to see Galway again.'

'You can go if you like,' said Gabriel coldly.

She looked at him for a moment, then turned to Mrs Malins and said:

'There's a nice husband for you, Mrs Malins.'

While she was threading her way back across the room Mrs Malins, without adverting to the interruption, went on to tell Gabriel what beautiful places there were in Scotland and beautiful scenery. Her son-in-law brought them every year to the lakes and they used to go fishing. Her son-in-law was a splendid fisher. One day he caught a beautiful fish and the man in the hotel cooked it for their dinner.

Gabriel hardly heard what she said. Now that supper was coming near he began to think again about his speech and about the quotation. When he saw Freddy Malins coming across the room to visit his mother Gabriel left the chair free for him and retired into the embrasure of the window. The room had already cleared and from the back room came the clatter of plates and knives. Those

---

65) row: [rau] 법석, 소동, 말다툼(=noisy or violent argument). cf. row [rou] : 줄, 열, 노(를 젓다).

who still remained in the drawing-room seemed tired of dancing and were conversing quietly in little groups. Gabriel's warm, trembling fingers tapped the cold pane of the window. How cool it must be outside! How pleasant it would be to walk out alone, first along by the river and then through the park! The snow would be lying on the branches of the trees and forming a bright cap on the top of the Wellington Monument.[66] How much more pleasant it would be there than at the supper-table![67]

He ran over the headings[68] of his speech: Irish hospitality, sad memories, the Three Graces,[69] Paris, the quotation from Browning. He repeated to himself a phrase he had written in his review: "One feels that one is listening to a thought-tormented music." Miss Ivors had praised the review. Was she sincere? Had she really any life of her own behind all her propagandism? There had never been any ill-feeling between them until that night. It unnerved him to think that she would be at the supper-table, looking up at him, while he spoke, with her critical quizzing[70] eyes. Perhaps she would not be sorry to see him fail in his speech. An idea came into his mind and gave him courage. He would say, alluding to Aunt Kate and Aunt Julia: 'Ladies and Gentlemen, the generation which is now on the wane among us may have had its faults, but for my part I think it had certain qualities of hospitality, of humor, of humanity, which the new and very serious and hyper-educated generation that is growing up around us seems to me to lack.' Very good: that was one for Miss Ivors. What did he care that his aunts were only two ignorant old women?[71]

---

66) Wellington Monument: 웰링턴 장군 기념비.

67) 하녀 릴리와 동창생 아이버스 양으로부터 마음이 상한 가브리엘 콘로이는 만찬이 임박하자 만찬 연설을 생각하면서 저녁 식탁보다는 혼자 강변을 걷거나 눈 덮인 공원을 산책하는 것이 훨씬 더 즐거울 것이라고 상상한다.

68) headings: 서두, 표제.

69) Graces: Zeus와 Eurynome의 세 딸. 미의 여신들로서 Aglaia(Brilliance-화려), Euphrosyne(Joy-기쁨), Thalia(Bloom-꽃) 등이다.

70) quiz: 시험(하다); 놀리다, 조롱하다, 비웃다.

A murmur in the room attracted his attention. Mr Browne was advancing from the door, gallantly escorting Aunt Julia, who leaned upon his arm, smiling and hanging her head. An irregular musketry[72] of applause escorted him her also as far as the piano and then, as Mary Jane seated herself on the stool, and Aunt Julia, no longer smiling, half turned so as to pitch her voice fairly into the room, gradually ceased. Gabriel recognized the prelude. It was that of an old song of Aunt Julia's— 'Arrayed for the Bridal'. Her voice, strong and clear in tone, attacked with great spirit the runs which embellish the air, and though she sang very rapidly she did not miss even the smallest of the grace notes.[73] To follow the voice, without looking at the singer's face, was to feel and share the excitement of swift and secure flight. Gabriel applauded loudly with all the others at the close of the song, and loud applause was borne in from the invisible supper-table. It sounded so genuine that a little colour struggled into Aunt Julia's face as she bent to replace in the music-stand the old leather-bound song-book that had her initials on the cover. Freddy Malins, who had listened with his head perched sideways to hear her better, was still applauding when everyone else had ceased and talking animatedly to his mother who nodded her head gravely and slowly in acquiescence.[74] At last, when he could clap no more, he stood up suddenly and hurried across the room to Aunt Julia whose hand he seized and held in both his hands, shaking it when words failed him or the catch in his voice proved too much for him.[75]

'I was just telling my mother,' he said, 'I never heard you sing so well, never. No, I never heard your voice so good as it is tonight. Now! Would you believe that now? That's the truth. Upon my word

---

71) What did he care~old women?: 자기 이모들이 무식한 노파라 한들 무슨 상관이겠는가?

72) musketry: 사격, 소총사격.

73) grace notes: 장식음.

74) acquiescence: 묵종, 묵인.

75) words failed~too much for him: 말로 표현을 못하거나, 아니면 목소리가 꽉 막혀 도저히 참을 수가 없었다.

and honour that's the truth. I never heard your voice sound so fresh and so...so clear and fresh, never.'

Aunt Julia smiled broadly and murmured something about compliments as she released her hand from his grasp. Mr Browne extended his open hand towards her and said to those who were near him in the manner of a showman introducing a prodigy to an audience:

'Miss Julia Morkan, my latest discovery!'

He was laughing very heartily at this himself when Freddy Malins turned to him and said:

'Well, Browne, if you're serious you might make a worse discovery. All I can say is I never heard her sing half so well as long as I am coming here. And that's the honest truth.'

'Neither did I,' said Mr Browne. 'I think her voice has greatly improved.'

Aunt Julia shrugged her shoulders and said with meek pride:

'Thirty tears ago I hadn't a bad voice as voices go.'[76)]

'I often told Julia,' said Aunt Kate emphatically, 'that she was simply thrown away in that choir. But she never would be said by me.'

She turned as if to appeal to the good sense of the others against a refractory[77)] child, while Aunt Julia gazed in front of her, a vague smile of reminiscence playing on her face.

'No,' continued Aunt Kate, 'she wouldn't be said or led by anyone, slaving there in that choir night and day, night and day. Six o'clock on Christmas morning! And all for what?'

'Well, isn't it for the honour of God, Aunt Kate?' asked Mary Jane, twisting round on the piano-stool and smiling.

Aunt Kate turned fiercely on her niece and said:

'I know all about the honour of God, Mary Jane, but I think it's not at all honourable for the Pope to turn out the women out of

---

76) 30년 전에는 목소리치고 나쁘지 않았어요.
77) refractory: 다루기 힘든, 순종하지 않는.

the choirs that have slaved there all their lives and put little whipper-snappers of boys over their heads. I suppose it is for the good of the Church, if the Pope does it. But it's not just, Mary Jane, and it's not right.'

She had worked herself into a passion and would have continued in defence of her sister, for it was a sore subject with her, but Mary Jane, seeing that all the dancers had come back, intervened pacifically.

'Now, Aunt Kate, you're giving scandal to Mr Browne, who is of the other persuasion.'[78)]

Aunt Kate turned to Mr Browne, who was grinning at this allusion to his religion, and said hastily:

'O, I don't question the Pope's being right. I'm only a stupid old woman and I wouldn't presume to do such a thing. But there's such a thing as common everyday politeness and gratitude. And if I were in Julia's place I'd tell that Father Healey straight up to his face...'

'And besides, Aunt Kate,' said Mary Jane, 'we really are all hungry and when we are hungry we are all very quarrelsome.'

'And when we are thirsty we are also quarrelsome,' added Mr Browne.

'So that we had better go to supper,' said Mary Jane, 'and finish the discussion afterwards.'

On the landing outside the drawing-room Gabriel found his wife and Mary Jane trying to persuade Miss Ivors to stay for supper. But Miss Ivors, who had put on her hat and was buttoning her cloak, would not stay. She did not feel in the least hungry and she had already overstayed her time.

'But only for ten minutes, Molly,' said Mrs Conroy. 'That won't delay you.'

'To take a pick[79)] itself,' said Mary Jane, 'after all your dancing.'

'I really couldn't,' said Miss Ivors.

'I am afraid you didn't enjoy yourself at all,' said Mary Jane

---

78) persuasion: 교파(=sect).
79) take a pick: 음식을 조금 들다.

hopelessly.

'Ever so much, I assure you,' said Miss Ivors, 'but you really must let me run off now.'

'But how can you get home?' asked Mrs Conroy.

'O, it's only two steps up the quay.'

Gabriel hesitated a moment and said:

'If you will allow me, Miss Ivors, I'll see you home[80] if you are really obliged to go.'

But Miss Ivors broke away from them.

'I won't hear of it,' she cried. 'For goodness' sake go in to your suppers and don't mind me. I'm quite well able to take care of myself.'

'Well, you're the comical girl, Molly,' said Mrs Conroy frankly.

'*Beannacht libh,*'[81] cried Miss Ivors, with a laugh, as she ran down the staircase.

Mary Jane gazed after her, a moody puzzled expression on her face, while Mrs Conroy leaned over the banisters to listen for the hall-door. Gabriel asked himself was he the cause of her abrupt departure.[82] But she did not seem to be in ill humour—she had gone away laughing. He stared blankly down the staircase.

At the moment Aunt Kate came toddling out of the supper-room, almost wringing her hands in despair.

'Where is Gabriel?' she cried. 'Where on earth is Gabriel? There's everyone waiting in there, stage to let, and nobody to carve the goose!'

'Here I am, Aunt Kate!' cried Gabriel, with sudden animation, 'ready to carve a flock of geese, if necessary.'

A fat brown goose lay at one end of the table, and at the other end, on a bed of creased paper strewn with sprigs of parsley, lay

---

80) see you home: 집까지 바래다주다.

81) *Beannacht libh*: 작별할 때 건네는 '안녕'이란 뜻의 아일랜드 말.

82) 직접 말한 "Am I the cause of your abrupt departure?"를 그냥 어순 그대로 간접화법으로 고친 문장이다.

a great ham, stripped of its outer skin and peppered over with crust crumbs, a neat paper frill round its shin, and beside this was a round of spiced beef. Between these rival ends ran parallel lines of side-dishes: two little minsters of jelly, red and yellow; a shallow dish full of blocks of blancmange and red jam, a large green leaf-shaped of purple raisins and peeled almonds, a companion dish on which lay a solid rectangle of Smyrna figs, a dish of custard topped with grated nutmeg, a small bowl full of chocolates and sweets wrapped in gold and silver papers and a glass vase in which stood some tall celery stakes. In the center of the table there stood, as sentries to a fruit-stand which upheld a pyramid of oranges and American apples, two squat old-fashioned decanters of cut glass, one containing port and the other dark sherry. On the closed square piano a pudding in a huge yellow dish lay in waiting, and behind it were three squads of bottles of stout and ale and minerals drawn up according to the colours of their uniforms, the first two black, with brown and red labels, the third and smallest squad white, with transverse green sashes.

Gabriel took his seat boldly at the head of the table and, having looked to the edge of the carver, plunged his fork firmly into the goose. He felt quite at ease now, for he was an expert carver and liked nothing better than to find himself at the head of a well-laden table.[83)]

'Miss Furlong, what shall I send you?' he asked, 'A wing or a slice of the breast?'

'Just a small slice of the breast.'

'Miss Higgins, what for you?'

'O, anything at all, Mr Conroy.'

While Gabriel and Miss Daly exchanged plates of goose and plates of ham and spiced beef, Lily went from guest to guest with a dish of hot floury potatoes wrapped in a white napkin. This was

83) 가브리엘 콘로이의 속물적 근성이 드러나는 부분이다. 잘 차려진 식탁 머리 상석에 앉는 것을 좋아한다.

Mary Jane's idea and she had also suggested apple sauce for the goose, but Aunt Kate had said that plain roast goose without any apple sauce had always been good enough for her and she hoped she might never eat worse. Mary Jane waited on her pupils and saw that they got the best slice, and Aunt Kate and Aunt Julia opened and carried across from the piano bottles of stout and ale for the gentlemen and bottles of minerals for the ladies. There was a great deal of confusion and laughter and noise, the noise of orders and counter-orders, of knives and forks, of corks and glass-stoppers. Gabriel began to carve second helping as soon as he had finished the first round without serving himself. Everyone protested loudly, so that he compromised by taking a long draught of stout, for he had found the carving hot work. Mary Jane settled down quietly to her supper, but Aunt Kate and Aunt Julia were still toddling round the table, walking on each other's heels, getting in each other's way and giving each other unheeded orders. Mr Browne begged of them to sit down and eat their suppers and so did Gabriel, but they said there was time enough, so that, at last, Freddy Malins stood up and, capturing Aunt Kate, plumped her down on her chair amid general laughter.

When everyone had been well served Gabriel said, smiling:

'Now, if anyone wants a little more of what vulgar people call stuffing let him or her speak.'

A chorus of voices invited him to begin his own supper, and Lily came forward with three potatoes which she had reserved for him.

'Very well,' said Gabriel amiably, as he took another preparatory draught, 'kindly forget my existence, ladies and gentlemen, for a few minutes.'

He set to his supper and took no part in the conversation with which the table covered Lily's removal of the plates. The subject of talk was the opera company which was then at the Theatre Royal. Mr Bartell D'Arcy, the tenor, a dark-complexioned young man with a smart moustache, praised very highly the leading contralto[84] of the company, but Miss Furlong thought she had a rather vulgar style of production. Freddy Malins said there was a Negro chieftain singing in the second part of the Gaiety[85] pantomime who had one of the finest tenor voices he had ever heard.

'Have you heard him?' he asked Mr Bartell D'Arcy across the table.

'No,' answered Mr Bartell D'Arcy carelessly.

'Because,' Freddy Malins explained, 'now I'd be curious to hear your opinion of him. I think he has a grand voice.'

'It takes Teddy to find out the really good things,' said Mr Browne familiarly to the table.

'And why couldn't he have a voice too?' asked Freddy Malins sharply. 'Is it because he's only a black?'

Nobody answered this question and Mary Jane led the table back to the legitimate opera. One of her pupils had given her a pass for *Mignon*.[86] Of course it was very fine, she said, but it made her think of poor Georgina Burns.[87] Mr Browne could go back farther still, to the old Italian companies that used to come to Dublin—Tietjens, Ilma de Murzka, Campanini, the great Trebelli, Giuglini, Ravelli, Aramburo. Those were the days, he said, when there was something like singing to be heard in Dublin. He told too of how the top gallery of the old Royal used to be packed night after night, of how one night an Italian tenor had sung five encores to 'Let me like a Soldier fall' introducing a high C every time, and of how the gallery boys would sometimes in their enthusiasm unyoke the horses from the carriage of some great *prima donna* and pull her themselves through the streets to her hotel. Why did they never play the grand old operas now, he asked, *Dinorah, Lucrezia Borgia*? Because they could not get the voices to sing them: that was why.

84) contralto: 여성의 가장 낮은 소리.
85) Gaiety: 더블린에 있는 극장 이름.
86) *Mignon*: 19세기 말 대단한 인기를 끌었던 프랑스 오페라.
87) Georgina Burns: 확인 안 되는 당시의 오페라 가수.

'O, well,' said Mr Bartell D'Arcy, 'I presume there are as good singers today as there were then.'

'Where are they?' asked Mr Browne defiantly.

'In London, Paris, Milan,' said Mr Bartell D'Arcy warmly. 'I suppose Caruso, for example, is quite as good, if not better than any of the men you have mentioned.'

'Maybe so,' said Mr Browne. 'But I may tell you I doubt it strongly.'

'O, I'd give anything to hear Caruso sing,' said Mary Jane.

'For me,' said Ant Kate, who had been picking a bone, 'there was only one tenor. To please me, I mean. But I suppose none of you ever heard of him.'

'Who was he, Miss Morkan?' asked Mr Bartell D'Arcy politely.

'His name,' said Aunt Kate, 'was Parkinson. I heard him when he was in his prime and I think he had then the purest tenor voice that was ever put into a man's throat.'

'Strange,' said Mr Bartell D'Arcy. 'I never even heard of him.'

'Yes, yes, Miss Morkan is right,' said Mr Browne. 'I remember hearing old Parkinson, but he's too far back for me.'[88)]

'A beautiful, pure, sweet, mellow English tenor,' said Aunt Kate with enthusiasm.

Gabriel having finished, the huge pudding was transferred to the table. The clatter of forks and spoons began again,

Gabriel's wife served out spoonfuls of the pudding and passed the plates down the table. Midway down they were held up by Mary Jane, who replenished them with raspberry or orange jelly or with blancmange and jam. The pudding was of Aunt Julia's making, and she received praises for it from all quarters. She herself said that it was not quite brown enough.

'Well, I hope, Miss Morkan,' said Mr Browne, 'that I'm brown enough for you because, you know, I'm all brown.'[89)]

---

88) he's too far back for me: 그 사람은 나에게 너무 옛날 사람이다.

89) I'm all frown: 나는 온통 갈색이다. 브라운이 자기 이름과 관련하여 던진 농담

All the gentlemen, except Gabriel, ate some of the pudding out of compliment to Aunt Julia. As Gabriel never ate sweets the celery had been left for him. Freddy Malins also took a stalk of celery and ate it with his pudding. He had been told that celery was a capital thing for the blood and he was just then under doctor's care. Mrs Malins, who had been silent all through the supper, said that her son was going down to Mount Melleray in a week or so. The table then spoke of Mount Mellery, how bracing the air was down there, how hospitable the monks were and how they never asked for a penny-piece from their guests.

'And do you mean to say,' asked Mr Browne incredulously, 'that a chap can go down there and put up there as if it were a hotel and live on the fat of the land[90] and then come away without paying anything?'

'O, most people give some donation to the monastery when they leave,' said Mary Jane.

'I wish we had an institution like that in our Church,' said Mr Browne candidly.

He was astonished to hear that the monks never spoke, got up at two in the morning and slept in their coffins. He asked what they did it for.

'That's the rule of the order,' said Aunt Kate firmly.

'Yes, but why?' asked Mr Browne.

Aunt Kate repeated that it was the rule, that was all. Mr Browne still seemed not to understand. Freddy Malins explained to him, as best he could, that the monks were trying to make up for the sins committed by all the sinners in the outside world. The explanation was not very clear, for Mr Browne grinned and said:

'I like that idea very much, but wouldn't a comfortable spring bed do them as well as a coffin?'

이지만, 그의 무기력한 성격을 드러내는 말이다. 조이스의 작품에서 갈색은 쇠퇴와 죽음, 무기력 등을 상징한다.

90) the fat of the land: 가장 좋은 소산물, 가장 좋은 것.

'The coffin,' said Mary Jane, 'is to remind them of their last end.'

As the subject had grown lugubrious[91] it was buried in a silence of the table, during which Mrs Malins could be heard saying to her neighbour in an indistinct undertone:

'They are very good men, the monks, very pious men.'

The raisins and almonds and figs and apples and oranges and chocolates and sweets were now passed about the table, and Aunt Julia invited all the guests to have either port or sherry. At first Mr Bartell D'Arcy refused to take either, but one of his neighbours nudged him and whispered something to him, upon which he allowed his glass to be filled. Gradually as the last glasses were being filled the conversation ceased. A pause followed, broken only by the noise of the wine and by unsettling of chairs. The Misses Morkan, all three, looked down at the tablecloth. Someone coughed once or twice, and then a few gentlemen patted the table gently as a signal for silence. The silence came and Gabriel pushed back his chairs and stood up.

The patting at once grew louder in encouragement and then ceased altogether. Gabriel leaned his ten trembling fingers on the tablecloth and smiled nervously at the company. Meeting a row of upturned faces he raised his eyes to the chandelier. The piano was playing a waltz tune and he could hear the skirts sweeping against the drawing-room door. People, perhaps, were standing in the snow on the quay outside, gazing up at the lighted windows and listening to the waltz music. The air was pure there. In the distance lay the park, where the trees were weighted with snow. The Wellington Monument wore a gleaming cap of snow that flashed westwards over the white field of Fifteen Acres.

He began:[92]

'Ladies and Gentlemen,

'It has fallen to my lot this evening, as in years past, to perform

---

91) lugubrious: 울적한, 우울한.
92) 가브리엘 콘로이의 만찬 연설이 시작된다.

a very pleasing task, but a task for which I am afraid my poor powers as a speaker are all too inadequate.'

'No, no!' said Mr Browne.

'But, however that may be, I can only ask you tonight to take the will for the deed,[93] and to lend me your attention for a few moments while I endeavour to express to you in words what my feelings are on this occasion.

'Ladies and Gentlemen, it is not the first time that we have gathered together under this hospitable roof, around this hospitable board. It is not the first time that we have been the recipients—or perhaps, I had better say, the victims—of the hospitality of certain good ladies.'

He made a circle in the air with his arm and paused. Everyone laughed or smiled at Aunt Kate and Aunt Julia and Mary Jane, who all turned crimson with pleasure. Gabriel went on more boldly:

'I feel more strongly with every recurring year that our country has no tradition which does it so much honour and which it should guard so jealously as that of its hospitality.

It is a tradition that is unique as far as my experience goes (and I have visited not a few places abroad) among the modern nations. Some would say, perhaps, that with us it is rather a failing than anything to be boasted of. But granted even that, it is, to my mind, a princely failing, and one that I trust will long be cultivated among us. Of one thing, at least, I am sure. As long as this one roof shelters the good ladies aforesaid—and I wish from my heart it may do so for many and many a long year to come—the tradition of genuine warm-hearted courteous Irish hospitality, which our forefathers have handed down to us and which we must hand down to our descendants, is still alive among us.'

A hearty murmur of assents ran round the table. It shot through Gabriel's mind that Miss Ivors was not there and that she had gone

---

93) take the will for the deed: 나의 행동이나 공적 대신 나의 뜻이나 의도를 이해해 주다.

away discourteously: and he said with confidence in himself:

'Ladies and Gentlemen,

'A new generation is growing up in our midst, a generation actuated by new ideas and new principles. It is serious and enthusiastic for these new ideas and its enthusiasm, even when it is misdirected, is, I believe, in the main sincere. But we are living in a sceptical and, if I may use the phrase, a thought-tormented age: and sometimes I fear that this new generation, educated or hyper-educated as it is, will lack those qualities of humanity, of hospitality, of kindly humour which belonged to an older day. Listening tonight to the names of all those great singers of the past it seemed to me, I must confess, that we were living in a less spacious age. Those days might, without exaggeration, be called spacious days: and if they are gone beyond recall, let us hope, at least, that in gatherings such as this we shall speak of them with pride and affection, still cherish in our hearts the memory of those dead and gone greats ones whose fame the world will not willingly let die.'

'Hear, hear!' said Mr Browne loudly.

'But yet,' continued Gabriel, his voice falling into a softer inflection, 'there are always in gatherings such as this sadder thoughts that will recur to our minds: thoughts of the past, of youth, of changes, of absent faces that we miss here tonight. Our path through life is strewn with[94] many such sad memories: and were we to brood upon them always we could not find the heart to go on bravely with our work among the living.[95] We have all of us living duties and living affections which claim, and rightly claim, our strenuous endeavours.

'Therefore, I will not linger on the past. I will not let any gloomy moralizing intrude upon us here tonight. Here we are gathered together for a brief moment from the bustle and rush of our everyday routine. We are met here as friends, in the spirit of good-fellowship,

94) is strewn with: is scattered with.
95) 가브리엘의 현실적 인생관이 드러난다. 인생은 슬픈 것이나, 지나간 일에 집착하면 용기를 잃는다는 것이다.

as colleagues, also to a certain extent, in the true spirit of *camaraderie*, and as the guests of—what shall I call them?—the Three Graces of the Dublin musical world.'

The table burst into applause and laughter at this allusion. Aunt Julia vainly asked each of her neighbours in turn to tell her what Gabriel had said.

'He says we are the Three Graces, Aunt Julia,' said Mary Jane.

Aunt Julia did not understand, but she looked up, smiling, at Gabriel, who continued in the same vein:

'Ladies and Gentlemen,

'I will not attempt to play tonight the part that Paris[96] played on another occasion. I will not attempt to choose between them. The task would be an invidious[97] one and one beyond my poor powers. For when I view them in turn, whether it be our chief hostess herself, whose good heart, whose too good heart, has become a byword with all who know her; or her sister, who seems to be gifted with perennial youth and whose singing must have been a surprise and revelation to us all tonight; or, last but not least, when I consider our youngest hostess, talented, cheerful, hardworking and the best of nieces, I confess, Ladies and Gentlemen, that I do not know to which of them I should award the prize.'

Gabriel glanced down at his aunts and, seeing the large smile on Aunt Julia's face and the tears which had risen to Aunt Kate's eyes, hastened to his close. He raised his glass of port gallantly, while every member of the company fingered a glass expectantly, and said loudly:

'Let us toast them all three together. Let us drink to their health, wealth, long life, happiness, and prosperity and may they long continue to hold the proud and self-won position which they hold in their profession and the position of honour and affection which

---

96) Paris: Troy의 왕자. Juno, Minerva, Venus의 세 여신 중에 Venus를 가장 아름다운 여신으로 지목하여 결국 Troy전쟁이 일어나게 함.

97) invidious: 화나게 만드는, 질투심을 일으키는.

they hold in our hearts.'

All the guests stood up, glass in hand, and turning towards the three seated ladies, sang in unison, with Mr Browne as leader:

For they are jolly gay fellows,
For they are jolly gay fellows,
For they are jolly gay fellows,
Which nobody can deny.

Aunt Kate was making frank use of her handkerchief and even Aunt Julia seemed moved. Freddy Malins beat time with his pudding-fork and the singers turned towards one another, as if in melodious conference, while they sang with emphasis:

Unless he tells a lie,
Unless he tells a lie.

Then, turning once more towards their hostesses, they sang:

For they are jolly gay fellows,
For they are jolly gay fellows,
For they are jolly gay fellows,
Which nobody can deny.

The acclamation which followed was taken up beyond the door of the supper room by many of the other guests and renewed time after time, Freddy Malins acting as officer with his fork on high.

*

The piercing morning air came into the hall where they were standing so that Aunt Kate said:

'Close the door, somebody. Mrs Malins will get her death of cold.'

'Browne is out there, Aunt Kate,' said Mary Jane.

'Browne is everywhere,' said Aunt Kate, lowering her voice.

Mary Jane laughed at her tone.

'Really,' she said archly, 'he is very attentive.'

'He has been laid on here like the gas,' said Aunt Kate in the same tone, 'all during the Christmas.'

She laughed herself this time good-humouredly and then added quickly:

'But tell him to come in, Mary Jane, and close the door. I hope to goodness he didn't hear me.'

At that moment the hall-door was opened and Mr Browne came in from the doorstep, laughing as if his heart would break. He was dressed in a long green overcoat with mock astrakhan cuffs and collar and wore on his head an oval fur cap. He pointed down the snow-covered quay from where the sound of shrill prolonged whistling was borne in.

'Teddy will have all the cabs in Dublin out,' he said.

Gabriel advanced from the little pantry behind the office, struggling into his overcoat and, looking round the hall, said.

'Gretta not down yet?'

'She's getting on her things, Gabriel,' said Aunt Kate.

'Who's playing up there?' asked Gabriel.

'Nobody. They're all gone.'

'O no, Aunt Kate,' said Mary Jane. 'Bartell D'Arcy and Miss O'Callaghan aren't gone yet.'

'Someone is fooling at the piano anyhow,' said Gabriel.

Mary Jane glanced at Gabriel and Mr Browne and said with a shiver:

'It makes me feel cold to look at you two gentlemen muffled up like that. I wouldn't like to face your journey home at this hour.'

'I'd like nothing better this minute,' said Mr Browne stoutly, 'than a rattling fine walk in the country or a fast drive with a good spanking[98] goer between the shafts.'

'We used to have a very good horse and trap at home,' said Aunt

98) spanking: strong.

Julia, sadly.

'The never-to-be-forgotten[99] Johnny,' said Mary Jane, laughing.

Aunt Kate and Gabriel laughed, too.

'Why, what was wonderful about Johnny?' asked Mr Browne.

'The late lamented Patrick Morkan, our grandfather, that is,' explained Gabriel, 'commonly known in his later years as the old gentleman, was a glue-boiler.'

'O, now, Gabriel,' said Aunt Kate, laughing, 'he had a starch mill.'

'Well, glue or starch,' said Gabriel, 'the old gentleman had a horse by the name of Johnny. And Johnny used to work in the old gentleman's mill, walking round and round in order to drive the mill. That was all very well; but now comes the tragic part about Johnny. One fine day the old gentleman thought he'd like to drive out with the quality to a military review in the park.'

'The Lord have mercy on his soul,' said Aunt Kate, compassionately.

'Amen,' said Gabriel. 'So the old gentleman, as I said, harnessed Johnny and put on his very best tall hat and his very best stock collar and drove out in grand style from his ancestral mansion somewhere near Back Lane, I think.'

Everyone laughed, even Mrs Malins, at Gabriel's manner, and Aunt Kate said:

'O, now, Gabriel, he didn't live in Back Lane, really. Only the mill was there.'

'Out from the mansion of his forefathers,' continued Gabriel, 'he drove with Johnny. And everything went on beautifully until Johnny came in sight of King Billy's statue: and whether he fell in love with the horse King Billy sits on or whether he thought he was back again in the mill, anyway he began to walk round the statue.'

Gabriel paced in a circle round the hall in his goloshes amid the laughter of the others.

'Round and round he went,' said Gabriel, 'and the old gentleman, who was a very pompous old gentleman, was highly indignant. "Go

99) never-to-be-forgotten: 결코 잊혀질 수 없는.

on sir! What do you mean, sir? Johnny! Johnny! Most extraordinary conduct! Can't understand the horse!" '

The peals of laughter which followed Gabriel's imitation of the incident were interrupted by a resounding knock at the hall door. Mary Jane ran to open it and let in Freddy Malins. Freddy Malins, with his hat well back on hid head and his shoulders humped with cold, was puffing and steaming after his exertions.

'I could only get one cap,' he said.

'O, we'll find another along the quay,' said Gabriel.

'Yes,' said Aunt Kate. 'Better not keep Mrs Malins standing in the draught.'[100]

Mrs Malins was helped down the front steps by her son and Mr Browne and, after many manoeuvres, hoisted into the cab. Freddy Malins clambered in after her and spent a long time setting her on the seat, Mr Browne helping him with advice. At last she was settled comfortably and Freddy Malins invited Mr Browne into the cab. There was a good deal of confused talk, and then Mr Browne got into the cab. The cabman settled his rug over his knees, and bent down for the address. The confusion grew greater and the cabman was directed differently by Freddy Malins and Mr Browne, each of whom had his head out through a window of the cab. The difficulty was to know where to drop Mr Browne along the route, and Aunt Kate, Aunt Julia, and Mary Jane helped the discussion from the doorstep with cross-directions and contradictions and abundance of laughter. As for Freddy Malins he was speechless with laughter. He popped his head in and out of the window every moment to the great danger of his hat, and told his mother how the discussion was progressing, till at last Mr Browne shouted to the bewildered cabman above the din of everybody's laughter:

'Do you know Trinity College?'

'Yes, sir,' said the cabman.

'Well, drive bang up against Trinity College gates,' said Mr

---

100) draught: wind.

Browne, 'and then we'll tell you whether to go. You understand now?'

'Yes, sir,' said the cabman.

'Make like a bird for Trinity College.'

'Right, sir,' said the cabman.

The horse was whipped up and the cab rattled off along the quay amid a chorus of laughter and adieux.

Gabriel had not gone to the door with the others. He was in a dark part of the hall gazing up the staircase. A woman was standing near the top of the first flight, in the shadow also. He could not see her face but he could see the terra-cotta and salmon-pink panels of her skirt which the shadow made appear black and white. It was his wife. She was leaning on the banisters, listening to something. Gabriel was surprised at her stillness and strained his ear to listen also. But he could hear little save the noise of laughter and dispute on the front steps, a few chords struck on the piano and a few notes of a man's voice singing.

He stood still in the gloom of the hall, trying to catch the air that the voice was singing and gazing up at his wife. There was grace and mystery in her attitude as if she were a symbol of something. He asked himself what is a woman standing on the stairs in the shadow, listening to distant music, a symbol of. If he were a painter he would paint her in that attitude. Her blue felt hat would show off the bronze of her hair against the darkness and the dark panels of her skirt would shadow off the light ones. *Distant Music* he would call the picture if he were a painter.

The hall-door was closed, and Aunt Kate, Aunt Julia, and Mary Jane came down the hall, still laughing.

'Well, isn't Freddy terrible?' said Mary Jane. 'He's really terrible.'

Gabriel said nothing, but pointed up the stairs towards where his wife was standing. Now that the hall-door was closed the voice and the piano could be heard more clearly. Gabriel held up his hand for them to be silent. The song seemed to be in the old Irish tonality[101)]

---

101) Irish tonality: 아일랜드 가락.

and the singer seemed uncertain both of his words and of his voice. The voice, made plaintive by distance and by the singer's hoarseness, faintly illuminated the cadence of the air with words expressing grief:

O, the rain falls on my heavy locks
And the dew wets my skin,
My babe lies cold ...

'O,' exclaimed Mary Jane. 'It's Bartell D'Arcy singing, and he wouldn't sing all the night. O, I'll get him to sing a song before he goes.'

'O, do, Mary Jane,' said Aunt Kate.

Mary Jane brushed past the others and ran to the staircase, but before she reached it the singing stopped and the piano was closed abruptly.

'O, what a pity!' she cried. 'Is he coming down, Gretta?'

Gabriel heard his wife answer yes and saw her come down towards them. A few steps behind her were Mr Bartell D'Arcy and Miss O'Callaghan.

'O, Mr D'Arcy,' cried Mary Jane, it's downright mean[102] of you to break off like that when we were all in raptures listening to you.'

'I have been at him all the evening,'[103] said Miss O'Callaghan, 'and Mr Conroy, too, and he told us he had a dreadful cold and couldn't sing.'

'O, Mr D'Arcy,' said Aunt Kate, 'now that was a great fib[104] to tell.'

'Can't you see that I'm as hoarse as a crow?' said Mr D'Arcy roughly.

He went into the pantry hastily and put on his overcoat. The

---

102) downright mean: 정말 치사한, 비열한.
103) I have been at him all the evening: 밤 내내 그를 졸랐다.
104) fib: 사소한 거짓말.

others, taken back by his rude speech, could find nothing to say. Aunt Kate wrinkled her brows and made signs to the others to drop the subject. Mr D'Arcy stood swathing his neck carefully and frowning.

'It's the weather,' said Aunt Julia, after a pause.

'Yes, everybody has colds,' said Aunt Kate readily, 'everybody.'

'They say,' said Mary Jane, 'we haven't had snow like it for thirty years, and I read this morning in the newspapers that the snow is general all over Ireland.'[105)]

'I love the look of snow,' said Aunt Julia sadly.

'So do I,' said Miss O'Callaghan. 'I think Christmas is never really Christmas unless we have the snow on the ground.'

'But poor Mr D'Arcy doesn't like the snow,' said Aunt Kate, smiling.

Mr D'Arcy came from the pantry, fully swathed and buttoned, and in a repentant tone told them the history of his cold. Everyone gave him advice and said it was a great pity and urged him to be very careful of his throat in the night air. Gabriel watched his wife, who did not join in the conversation. She was standing right under the dusty fanlight and the flame of the gas lit up the rich bronze of her hair, which he had seen her drying at the fire a few days before. She was in the same attitude and seemed unaware of the talk about her. At last she turned towards them and Gabriel saw that there was colour on her cheeks and that her eyes were shining. A sudden tide of joy went leaping out of his heart.

'Mr D'Arcy,' she said, 'what is the name of that song you were singing?'

'It's called "The Lass of Aughrim,'[106)] said Mr D'Arcy, 'but I couldn't remember it properly. Why? Do you know it?'

'The Lass of Aughrim,' she repeated. I couldn't think of the

---

105) the snow is general all over Ireland: 눈이 아일랜드 전국에 걸쳐 내린다.
106) The Lass of Aughrim: 민요 '오림의 처녀'. 귀족의 아들을 낳고 버림받은 줄 알고 바다에 빠져 죽는다는 내용.

name.'

'It's a very nice air,' said Mary Jane. 'I'm sorry you were not in voice tonight.'

'Now, Mary Jane,' said Aunt Kate, 'don't annoy Mr D'Arcy. I won't have him annoyed.'

Seeing that all were ready to start she shepherded them to the door, where good night was said:

'Well, good night, Aunt Kate, and thanks for the pleasant evening.'

'Good night, Gabriel. Good night, Gretta!'

'Good night, Aunt Kate, and thanks ever so much. Good night, Aunt Julia.'

'O, good night, Gretta, I didn't see you.'

'Good night, Mr D'Arcy. Good night, Miss O'Callaghan.'

'Good night, Miss Morkan.'

'Good night, again.'

'Good night, all. Safe home.'

'Good night. Good night.'

The morning was still dark. A dull, yellow light brooded over the houses and the river; and the sky seemed to be descending. It was slushy underfoot, and only streaks and patches of snow lay on the roofs, on the parapets of the quay and on the area railings. The lamps were still burning redly in the murky air and, across the river, the palace of the Four Courts stood out menacingly against the heavy sky.

She was walking on before him with Mr Bartell D'Arcy, her shoes in a brown parcel tucked under one arm and her hands holding her skirt up from the slush. She had no longer any grace of attitude, but Gabriel's eyes were still bright with happiness. The blood went bounding along his veins and the thoughts went rioting through his brains, proud, joyful, tender, valorous.

She was walking on before him so lightly and so erect that he longed to run after her noiselessly, catch her by the shoulders and say something foolish and affectionate into her ear. She seemed to him so frail that he longed to defend her against something and then to be alone with her. Moments of their secret life together burst like stars upon his memory. A heliotrope envelope was lying beside his breakfast-cup and he was caressing it with his hand. Birds were twittering in the ivy and the sunny web of the curtain was shimmering along the floor: he could not eat for happiness. They were standing on the crowded platform and he was placing a ticket inside the warm palm of her glove. He was standing with her in the cold, looking in through a grated window at a man making bottles in a roaring furnace. It was very cold. Her face, fragrant in the cold air, was quite close to his, and suddenly he called out to the man at the furnace:

'Is the fire hot, sir?'

But the man could not hear with the noise of the furnace.[107)] It was just as well. He might have answered rudely.

A wave of yet more tender joy escaped from his heart and went coursing in warm flood along his arteries. Like the tender fire of stars moments of their life together, that no one knew of or would ever know of, broke upon and illumined his memory. He longed to recall to her those moments, to make her forget the years of their dull existence together and remember only their moments of ecstasy. For the years, he felt, had not quenched his soul or hers. Their children, his writing, her household cares had not quenched all their souls' tender fire. In one letter that he had written to her then he had said: 'Why is it that words like these seem to me so dull and cold? Is it because there is no word tender enough to be your name?'

Like distant music these words that he had written years before were borne towards him from the past. He longed to be alone with her. When the others had gone away, when he and she were in the room in their hotel, then they would be alone together. He would

---

107) with the noise of the furnace: 용광로 소리 때문에.

call her softly:

'Gretta!'

Perhaps she would not hear at once: she would be undressing. Then something in his voice would strike her. She would turn and look at him....

At the corner of Winetavern Street they met a cab. He was glad of its rattling noise as it saved him from conversation. She was looking out of the window and seemed tired. The others spoke only a few words, pointing out some building or street. The horse galloped along wearily under the murky morning sky, dragging his old rattling box after his heels, and Gabriel was again in a cab with her, galloping to catch the boat, galloping to their honeymoon.

As the cab drove across O'Connell Bridge Miss O'Callaghan said:

'They say you never cross O'Connell Bridge without seeing a white horse.'

'I see a white man this time,' said Gabriel.

'Where?' asked Mr Bartell D'Arcy.

Gabriel pointed to the statue, on which lay patches of snow. Then he nodded familiarly to it and waved his hand.

'Good night, Dan,' he said gaily.

When the cab drew up before the hotel, Gabriel jumped out and, in spite of Mr Bartell D'Arcy's protest, paid the driver. He gave the man a shilling over his fare. The man saluted and said:

'A prosperous New Year to you, sir.'

'The same to you,' said Gabriel cordially.

She leaned for a moment on his arm in getting out of the cab and while standing at the kerb-stone,[108] bidding the others good night. She leaned lightly on his arm, as lightly as when she had danced with him a few hours before. He had felt proud and happy then, happy that she was his, proud of her grace and wifely carriage. But now, after the kindling again of so many memories, the first touch of her body, musical and strange and perfumed, sent

---

108) kerb-stone: 보도와 차도를 구분 짓는 가장 자리 돌, 연석(=curbstone).

through him a keen pang of lust. Under cover of her silence he pressed her arm closely to his side, and, as they stood at the hotel door, he felt that they had escaped from their lives and duties, escaped from home and friends and run away together with wild and radiant hearts to a new adventure.

An old man was dozing in a great hooded chair in the hall. He lit a candle in the office and went before them to the stairs. They followed him in silence, their feet falling in soft thuds on the thickly carpeted stairs. She mounted the stairs behind the porter, her head bowed in the ascent, her frail shoulders curved as with a burden, her skirt girt tightly about her. He could have flung his arms about her hips and held her still, for his arms were trembling with desire to seize her and only the stress of his nails against the palms of his hands held the wild impulse of his body in check. The porter halted on the stairs to settle his guttering candle. They halted, too, on the steps below him. In the silence Gabriel could hear the falling of molten wax into tray and the thumping of his own heart against his ribs.

The porter led them along a corridor and opened a door. Then he set his unstable candle down on a toilet-table and asked at what hour they were to be called in the morning.

'Eight,' said Gabriel.

The porter pointed to the tap of the electric-light and began a muttered apology, but Gabriel cut him short.

'We don't want any light. We have light enough from the street. And I say,' he added, pointing to the candle, 'you might remove that handsome article, like a good man.'

The porter took up his candle again, but slowly, for he was surprised by such a novel idea. Then he mumbled good night and went out. Gabriel shot the lock to.

A ghastly light from the street lamp lay in a long shaft from one window to the door. Gabriel threw his overcoat and hat on a cough and crossed the room towards the window. He looked down into the street in order that his emotion might calm a little. Then he turned and leaned against a chest of drawers with his back to the light. She had taken off her hat and cloak and was standing before a large swinging mirror, unhooking her waist. Gabriel paused for a few moments, watching her, and then said:

'Gretta!'

She turned away from the mirror slowly and walked along the shaft of light towards him. Her face looked so serious and weary that the words would not pass Gabriel's lips. No, it was not the moment yet.

'You looked tired,' he said.

'I am a little,' she answered.

'You don't feel ill or weak?'

'No, tired: that's all.'

She went on to the window and stood there, looking out. Gabriel waited again and then, fearing that diffidence was about to conquer him, he said abruptly:

'By the way, Gretta!'

'What is it?'

'You know that poor fellow Malins?' he said quickly.

'Yes, What about him?'

'Well, poor fellow, he's a decent sort of chap, after all,'continued Gabriel in a false voice. 'He gave me back that sovereign I lent him, and I didn't expect it, really. It's a pity he wouldn't keep away from that Browne, because he's not a bad fellow, really.'

He was trembling now with annoyance. Why did she seem so abstracted? He did not know how he could begin. Was she annoyed, too, about something? If she would only turn to him or come to him of her own accord![109] To take her as she was would be brutal. No, he must see some ardour in her eyes first. He longed to be master of her strange mood.

'When did you lend him the pound?' she asked, after a pause.

---

109) of her own accord: 아내 스스로, 자진해서.

Gabriel strove to restrain himself from breaking out into brutal language about the sottish Malins and his pound. He longed to cry to her from his soul, to crush her body against his, to overmaster her. But he said:

'O, at Christmas, when he opened that little Christmas-card shop, in Henry Street.'

He was in such a fever of rage and desire that he did not hear her come from the window. She stood before him for an instant, looking at him strangely. Then, suddenly raising herself on tiptoe and resting her hands lightly on his shoulders, she kissed him.

'You are a very generous person, Gabriel,' she said.

Gabriel, trembling with delight at her sudden kiss and at the quaintness of her phrase, put his hands on her hair and began smoothing it back, scarcely touching it with his fingers. The washing had made it fine and brilliant. His heart was brimming over with happiness. Just when he was wishing for it she had come to him of her own accord. Perhaps her thoughts had been running with his. Perhaps she had felt the impetuous desire that was in him, and then the yielding mood had come upon her. Now that she had fallen to him so easily, he wondered why he had been so diffident.

He stood, holding her head between his hands. Then, slipping one arm swiftly about her body and drawing her towards him, he said softly:

'Gretta, dear, what are you thinking about?'

She did not answer nor yield wholly to his arm. He said again, softly:

'Tell me what it is, Gretta. I think I know what is the matter. Do I know?'

She did not answer at once. Then she said in an outburst of tears:

'O, I am thinking about that song, 'The Lass of Aughrim.'

She broke loose from him and ran to the bed and, throwing her arms across the bed-rail, hid her face. Gabriel stood stock-still for a moment in astonishment and then followed her. As he passed in the way of the cheval-glass he caught sight of himself in full length, his broad, well-filled shirtfront, the face whose expression always puzzled him when he saw it in a mirror, and his glimmering gilt-rimmed eyeglasses. He halted a few paces from her and said:

'What about the song? Why does that make you cry?'

She raised her head from her arms and dried her eyes with the back of her hand like a child. A kinder note than he had intended went into his voice.

'Why, Gretta?' he asked.

'I am thinking about a person long ago who used to sing that song.'

'And who was the person long ago?' asked Gabriel, smiling.

'It was a person I used to know in Galway when I was living with my grandmother,' she said.

The smile passed away from Gabriel's face. A dull anger began to gather again at the back of his mind and the dull fires of his lust began to glow angrily in his veins.

'Someone you were in love with?' he asked ironically.

'It was a young boy I used to know,' she answered, 'named Michael Furey. He used to sing that song,' 'The Lass of Aughrim.' He was very delicate.'

Gabriel was silent. He did not wish her to think that he was interested in this delicate boy.

'I can see him so plainly,' she said, after a moment. 'Such eyes as he had: big, dark eyes! And such an expression in them—an expression!'

'O, then, you were in love with him?' said Gabriel.

'I used to go out walking with him,' she said, 'when I was in Galway.'

A thought flew across Gabriel's mind.

'Perhaps that was why you wanted to go to Galway with that Ivors girl?' he said coldly.

She looked at him and asked in surprise:

'What for?'

Her eyes made Gabriel feel awkward. He shrugged his shoulders and said:

'How do I know? To see him, perhaps.'

She looked away from him along the shaft of light towards the window in silence.

'He is dead,' she said at length. 'He died when he was only seventeen. Isn't it a terrible thing to die so young as that?'

'What was he?' asked Gabriel, still ironically.

'He was in the gasworks,' she said.

Gabriel felt humiliated by the failure of his irony and by the evocation of this figure from the dead, a boy in the gasworks. While he had been full of memories of their secret life together, full of tenderness and joy and desire, she had been comparing him in her mind with another. A shameful consciousness of his own person assailed him. He saw himself as a ludicrous figure, acting as a penny-boy for his aunts, a nervous, well-meaning sentimentalist, orating to vulgarians and idealizing his own clownish lusts, the pitiable fatuous fellow he had caught a glimpse of in the mirror.[110] Instinctively he turned his back more to the light lest she might see the shame that burned upon his forehead.

He tried to keep us his tone of cold interrogation, but his voice when he spoke was humble and indifferent.

'I suppose you were in love with this Michael Furey, Gretta,' he said.

'I was great with him at that time,' she said.

Her voice was veiled and sad. Gabriel, feeling now how vain it

---

110) He saw himself as a ludicrous figure~in the mirror: 가브리엘 콘로이가 에피파니의 순간을 경험한다. 파티를 마치고 호텔로 돌아오는 도중에 아내를 향해 강렬한 욕정을 느끼다가 아내의 고백을 통해 소녀 시절의 연애사건을 듣게 되고, 거기에 대해 빈정대며 냉소적으로 반응하면서 질투심에 사로잡히다가 상대가 어린 소년이었고 한낱 가스공장에 근무하던 직공이었음을 듣게 되면서 자신의 우스꽝스런 모습을 발견한다.

would be to try lead her whither he had purposed, caressed one of her hands and said, also sadly:

'And what did he die of so young, Gretta? Consumption, was it?'

'I think he died for me,' she answered.

A vague terror seized Gabriel at this answer, as if, at that hour when he had hoped to triumph, some impalpable and vindictive being was coming against him, gathering forces against him in its vague world. But he shook himself free of it with an effort of reason and continued to caress her hand. He did not question her again, for he felt that she would tell him of herself. Her hand was warm and moist: it did not respond to his touch, but he continued to caress it just as he had caressed her first letter to him that spring morning.

'It was in the winter,' she said, 'about the beginning of the winter when I was going to leave my grandmother's and come up here to the convent. And he was ill at the time in his lodgings in Galway and wouldn't be let out, and his people in Oughterard[111] were written to. He was in decline, they said, or something like that. I never knew rightly.'

She paused for a moment and sighed.

'Poor fellow,' she said. 'He was very fond of me and he was such a gentle boy. We used to go out together, walking, you know, Gabriel, like the way they do in the country. He was going to study singing only for his health. He had a very good voice, poor Michael Furey.'

'Well: and then?' asked Gabriel.

'And then when it came to the time for me to leave Galway and come up to the convent he was much worse and I wouldn't be let see him, so I wrote him a letter saying I was going up to Dublin and would be back in the summer, and hoping he would be better then.'

She paused for a moment to get her voice under control, and

---

111) Oughterard: 오테라드. Galway에서 17마일 떨어져 있는 소읍.

then went on:

'Then the night before I left, I was in my grandmother's house in Nuns' Island, packing up, and I heard gravel thrown up against the window. The window was so wet I couldn't see, so I ran downstairs as I was[112] and slipped out the back into the garden and there was the poor fellow at the end of the garden, shivering.'

'And did you not tell him to go back?' asked Gabriel.

'I implored of him to go home at once and told him he would get his death in the rain. But he said he did not want to live. I can see his eyes as well as well! He was standing at the end of the wall where there was a tree.'

'And did he go home?' asked Gabriel.

'Yes, he went home. And when I was only a week in the convent he died and he was buried in Oughterard, where his people came from. O, the day I heard that, that he was dead!'

She stopped, choking with sobs, and, overcome by emotion, flung herself face downward on the bed, sobbing in the quilt. Gabriel held her hand for a moment longer, irresolutely, and then, shy of intruding on her grief, let it fall gently and walked quietly to the window.

She was fast asleep.[113]

Gabriel, leaning on his elbow, looked for a few moments unresentfully on her tangled hair and half-open mouth, listening to her deep-drawn breath. So she had had that romance in her life: a man had died for her sake. It hardly pained him now to think how poor a part he, her husband, had played in her life.[114] He watched her while she slept, as though he and she had never lived together as man and wife. His curious eyes rested upon her face and on her hair: and as he thought of what she must have been

---

112) as I was: 입은 그대로.

113) 아내 그레타는 가슴 아픈 첫사랑의 추억을 고백한 후 깊은 잠에 빠져들었다.

114) 매우 이기적이었던 가브리엘이, 아내의 마음속에서 남편인 자기가 차지한 자리가 별 것 아니었음을 알고도 마음의 고통을 느끼지 않는 변화된 모습을 보여준다. 상대방을 이해하고 포용하는 관대한 사람으로 변모해가는 중이다.

then, in that time of her first girlish beauty, a strange, friendly pity for her entered his soul. He did not like to say even to himself that her face was no longer beautiful, but he knew that it was no longer the face for which Michael Furey had braved death.

Perhaps she had not told him all the story. His eyes moved to the chair over which she had thrown some of her clothes. A petticoat string dangled to the floor. One boot stood upright, its limp upper fallen down: the fellow of it lay upon its side. He wondered at his riot of emotions of an hour before. From what had it proceeded? From his aunt's supper, from his own foolish speech, from the wine and dancing, the merry-making when saying good night in the hall, the pleasure of the walk along the river in the snow. Poor Aunt Julia! She, too, would soon be a shade with the shadow of Patrick Morkan and his horse. He had caught that haggard look upon her face for a moment when she was singing 'Arrayed for the Bridal'. Soon, perhaps, he would be sitting in that same drawing-room, dressed in black, his silk hat on his knees. The blinds would be drawn down and Aunt Kate would be sitting beside him, crying and blowing her nose and telling him how Julia had died. He would cast about in his mind for some words that might console her, and would find only lame and useless ones. Yes, yes: that would happen very soon.[115)]

The air of the room chilled his shoulders. He stretched himself cautiously along under the sheets and lay down beside his wife. One by one, they were all becoming shades. Better pass boldly into that other world, in the full glory of some passion, than fade and wither dismally with age. He thought of how she who lay beside him had locked in her heart for so many years that image of her lover's eyes when he had told her that he did not wish to live.

Generous tears filled Gabriel's eyes. He had never felt like that himself towards any woman, but he knew that such a feeling must

---

115) 가브리엘은 연로한 이모들의 죽음을 예감한다. 그는 죽음의 그림자 앞에서 겸손해지며 죽을 수밖에 없는 인간의 보편적 운명을 느낀다.

be love. The tears gathered more thickly in his eyes and in the partial darkness he imagined he saw the form of a young man standing under a dripping tree. Other forms were near. His soul had approached that region where dwell the vast hosts of the dead. He was conscious of, but could not apprehend, their wayward and flickering existence. His own identity was fading out into a grey impalpable world: the solid world itself, which these dead had one time reared and lived in, was dissolving and dwindling.

A few light taps upon the pane made him turn to the window. It had begun to snow again. He watched sleepily the flakes, silver and dark, falling obliquely against the lamplight. The time had come for him to set out on his journey westward.[116] Yes, the newspapers were right: snow was general all over Ireland. It was falling on every part of the dark central plain, on the treeless hills, falling softly upon the Bog of Allen and, farther westward, softly falling into the dark mutinous Shannon waves. It was falling, too, upon every part of the lonely churchyard on the hill where Michael Furey lay buried. It lay thickly drifted on the crooked crosses and headstones, on the spears of the little gate, on the barren thorns. His soul swooned slowly as he heard the snow falling faintly through the universe and faintly falling, like the descent of their last end, upon all the living and the dead.

---

116) journey westward: 집으로 가는 여행, 죽음으로의 여행, 아일랜드 민족주의로의 여행, 이타적인 사랑으로의 여행 등의 의미가 다 포함된다.

Critical Essays

Storytelling is a basic human activity[1)]

Storytelling is a basic human activity. The urge to tell stories and the desire to hear them is so primal that it is difficult to imagine a time in human existence without them. The gift of narrative—whether in myth, parable, epic, film, or short story—is so deep and universal that it seems one of the attributes that most clearly separates humanity from other species. Dolphins may have a vocabulary, but they do not create novels or short stories.

Why humans tell stories may differ from case to case, but whether the narrator speaks around a tribal fire or through the printed letters of a book, certain general impulses usually apply. Stories exist to delight, instruct, or console us. Some stories warn; others enlighten. At the root of the narrative urge, however, is the conviction that there are some truths we can only tell one another as stories. Conveyed in any other form, these insights evaporate into airy and intangible abstractions.

Storytelling also affects us differently from other modes of language. We hear or read a story with the fullness of our humanity—not merely with our intellects, but also our emotions, intuition and physical senses. A strong story has the ability to reach us in ways that logic alone cannot match. "A book," wrote Franz Kafka, "must be the axe for the frozen sea inside us." Religious leaders and philosophers have long understood the deep power of narrative. Jesus instructed his followers with parables. The right story encountered at the right moment should be able to change your life—perhaps only in a small way but sometimes in a larger sense.

---

1) X. J. Kennedy and Dana Gioia, *An Introduction to Fiction*(Harlow: Longman, 1999), xix.

A Word about Careers[2)]

Most students agree that to read celebrated writers such as William Faulkner or Willa Cather is probably good for the spirit. Most students even take some pleasure in the experience. But many, not planning to teach English and impatient to begin some other career, wonder whether the study of literature, however enjoyable, is a waste of time—or, at least, an annoying obstacle.

This objection may seem reasonable at first glance, but it rests on a shaky assumption. It can be convincingly argued that success in a career is not merely a matter of learning the specialized information and skills required to join a profession. In most careers, according to one senior business executive, people often fail not because they don't understand their jobs, but because they don't understand their coworkers, their clients, or their customers. They don't ever see the world from another person's point of view. Their problem is a failure of imagination.

To leap over the wall of self, to look through another's eyes—this is valuable experience, which literature offers....

....

Plodding single-mindedly toward careers, some people resemble horses wearing blinders. For many, the goals looked fixed and predictable. Competent nurses, accountants, and dental technicians seem always in demand. Others may find that in our society some careers, like waves in the sea, rise or fall unexpectedly. Think how many profession we now take for granted, which a few years ago didn't even exist: computer programming, energy conservation, tofu manufacture, digital editing and website design. Others that once looked like lifetime meal tickets have been cut back and nearly ruined: shoe repairing, commercial fishing, railroading.

In a perpetually changing society, it may be risky to lock your-

---

2) *Ibid.*, xx-xxi.

self on one track to a career, refusing to consider any other. "We are moving," writes John Naisbitt in *Megatrends*, a study of our changing society, "from the specialist, soon obsolete, to the generalist who can adapt." Perhaps the greatest opportunity in your whole life lies in a career that has yet to be invented. If you do change your career as you go along, you will be like most people. According to U. S. Department of Labor statistics, the average person in a working life changes occupations three times. When for some unforeseen reason you have to make such a change, basic skills—and a knowledge of humanity may be your most valuable credentials.

Literature has much practical knowledge to offer you. An art of words, it can help you become more sensitive to language, both your own and other people's. It can make you aware of the difference between the word that is exactly right and the word that is merely good enough....

Many careers today, beside law, call for close reading and clear writing—as well as careful listening and thoughtful speech. Lately, college placement directors have reported more demand for graduates who are good readers and writers. The reason is evident: employers need people who can handle words. In a survey conducted by Cornell University, business executives were asked to rank in importance the traits they look for when hiring. Leadership was first, but skill in writing and speaking came in fourth, ahead managerial skill and analytical skill. Times change, but to think cogently and to express yourself well will always be the abilities the world needs.

Twice-Told Tales, by Nathaniel Hawthorne[1)]
A Review

* * *

But it is of his tales that we desire principally to speak. The tale proper, in our opinion, affords unquestionably the fairest field for the exercise of the loftiest talent, which can be afforded by the wide domains of mere prose. Were we bidden to say how the highest genius could be more advantageously employed for the best display of its own powers, we should answer, without hesitation—in the composition of a rhymed poem, not to exceed in length what might be perused in an hour. Within this limit alone can the highest order of true poetry exist. We need only here say, upon this topic, that, in almost all classes of composition, the unity of effect or impression is a point of the greatest importance. It is clear, moreover, that this unity cannot be thoroughly preserved in productions whose perusal cannot be completed at one sitting. We may continue the reading of a prose composition, from the very nature of prose itself, much longer than we can persevere, to any good purpose, in the perusal of a poem. This latter, if truly fulfilling the demands of the poetic sentiment, induces an exaltation of the soul which cannot be long sustained. All high excitements are necessarily transient. Thus a long poem is a paradox. And, without unity of impression, the deepest effects cannot be brought about. Epics were offspring of an imperfect sense of Art, and their reign is no more. A poem too brief may produce a vivid, but never an intense or enduring impression. Without a certain continuity of effort—without a certain duration or

1) This is one of Poe's most important critical articles. In the fourth paragraph begins the famous formulation of the short story as a literary *genre*, which Poe was the first to define, and was already illustrating in his own stories, at the height of his maturity. Apart from this, of course, the essay is one of poe's most characteristic critiques. It first appeared in *Graham's Magazine* for May, 1842, although Poe had printed a brief notice of five paragraphs in the April issue.

repetition of purpose—the soul is never deeply moved. There must be the dropping of the water upon the rock. De Beranger[2] has wrought brilliant things—pungent and spirit-stirring—but, like all immassive bodies, they lack momentum, and thus fail to satisfy the Poetic Sentiment. They sparkle and excite, but, from want of continuity, fail deeply to impress. Extreme brevity will degenerate into epigrammatism; but the sin of extreme length is even more unpardonable. In medio tutissimus ibis.[3]

Were we called upon, however, to designate that class of composition which, next to such a poem as we have suggested, should best fulfil the demands of high genius—should afford it the most advantageous field of exertion—we should unhesitatingly speak of the prose tale, as Mr. Hawthorne has here exemplified it. We allude to the short prose narrative, requiring from a half-hour to one or two hours in its perusal. The ordinary novel is objectionable, from its length, for reasons already stated in substance. As it cannot be read at one sitting, it deprives itself, of course, of the immense force derivable from *totality*. Worldly interests intervening during the pauses of perusal, modify, annul, or counteract, in a greater or less degree, the impressions of the book. But more simple cessation in reading would, of itself, be sufficient to destroy the true unity. In the brief tale, however, the author is enabled to carry out the fullness of his intention, be it what it may. During the hour of perusal the soul of the reader is at the writer's control. There are no external or extrinsic influences—resulting from weariness or interruption.

A skilful literary artist has constructed a tale. If wise, he has not fashioned his thoughts to accommodate his incidents; but having conceived, with deliberate care, a certain unique or single *effect* to be wrought out, he then invents such incidents—he then combines

---

2) Pierre Jean de Beranger(1780-1857): French lyric poet.

3) "You travel most safely in the middle [moderate] course"; Ovid, in the *Metamorphoses*; the advice of Helios to his son Phaethon, who insists on driving the chariot of the sun for a day, and nearly burns up the earth by neglecting his father's injunction.

such events as may best aid him in establishing this preconceived effect. If his very initial sentence tend not to the outbringing of this effect, then he has failed in his first step. In the whole composition there should be no word written, of which the tendency, direct or indirect, is not the one pre-established design. And by such means, with such care and skill, a picture is at length, painted which leaves in the mind of him who contemplates it with a kindred art, a sense of the fullest satisfaction. The idea of the tale has been presented unblemished, because undisturbed; and this is an end unattainable by the novel. Undue brevity is just as exceptionable here as in the poem; but undue length is yet more to be avoided.

We have said that the tale has a point of superiority even over the poem. In fact, while the *rhythm* of this latter is an essential aid in the development of the poem's highest idea—the idea of the Beautiful—the artificialities of this rhythm are an inseparable bar to the development of all points of thought or expression which have their basis in *Truth.* But Truth is often, and in very great degree, the aim of the tale. Some of the finest tales are tales of ratiocination. Thus the field of this species of composition, if not in so elevated a region on the mountain of Mind, is a table-land of far vaster extent than the domain of the mere poem. Its products are never so rich, but infinitely more numerous, and more appreciable by the mass of mankind. The writer of the prose tale, in short, may bring to his theme a vast variety of modes or inflections of thought and expression—(the ratiocinative, for example, the sarcastic, or the humorous) which are not only antagonistical to the nature of the poem, but absolutely forbidden by one of its most peculiar and indispensable adjuncts; we allude, of course, to rhythm. It may be added here, *par parenthese,*[4] that the author who aims at the purely beautiful in a prose tale is laboring at a great disadvantage. For Beauty can be better treated in the poem. Not so with terror, or passion, or horror, or a multitude of such other points. And here it will be

4) parenthetically.

seen how full of prejudice are the usual animadversions against those *tales of effect*, many fine examples of which were found in the earlier numbers of *Blackwood*. The impressions produced were wrought in a legitimate sphere of action, and constituted a legitimate although sometimes an exaggerated interest. They were relished by every man of genius: although there were found many men of the genius who condemned them without just ground. The true critic will but demand the means most advantageously applicable.

We have very few American tales of real merit—we may say, indeed, none, with the exception of *The Tales of a Traveller of* Washington Irving, and these *Twice-Told Tales of Mr. Hawthorne.* Some of the pieces of Mr. John Neal abound in vigor and originality; but, in general, his compositions of this class are excessively diffuse, extravagant, and indicative of an imperfect sentiment of Art. Articles at random are, now and then, met with in our periodicals which might be advantageously compared with the best effusions of the British Magazines; but, upon the whole, we are far behind our progenitors in this department of literature.

Of Mr. Hawthorne's tales we should say, emphatically, that they belong to the highest region of Art—an Art subservient to genius of a very lofty order. We had supposed, with good reason for so supposing, that he had been thrust into his present position by one of the impudent *cliques* which beset our literature, and whose pretensions it is our full purpose to expose at the earliest opportunity; but we have been most agreeably mistaken. We know of few compositions which the critic can more honestly commend than these *Twice-Told Tales.* As Americans, we feel proud of the book.

Mr. Hawthorne's distinctive trait is invention, creation, imagination, originality—a trait which, in the literature of fiction, is positively worth all the rest. But the nature of the originality, so far as regards its manifestation in letters, is but imperfectly understood. The inventive or original mind as frequently displays itself in novelty of *tone* as in novelty of matter. Mr. Hawthorne is original at all points.

The Short Story[1)]

The teller of a tale relies heavily upon the method of summary: terse, general narration. But in a short story, a form more realistic than the tale and of modern origin, the writer usually presents the main events in greater fullness. Fine writers of short stories, although they may use summary at times (often to give some portion of a story less emphasis), are skilled in rendering a scene: a vivid or dramatic moment described in enough detail to create the illusion that the reader is practically there. Avoiding long summary, they try to show rather than simply to *tell.*

A short story is more than just a sequence of happenings. A finely wrought short story has the richness and conciseness of an excellent lyric poem. Spontaneous and natural as the finished story may seem, the writer has written it so artfully that there is meaning in even seemingly casual speeches and apparently trivial details. If we skim it hastily, skipping the descriptive passages, we miss significant parts. Some literary short stories, unlike commercial fiction in which the main interest is in physical action or conflict, tell of an epiphany: some moment of insight, discovery, or revelation by which a character's life, or view of life, is greatly altered. Other short stories tell of a character initiated into experience or maturity: one such story of initiation is William Faulkner's "Barn Burning", in which a boy finds it necessary to defy his father and suddenly to grow into manhood.

The fable and the tale are ancient forms; the short story is of more recent origin. In the nineteenth century, writers of fiction were encouraged by a large, literate audience of middle-class readers who wanted to see their lives reflected in faithful mirrors. Skillfully representing ordinary life, many writers perfected the art of the

---

1) X. J. Kennedy and Dana Gioia, *An Introduction to Fiction*(1999). pp.11-12.

short story: in Russia, Anton Chekhov; in France, Honore de Balzac, Gustave Flaubert, and Guy de Maupassant; and in America, Nathaniel Hawthorne and Edgar Allan Poe(although the Americans seem less fond of everyday life than of dream and fantasy). It would be false to claim that, in passing from the fable and the tale to the short story, fiction has made a triumphant progress; or to claim that, because short stories are modern, they are superior to fables and tales. Fable, tale, and short story are distinct forms, each achieving its own effects. (Incidentally, fable and tale are far from being extinct today.) Lately, in the hands of Jorge Luis Borges, Joyce Carol Oates, John Barth, and other innovative writers, the conventions of the short story have been changing; and at the moment, stories of epiphany and initiation have become scarcer.

The Short Story[1)]

Although most of the points covered so far apply equally to the short story or to the novel, the genres are different, after all, and their differences affect our approach to each. The most obvious difference is length: normally the maximum for short stories is about fifteen thousand words, or fifty pages, and the minimum for novels is about thirty thousand words, or one hundred pages. The in-between forms are variously called long short stories, novellas (or nouvelles or novelettes), and short novels. Differences other than length are hard to identify, but they must exist. Hemingway's *The Old Man and the Sea* is usually called a novel, and Conrad's *Heart of Darkness* is sometimes called a long short story; and yet Hemingway's story is considerably the shorter. We are sometimes told that a certain short story should have been developed into a novel, or that a certain novel is no more than a short story stretched out. These judgments obviously invoke criteria other than length. The difficulty in identifying these criteria is that unlike sonnets and symphonies, fiction types have no fixed patterns. Their differences, like those between large paintings and small paintings, have evolved naturally from their differences in scale. For example, the length of the novel enables it to treat certain subjects such as the history of a family, which a short story cannot handle. Even the limitations of a form may contribute to its effect; artists have always enjoyed turning limitations into virtues. Thus the very confinement of the short story has forced artists to find ways of transcending its limits, of saying more than one would think possible in the space. Over the years, as authors have exploited the opportunities and overcame the limitations peculiar to various fictional lengths, each genre has developed typical features, earmarks, which are closely related to its spe-

1) Robert Stanton, *An Introduction to Fiction*(1965), pp. 37-43.

cial problems and rewards. An acquaintance with these earmarks of each genre will contribute to the reader's understanding and pleasure. In this chapter, we shall consider some typical features of the short story.

First of all, it is obvious that a short story must be *compressed*; it must accomplish more than the same number of words within a novel. A novelist can begin his crucial chapters with the characters already introduced and the battle-lines already drawn. But a short story author must create and people his world and plunge us into the action simultaneously. As a rule, therefore, his style, especially at the beginning, must be more densely packed with meaning than that of a novelist. For example, here is the opening paragraph of Hemingway's "The Undefeated":

> Manuel Garcia climbed the stairs to Don Miguel Retana's office. He set down his suitcase and knocked on the door. There was no answer. Manuel, standing in the hallway, felt there was someone in the room.

This passage may seem poorly chosen as an illustration of a dense style. It is dense with action, but apparently not with anything else. Hemingway does not pause even to introduce Manuel: he lets the conversation that follows (in Retana's office) tell us that Manuel is a second-rate matador just released form hospital and that he has come to ask Retana for a booking. Even so, the opening contains a few implications. It suggests that the setting is a city in Spain or Mexico; we soon learn that it is Madrid. Why does no one answer Manuel's knock? When Retana finally admits him, we learn that Manuel is looking for a bullfighting match and that Retana is reluctant to employ him. Retana pretends to be out, therefore, because he has seen Manuel's approach and hates to refuse him to his face. Why is Manuel carrying his suitcase? Why hasn't he checked into a hotel first and left the suitcase there? This is explained when he asks Retana for a small advance on his salary; evidently he hasn't the money for a hotel. Perhaps the first two sentences suggest, very slightly, that Manuel is weak or tired (from his injury or his stay in the hospital). Finally, the simplicity of Manuel, from whose point of view these events are described.

It is perfectly true that without later information most of these "implications" are tentative or ambiguous or unrecognizable. But assuming the reader's knowledge of the later information, the implications are present, and thus the opening paragraph accomplishes a good deal more than introducing the action. Evidently the reader of a short story not only should be sensitive to implication, but should be able to store away details for future understanding. And evidently he should read the story more than once.

Another evidence of the short story's compression is its use of symbolism. Novels use symbolism, too, but seldom with such frequency or centrality; a reader can understand *A Farewell to Arms* without knowing that rain symbolizes death, but he cannot understand Hemingway's "The Snows of Kilimanjaro" without knowing that the mountain (toward which the dying writer imagines himself flying at the end) symbolizes lost integrity. Even a perfectly realistic story may contain symbols: for example, the setting, the sleeping suits, and the hat in Conrad's "The Secret Sharer." At the other extreme, an entire story may be symbolic, whether its surface treatment be realistic (as in Shirley Jackson's "The Lottery") or fantastic (as in Franz Kafka's tales).

Since the typical short story can be read within an hour, it is poorly equipped to present in detail the development of a character, or a large complex social situation, or a relationship involving many characters, or a complicated event covering many years. What is it equipped to do? According to Edgar Allan Poe's 1842 review of Hawthorne's *Twice-Told Tales*, the short story's chief advantage over the novel is that it can be read in one uninterrupted sitting, and is therefore capable of an intense unity of effect. To achieve this effect, said Poe, the author must waste nothing: "If his very initial sentence tend not to the outbringing of this effect, then he has failed in his first step. In the whole composition there should be no word written, of which the tendency, direct or indirect, is not to the one pre-established design." Poe described two "effects" appropriate to the short story: passion, by which he meant chiefly horror; and truth, by which he meant an appeal to the intellect as in the detective story.

Poe's rule of unity has remained valid. Otherwise, the short story changed considerably after his time, until by the end of the nineteenth century it had acquired substantially its present form. Its history has been complex, partly because the stages overlap, partly because the form has been continually influenced by other genres and the fiction of other countries. So instead of trying to trace its history, we shall simply describe three differences between modern short stories and those by Poe.

First, according to Poe's theory, the story was to be unified around an "effect" of horror or ingenuity, that is, an exercising of the reader's emotions or intellect. But the very stories his essay reviewed, by Hawthorne, and most serious stories since then have been unified around a *theme;* they aim at not only effect, but understanding, especially of some problem of values. Actually, even Poe's own stories are organized around themes. In "The Black Cat," the theme is sadism; in "The Fall of the House of Usher," it is decadence; in "The Cask of Amontillado," it is revenge. But these are the themes of bizarre experiences; it is well that someone has explored them, but one Poe is enough. In Hawthorne's fiction, although the literal situations are as fantastic as Poe's, the themes belong to real and even common experiences; "Young Goodman Brown" literally describes a young Puritan attending a black communion in the forest; thematically, it describes the loss of an idealistic faith in human goodness.

A second difference is that since the late nineteenth century, most short stories have been realistic in style: the dialogue is true to life, the settings detailed and recognizable, the situations probable. This difference appears to have arisen from a changed idea of the function of the short story. Originally it was simply a tale to amuse an audience, and Poe's stress upon "effect" can be seen as a refinement of this view. Hawthorne treated the story as a symbolic meditation upon some problem, usually moral. Both views implied that the story's prime aim was outside or beneath or beyond the surface of actuality. Its events were means to this aim, and so there was no need for verisimilitude. But most modern authors consider the story an exploration of a specific experience, and since most experience consists of an encounter with and reaction to actual events, most stories today reproduce the surface of actuality. There is a satisfaction in the precision and solidity of good realism that is missing in even the best fantasy—as in this paragraph from Hemingway's "A Day's Wait":

> It was a bright, cold day, the ground covered with a sleet that had frozen so that it seemed as if all the bare trees, the bushes, the cut brush and all the grass and the bare ground had been varnished with ice. I took the young Irish setter for a little walk up the road and along a frozen creek, but it was difficult to stand or walk on the glassy surface and the red dog slipped and slithered and I fell twice, hard, once dropping my gun and having it slide away over the ice.

It must not be supposed that realism is a mere matter of style, a coat of verisimilitude that could be painted over any story. The difference is more fundamental. When we read Poe or Hawthorne, we are aware that they have invented these incidents, built them up, so as to establish a theme or emotional effect. But a realistic story seems to soak into a particular incident as a microscopist's stain soaks into a specimen, so as to reveal the incident's structure of feeling and meaning. This is not to say that a realistic story merely records some actual happening, although it has probably begun with one. Even when it has, the realist must reveal its meaning by filling out the incident with significant details, and by developing it into a resolved conflict, a finished plot, without violating its verisimilitude. Thus the story is realistic twice over—it explores reality, and it has the air of reality—and yet inside it may contain just as much artifice and meaning as, say, an allegory.

The third difference applies only to certain modern stories, perhaps fewer than half. For some readers, these stories are to fiction as the lyric is to poetry or as string quarters are to music: they illustrate the genre at its purest and best. But to a reader encountering them for the first time, they may seem plotless and pointless, because they do not have the neat external pattern found in most fiction. Their plots appear fragmentary, even trivial, with inconclusive endings; only slowly does one realize that inside, in the understanding of character or mood or emotional relationship, their pattern is coherent and complete. The author most responsible for this type of story is Anton Chekhov. Here is Virginia Woolf's description of Chekhov's story "Gusev":

> Some Russian soldiers lie ill on board a ship which is taking them back to Russia. We are given a few scraps of their talk and some of their thoughts; then one of them dies and is carried away; the talk goes on among the others for a time, until Gusev himself dies, and looking "like a carrot or a radish" is thrown overboard. The emphasis is laid upon such unexpected places that at first it seems as if there were no emphasis at all; and then, as the eyes accustom themselves to twilight and discern the shapes of things in a room we see how complete the story is, how profound, and how truly in obedience to his vision Tchekov has chosen this, that, and the other, and placed them together to compose something new.

Chekhov's characters speak and act with as much spontaneity

and unpredictability as any living beings; they are never the victims of the plot. And his stories are built around incidents of a special type. For example, one of his notebooks records this scrap of conversation between two actors at a rehearsal: the wife said, "How does that melody in Pagliacci go? Whistle it," and her husband replied, "One must not whistle on the stage; the stage is a temple."

James Joyce would have called Chekhov's note an "epiphany"; he meant by the term an incident or spectacle or phrase containing "a sudden spiritual manifestation." Many of Chekhov's stories have evidently grown out of such a moment luminous with meaning, a microcosm, a little world revealing a great world. For an author, the advantage of building a story around such a moment is that it enables him to transcend the limitation of the story's brevity. Chekhov's little anecdote, for example, reveals a profound misunderstanding between husband and wife; an equally small incident seen in a certain way reveal a paradox in one's character, a fundamental change in one's personality, or a broad social problem. This does not mean that in any ordinary sense such an incident is "typical." Almost certainly it is not typical, or it would not catch the artist's imagination. Its meaningfulness—epiphany, luminosity, whatever one calls it—appears as a unique quality of the unique incident, a quality that only the artist sees until he has turned it into a story. We cannot be sure, for example, whether Chekhov saw the husband in his anecdote as a dedicated artist or a pompous ass.

The point here is the *type* of incident, particularly as it appears in the finished story, not the mere fact that Chekhov's stories are based upon actuality. Henry James, for example, often began with a small incident (which he called the "germ"), and yet his finished stories are outwardly complete, symmetrical, fully developed. In spite of his difficult style, a careful and reasonably sensitive reader can usually understand his stories without needing the flash of insight described above. James illustrates what is called the planned story. But in a Chekhovian story, we see at first only an apparently fragmentary incident. We go on faith: there must be a way of looking at these facts that will give them a meaningful arrangement. When we recognize their meaning, we see that everything has pointed to it, even the style; and the meaning is so much larger than the facts themselves that the effect is a sudden illumination, almost a shock. According to some writers, the distinction between the Chekhovian story and the planned story is basic in modern fiction. Assuming that both types grow from a fragment of actual experience, the Chekhovian author considers that this fragment contains its own truth, and that his function is to let it reveal itself without distortion. To help it do so, he invents and arranges details, but only in so far as these details are true to life as it is—and life often seems contradictory and incongruous. Frank O'Connor expresses a version of the Chekhovian philosophy when he says, "I think I like the instinctual as against the intellectual... As a writer I like the feeling I get when some story that I've been trying to bring up in the right way gets on its own feet and tells me to go to hell." The author of a planned story, on the other hand, is concerned with communicating the meaning of his incident. He feels that his characters and events should seem real, but since he is an artist rather than a reporter, and since his story is art rather than fact, he sees no reason why he should reproduce all the confusion of reality. We might say that like a chess player, he enjoys keeping the game under his control, whereas the Chekhovian author, like a poker player, enjoys dealing with chance. Of course, the distinction is not absolute. If a story has no plan, it is meaningless; if its plan is too conspicuous, it is dead.

Now let us see how this method is used in a modern story, William Carlos Williams' "The Use of Force." A physician is called to visit a sick child, a beautiful little girl. The child is terrified and fights him off, and her parents are helpless, but he finally succeeds in examining her throat and detects the symptoms of diphtheria. That is the plot; stated thus, it sounds pointless and trivial. But near the end of the story, the physician-narrator says:

> Perhaps I should have desisted and come back in an hour or more. No doubt it would have been better. But I have seen at least two children lying dead in bed of neglect in such cases, and feeling that I must get a diagnosis now or never I went at it again. But the worst of it was that I too had got beyond reason. I could have torn the child apart in my own fury and enjoyed it. It was a pleasure to attack her. My face was burning with it.

Here, we realize, is what the story is about. In the face of the child's resistance, the doctor's "use of force" has aroused his anger and a desire to conquer the child, a pleasure in the use of force for its own sake. His actions remain exactly those of one moved by compassion or duty, and his ultimate motive is good; but the use of force has corrupted his immediate motive. *This* situation, this shift of motive, is not at all trivial. It is relevant to a wide variety of human behavior, including that of parents, teachers, employers, and governments. Every detail of the story points to this view of the experience. Because the central character is professionally dedicated to alleviating pain, the issue is sharpened by irony. The beauty of the child should inspire pity or affection, but instead encourages the shift in motives: there is even a hint of sexual pleasure in the doctor's thoughts, as there is in all pleasurable cruelty. Yet the doctor is not at all a monster. That is the point: this comparatively ordinary experience of a comparatively ordinary man contains a pattern applicable to various and extraordinary situations—if one can see that pattern. Williams (a physician himself) has seen it, and through his story we see it.

Beginning, then, with the author's need to exploit the advantages and overcome the limitations of the short story's brevity, we have seen that the genre has developed several distinctive features. It is conspicuously unified in theme and effect. Its style is compressed, one common means of compression being its use of symbolism. it is multileveled, appealing simultaneously to the reader's sense of realism, his understanding, his emotions, and his moral sense. It is incapable of microcosmic effect, enfolding large significance within a trivial incident. Although none of these features is its exclusive property, nor does every short story contain them all, they are typical of the genre and well worth the reader's conscious attention.

According to William Faulkner, "Maybe every novelist wants to write poetry first, finds he can't, and then tries the short story, which is the most demanding form after poetry. And, failing at that, only then does he take up novel writing." Whether or not this is true, we are generally more conscious of craftsmanship and artistry in the short story than in the novel. The fact that an admiration for skill is usually an acquired taste probably explains why more of the public enjoy novels than short stories, just as more people enjoy symphonies than chamber music. But any really mature literally enjoyment requires an appreciation of the author's artistry, and short stories offer, in addition to their own value as literature, an ideal training ground for this appreciation.

A Critical History of "The Dead"

I

"The Dead," composed in 1907, was the last story Joyce completed for his collection *Dubliners*. Joyce had planned the story in Rome in 1906-07, but it was completed while he was living in Trieste. Prior to adding "the Dead," Joyce wrote to Grant Richards, a London publisher, on May 5, 1906:

> My intention was to write a chapter of the moral history of my country and I chose Dublin for the scene because that city seemed to me the centre of paralysis. I have tried to present it to the indifferent public under four of its aspects: childhood, adolescence, maturity and public life. The stories are arranged in this order. I have written it for the most part in a style of scrupulous meanness and with the conviction that he is a very bold man who dares to alter in the presentment, still more to deform, whatever he has seen and heard.[1)]

If in a sense the major character of Dubliners, including "The Dead," is the city of Dublin, the major antagonists are the British presence in Ireland and the Roman Catholic church in which Joyce was educated. He wrote to Nora in August 1904: "My mind rejects the whole present social order and Christianity—home, the recognized virtues, classes of life, and religious doctrines."[2)] In *Ulysses*, the semi-autobiographical Stephen Dedalus says, "I am a servant of two masters...an English and Italian...the imperial British state...and the holy Roman Catholic and apostolic church"(171).

---

1) Richard Ellmann, ed., *The Letters of James Joyce*, vol. 2 (New York: Viking, 1966) 132.

2) Richard Ellmann, *James Joyce*, 1984 ed. (New York: Oxford UP, 1959; new and rev. 1984) 165.

Joyce struggled for nine years to get his book published after it was first accepted by Grant Richardsin early 1906 before he wrote "The Dead," the fifteenth and last story. Asking if he might submit it originally as a collection of twelve stories, he wrote Richards:

> I do not think that any writer has yet presented Dublin to the world. It has been a capital of Europe for thousands of years; it is supposed to be the second city of the British Empire and it is nearly three times as big as Venice. Moreover, on account of many circumstances which I cannot detail here, the expression "Dubliner" seems to me to have some meaning and I doubt whether the same can be said for such words as "Londoner" and "Parisian" both of which have been used by writers as titles. *(Letters* 2:122)

In "Gabriel and Michael: The Conclusion of 'The Dead' " Florence L. Walzl explains the structure of *Dubliners* in 1906 prior to the addition of "The Dead":

> The 1905 version was highly symmetrical, consisting of an opening triad of stories of individual children ("The Sisters," "An Encounter," and "Araby"), a quartet of stories dealing with youthful men and women ("Eveline," "After the Race," "Two Gallants," and "The Boarding House"), another quartet picturing mature characters ("A Little Cloud," "Counterparts," "Clay," and "A Painful Case"), and a final triad dealing with public groups in public institutions ("Ivy Day in the Committee Room," "A Mother," and "Grace"). The first and final triads obviously balance individuals and groups, and all the stories in the middle quartets are arranged in pairs contrasting sex, age, and social type or status. Also, the characterizations have a patterning that is unusual in short story collections. Though the protagonist of each story is a different character, all—children or adults—are variants of a basic type, a central everyman figure. Since each main character is older in the first eleven tales, a life cycle is presented. This chronological structure is matched

> to a thematic one of hemiplegia. The result is a progression in which children are depicted as disillusioned, youths as frustrated or trapped, men and women as passive and non-productive, and social groups as completely static. The central image of the book is a creeping paralysis that ends in a dead society.[3)]

But "The Dead" extended the implications of moral and spiritual paralysis to the urban, bourgeoisie Dublin culture, even as it offered the possibility of love as an escape from that condition.

Even before "The Dead" was added in 1907, Richards's objections to certain passages as obscene drastically delayed publication. In particular, Richards objected to the story "Two Gallants," a passage in "Counterparts," and the word "bloody":

> Personally I prefer the word "bloody" in the places in which it occurs to any word you could substitute for it since it is, as you say, the right word; on the other hand a publisher has to be influenced by other considerations. Personally I have no objection to the other stories we have discussed, although I may use that in their present form they would damage their publisher.(274-75)

Joyce and Richards could not agree on changes, and in 1909 he entered into a publishing agreement with Messrs Maunsel, an Irish publisher, but that agreement got bogged down in a debate about a passage referring to Edward VII in "Ivy Day in the Committee Room." Later Messrs Maunsel wished him to omit "An Encounter," with its homosexual overtones; certain passages in "Two Gallants"; "The Boarding House"; and "A Painful Case"; and all references to names of businesses in Dublin. Eventually the book was printed according to Messrs Maunsel's stipulations; but when Joyce and the publisher couldn't come to an agreement about terms, all the copies

---

3) Florence L. Walzl, "Gabriel and Michael: The Conclusion of 'The Dead,' " *James Joyce Quarterly* 4 (1966): 17-31; see esp. 18.

were burned. Joyce retained the printed proof, which he submitted to Richards who finally published it in 1914.

II

Important to *Dubliners* and "The Dead" in particular is Joyce's concept of epiphany. In *Stephen Hero*, Joyce's earlier version of *A Portrait of the Artist as a Young Man,* Joyce defines the concept of epiphany:

> By an epiphany he meant a sudden manifestation, whether in the vulgarity of speech or of gesture or in a memorable phase of the mind itself....The three things requisite for beauty are, integrity, a wholeness, symmetry and radiance.... That is the first quality of beauty: it is declared in a simple sudden synthesis of the faculty which apprehends. What then? Analysis then. The mind considers the object in whole and in part, in relation to itself and to other objects, examines the balance of its parts, contemplates the form of the object, traverses every cranny of the structure. So the mind receives the impression of the symmetry of the object. The mind recognises that the object is in the strict sense of the word, a *thing*, a definitely constituted entity. You see?... Now for the third quality.... First recognise that it is an organised composite structure, a *thing* in fact: finally, when the relation of the parts is exquisite, when the parts are adjusted to the special point, we recognise that it is *that* thing which it is. Its soul, its whatness, leaps to us from the vestment of its appearance. The soul of the commonest object, the structure of which is so adjusted, seems to us radiant. The object achieves its epiphany.[4)]

This concept comes from the manifestation of Christ to the gentiles in the person of the Magi or Wise Men, a manifestation celebrated by the Feast of the Epiphany. In the Greek drama, it refers

4) Chester G. Anderson, ed., *A Portrait of the Artist as a Young Man: Text, Criticism, and Notes* (New York: Viking, 1968) 288-89.

to the moment when a god appears and imposes order on a chaotic or turbulent situation. While some critics have emphasized only the character's moment of awareness within the text, Joyce expected the reader to have her or his own revelatory moment of awareness that went beyond the character's and to see the plight of the central character from a larger and often ironic perspective.

In many stories, including "The Dead," the reader's epiphany is different from the character's epiphany; indeed, the reader's epiphany is an *awareness* of the limitations of the character's epiphany. Thus we understand that the retrospective narrator of "Araby" is reverting to the very Catholic epistemology that inscribed his conscience with guilt and anxiety: "gazing up into the darkness I saw myself as a creature driven and derided by vanity; and my eyes burned with anguish and anger"(*Dubliners* 35) and we understand that in "Evelin" Evelin's epiphany is a catatonic moment and really no epiphany at all: "He rushed beyond the barrier and called to her to follow. He was shouted at to go on but he still called to her. She set her white face to him, passive, like a helpless animal. Her eyes gave him no sign of love or farewell or recognition"(41).

In "The Dead" Gabriel, after becoming aware of his limitations as a lover and public figure, lapses out of his paralytic self-consciousness to become part of the reality of being. In a sense, his epiphany is a necessary prelude to his suspension of ego and will. But the reader is aware that Joyce is performing the suspension of consciousness and moving beyond Gabriel's awareness to imply the value of human love, particularly between a man and a woman (a theme that is central to his later *Ulysses*). And Gabriel's moment of transcendence ironically joins him to all the actual dead, including Michael Furey, who have lived passionately, and all those living dead in the *Dubliners* who, like himself, have been constrained by Dublin's social and political milieu, including a debilitating Catholic education, the British presence in Ireland, and the Irish capacity for self-delusion.

III

"The Dead" has been read as the last story of a closely integrated collection entitled *Dubliners* and as a separate story in its own right. Undoubtedly stimulated by *Ulysses* and the publication of Joyce's schema by Stuart Gilbert in his 1930 study *James Joyce's Ulysses: A Study*—which Joyce influenced—Richard Levin and Charles Shattuck in "First Flight to Ithaca"[5] stress parallels to the *Odyssey*. In 1931 Edmund Wilson in his chapter on James Joyce in *Axel's Castle* spoke of *Dubliners* as "a strong work of naturalistic fiction." Brewster Ghiselin's innovative 1956 essay argued convincingly for the unity of *Dubliners:*

> When the outlines of the symbolic pattern have been grasped, the whole unifying development will be discernible as a sequence of events in a moral drama, an action of the human spirit struggling for survival under peculiar conditions of deprivation, enclosed and disabled by a degenerate environment that provides none of the primary necessities of spiritual life. So understood, *Dubliners* will be seen for what it is, in effect, both a group of short stories and a novel, the separate histories of its protagonists composing one essential history, that of the soul of a people which has confused and weakened its relation to the source of spiritual life and cannot restore it.[6]

Also attentive to the unity of *Dubliners,* in 1969 Edward Brandabur wrote of the relationship of the first three stories to what follows: "In the first three stories of *Dubliners,* Joyce adumbrates the character of his book as an evaluation of motive. 'The Sisters,' 'An Encounter,' 'Araby,' all portray specific quests by sensitive young Dubliners who stand off from a perverse environment with a degree

---

5) Richard Levin and Charles Shattuck, "First Flight to Ithaca," *Two Decades of Criticism,* ed. Seon Givens (New York: Vanguard, 1948, 1963) 47-94.

6) Brewster Ghiselin, "The Unities of Joyce's *Dubliners,*" *Accent* 16 (1956) 75-88 and 196-213; see esp. 76.

of disengagement resembling that of Joyce himself."[7]

The interpretive history of a text tells us as much about the values of the critics at a particular time as it does about the text, and a major text like "The Dead" becomes a way of seeing how critical fashions change and contend. In the 1940-60 period, formalists like Allen Tate and Kenneth Burke read "The Dead" in terms of its patterns of language and internal structures, while under the influence of Richard Ellmann's monumental biography *James Joyce*, published in 1959 and revised in 1982, historical and biographical scholars focused on Joyce's life and the world in which he lived.

New Criticism, dominant in the 1950s and 1960s, saw a literary work as an autonomous object—a "well-wrought urn"—and rejected information about the author's life as biographical fallacy. In *The House of Fiction*, a much used and admired anthology, Allen Tate writes a classic New Critical essay that praised "The Dead" as an example of a work that used showing rather than telling: "All...we see is dramatized; it is all made active. Nothing is given us from the externally omniscient point of view."[8] New Critics believed that the unity and meaning of a work are discovered by a close reading of its image patterns and that the more a novel employed the aesthetic of consistent, dramatized point of view—the aesthetic of Henry James—the better the work. In the formalist mode of the New Critics that values showing rather than telling, Tate writes:

> In fact, from the beginning to the end of the story we are never told anything; we are shown everything. We are not told, for example, that the *milieu* of the story is the provincial, middle-class, "cultivated" society of Dublin at the turn of the century; we are not told that Gabriel represents its emotional sterility (as contrasted with the "peasant" richness

---

7) Robert Scholes and A. Walton Litz, eds., *James Joyce, Dubliners: Text, Criticism, and Notes* (New York: Viking, 1969) 333.

8) Allen Tate and Caroline Gordon, *The House of Fiction* (New York: Scribner's, 1950) 280.

> of his wife Gretta), ts complacency, its devotion to genteel culture, its sentimental evasion of "reality." All this we see dramatized; it is all made active.[9]

Many of the formalist critics of "The Dead" writing in the 1950s and 1960s—including Tate, Ghiselin, and Walzl—stressed the symbolic aspects of the text.

Aristotelian critics were more concerned with the evolving *agon* as it enacted the tale's values and the structure of effects and tended to be somewhat less interested in symbolism. Working in an Aristotelian mode, Kenneth Burke focuses on the effects of the text and its progress as a tripartite structure of effects as it moves from beginning to middle to end:

> In the first of its three parts, the keynote is expectancy, which is amplified by many appropriate details: talk of preparations, arrivals, introductions, apprehensions, while fittingly the section ends on an unfinished story....
>
> The second stage, dealing with the party at its height, could be analysed almost as a catalogue of superficial socialities, each in its way slightly false or misfit.
>
> ...But the third section concerns initiation into a mystery. It is to take us beyond the realm of realism, as so conceived, into the realm of *ideality.*[10]

Burke's focus is on what he calls significant form.

C. C. Loomis, in an important March 1960 *PMLA* essay entitled "Structures and Sympathy in 'The Dead'" builds on Burke's work on the structure of "The Dead." Writing in the formalist mode of the 1950s and 1960s, and using the vocabulary that values a dialogue between the particular and the general, he concludes,

---

9) Tate and Gordon 405.

10) Kenneth Burke, *Perspectives by Incongruity*, ed. Stanley Edgar Hymn and Barbara Karmiller (Bloomington: Indiana UP, 1954) 145-47.

> "The Dead" follows a logical pattern; we move from the general to the particular, then to a final universal. We see Gabriel's world generally; then we focus down to the particular, and from the combination of the general and particular we are given a universal symbol in the vision itself.
>
> The logic of "The Dead," however, is not the logic of mere intellect; it is the logic which exists on a plane where intellectual perception and emotional intuition, form and content, blend.[11)]

Any survey of Joyce criticism must acknowledge the eclectic criticism of Hugh Kenner. Beginning with *Dublin's Joyce* (1956) and including *Joyce's Voices* (1978), Hugh Kenner has contributed to our understanding of Joyce. Kenner finds in the latter part of *Dubliners* a "multiplication of spectres, of choices negated, passions unexplored, opportunities missed, aspects of the self denied" (*Dublin's Joyce* 480). Kenner coined what he called his "Uncle Charles principle" to argue that "the narrative idiom need not be the narrator's" (*Joyce's Voices* 18). When Joyce wants his narrator to show us how a character thinks or feels, his description of a character modifies the voice that is describing that character. Thus, the narrator would want us to see that it is Lily, not the narrator, who would use the word "literally" when "figuratively" is the proper word in the first sentence of "The Dead": "Lily, the caretaker's daughter, was literally run off her feet."

In part because *Ulysses* depends on what T. S. Eliot calls "the mythic method" to give a "shape and significance to the immense panorama of futility and anarchy which is contemporary history," critics have sought to discover structuring patterns of allusions in "The Dead."[12)] Northrop Frye's influence in the late 1950s and 1960s was another

11) C. C. Loomis, Jr., "Structure and Sympathy in Joyce's 'The Dead,'" *PMLA* 35 (1960): 149-51; see esp. 151.

12) T. S. Eliot, "*Ulysses*, Order, and Myth," *Dial* 75 (1923): 480-83; rpt. as "Myth and Literary Classicism" in *The Modern Tradition: Backgrounds of Modern Literature*, ed. Richard Ellmann and Charles Feidelson, Jr. (New York: Oxford UP, 1965) 675-81.

stimulus to the search for recurring archetypes: his *Anatomy of Criticism* appeared 1967. Florence L. Walzl's 1966 essay on the conclusion shows how, as the final story of *Dubliners*, "The Dead" is a crystllization of preceding themes and a story in its own right:

> In contrast to the stern role of the archangel Michael, Gabriel is a messenger angel associated with God's beneficience. In the Old testament he is the angel sent to Daniel to interpret two great visions of salvation, one of them a Messianic prophecy.
>
> ...The recollections of Christ's passion in the spears and thorns are reminders that sacrifice of self is the condition of revival. The judgment that Michael brings is a salvation, and Gabriel's swoon is a symbolic death from which he will rise revivified. Gabriel is rightly named: he is a figure of annunciation and new life. (29-30)

Written at a time when ambiguity—a kind of charged ambiguity that allowed for contradictory readings—was a value, Walzl's essay argues for a reading that stresses *both* Gabriel's acceptance of his material conditions *and* his spiritual redemption: "*Dubliners* as a whole work suggests that Ireland betrays its children. 'The Dead' in this symbolic identification seems to imply that the Dubliner betrays Ireland. This is only one of the ambiguities that 'The Dead' offers" (27). In 1981 Donald T. Torchian argued that Gabriel's life closely parallels that of St. Patrick and that at the end, unlike St. Patrick who converted the Irish, he undergoes a conversion by the Irish.[13)]

VI

Richard Ellmann develops the crucial relationship between Joyce's life and work:

---

13) Donald T. Torchiana, "The Ending of 'The Dead': I Follow St. Patrick," *James Joyce Quarterly* 18 (1981): 123-32.

> In Gretta's old sweetheart, in Gabriel's letter, in the book reviews and the discussion of them, as well as in the physical image of Gabriel with hair parted in the middle and rimmed glasses, Joyce drew directly upon his own life.... Gabriel's quarrels with his mother, who never accepted her son's marriage to a woman of lower station.[14)]

One of the great literary biographies of our time, Ellmann's study shows conclusively how Joyce's art draws upon his own experience growing up in Ireland. That we need to know about the author to know the work is often called expressionist criticism, a criticism that seeks to establish that the work is a psychic and moral gesture of the author's own emotional life. Relating the artist's life to his work is only one method and one that has often been called into question in the last several decades by both New Criticism and deconstruction. However, Joyce himself argued for the centrality of this approach in the crucial "Scylla and Charybdis" chapter of *Ulysses* where he and Stephen Dedalus read Shakespeare in expressionistic terms. Joyce believed that the writer of genius—such as Shakespeare or *himself* (Joyce did not suffer from paroxysms of false modesty)—"found in the world without as actual what was in his world within as possible" (*Ulysses* 9.1041-42) and that "his errors were volitional and the portals of discovery." It is worth noting that Joyce wrote at a time when such an expressionistic approach was more in vogue. Indeed, contemporary Irish writers, and in particular Yeats who was a towering figure when Joyce reached maturity in 1898-1904, drew upon a wide range of personal and cultural references.

Of "The Dead" Ellmann writes:

> Although the story dealt mainly with three generations of his family in Dublin, it drew also upon an incident in Galway in 1903. There Michael ("Sonny") Bodkin courted Nora Barnacle; but he contracted tuberculous and had to be confined to bed.

14) Ellmann 247.

> Shortly afterwards Nora resolved to go Dublin, and Bodkin stole out of his sickroom, in spite of the rainy weather, to sing to her under an apple tree and bid her good-by. In Dublin Nora soon learned that Bodkin was dead, and when she met Joyce she was first attracted to him, as she told a sister, because he resembled Sonny Bodkin.[15]

Certainly Joyce's wonder at and passion for Nora, a simple country girl who was socially beneath the pretensions of the Joyce family, find their way into the portrait of Gretta and into her relationship with Gabriel. Joyce's unjustified and irrational jealousy of possible rivals for Nora is repeated in the text. When Joyce wrote "The Dead" Gabriel, a high school teacher and writer of minor reviews, was the kind of bourgeois figure Joyce feared becoming. Of the ending, Ellmann writes,

> From a biographical point of view, these final pages compose one of Joyce's several tributes to his wife's artless integrity. Nora Barnacle, in spite of her defects of education, was independent, unselfconscious, instinctively right. Gabriel acknowledges the same coherence in his own wife, and he recognizes in the west of Ireland, in Michael Furey, a passion he has himself always lacked.[16]

Brenda Maddox's important *Nora: The Real Life of Molly Bloom* also offers insight on the relationship between the fictional Gretta and the actual Nora:

> If Nora did go direct from her late grandmother's house to the Presentation Convent, it means that the events upon which Joyce drew for the background of his most famous short story, "The Dead," took place just before her thirteenth birthday. The details of her life in that year fit the story

15) Ellmann 243.
16) Ellmann 249.

> well....
>
> The proximity of Michael Feeney's death in February to that of Nora's grandmother on New Year's Day and the occasion of her leaving her grandmother's home make Feeney a closer model for the fictional Michael Furey than Nora's late admirer, Michael Bodkin, who has been widely cast in the part....
>
> In all likelihood, Joyce fused Nora's memories of her two last friends.[17]

Over the past fifty years, literary criticism has oscillated between the poles of formalism (close scrutiny of the text as an independent imagined ontology) and contextualism (placing a work in the context of cultural, historical, biographical, and socioeconomical contexts). Recently, as deconstructive formalism has receded, more emphasis has been placed on historical and literary contexts. Because of Ellmann's work, the emphasis on the world in which Joyce lived, was never neglected as much as the world of many other modernists. Important studies stressing cultural contexts include Donald T. Torchiana's *Backgrounds for Joyce's "Dubliners"*(1986). R. B. Kershner has put "The Dead" in the context of popular culture in *Joyce, Bakhtin, and Popular Culture*(1989). For example, Kershner points out a parallel between Bret Harte's *Gabriel Conroy*(1871) and the three operas invoked by Mary Jane and Mr. Browne, *Mignon, Dinorah,* and *Lucrezia Borgia,* and reminds us that they

> turn upon the figure of the passionate, unrecognized woman whose love is not reciprocated; in all three death threatens as a result of the young man's failure to recognize the woman and her passion....The main force of the operatic interests, like that of Hart's novel, is to suggest that there is a fundamental sexual reversal in 'The Dead'; once Gabriel learns to speak as Woman, the intertextual tensions are resolved, though perhaps at the price of "the descent of their last end, upon all the living and

17) Brenda Maddox, *Nora: The Real LIfe of Molly Bloom* (Boston: Houghton, 1988) 16-17.

the dead."[18)]

The movement away from pure formalism has been stimulated by the rediscovery of the work of the Russian critic M. Bakhtin. Bakhtin argues that a text is a contending field where diverse ways of telling to which the author was exposed interact; this interaction or dialogism is called *heteroglossia*:

> Thus at any given moment of its historical existence, language is heteroglot from top to bottom: it represents the co-existence of socio-ideological contradictions between the present and the past, between differing epochs of the past, between different socio-idological groups in the present, between tendencies, schools, circles and so forth, all given a bodily form. These "languages" of heteroglossia intersect each other in a variety of ways, forming new socially typifying "languages."
>
> Each of thse "languages" of heteroglossia requires a methodology very different from the others; each is grounded in a completely different principle for making differences and for establishing units (for some this principle is functional, in others it is the principle of theme and content, in yet others it is, properly speaking, a socio-dialectological principle). Therefore languages do not exclude each other, but rather intersect with each other in many different ways....
>
> ...All languages of heteroglossia, whatever the principle underlying and making each unique, are specific points of view on the world, forms for conceptualizing the world in words, specific world views, each characterized by its own objects, meanings and values. As such they all may be juxtaposed to one another, mutually supplement one another, contradict one another and be interrelated dialogically. As such they encounter one another and co-exist in the consciousness of real people —first and foremost, in the creative consciousness of people who write novels. As such, these languages live a real life, they

18) R. B. Kershner, *Joyce, Bakhtin, and Popular Literature: Chronicles of Disorder* (Chapel Hill and Lodon: U of North Carolina P, 1989) 150.

> struggle and evolve in an environment of social heteroglossia. Therefore they are all able to enter into the unitary plane of the novel, which can unite in itself parodic stylizations of generic languages, various forms of stylizations and illustrations of professional and period-bound languages, the languages of particular generations, of social dialects and others (as occurs, for example, in the English comic novel). They may all be drawn in by the novelist for the orchestration of his themes and for the refracted (indirect) expression of his intentions and values.[19)]

In "The Dead" we see multiple kinds of discourse in a dialogue in which they struggle for position and interaction; remnants of Gabriel's Catholic education; his university education, including Elizabethan language; the language of Irish music; performative, non-syntactical languages; the language of fastidious manners as well as the language of passion; the language of nineteenth-century literary materialism and its opposite, aestheticism; the discourse of Irish nationalism and the Celtic Renaissance, including the Celtic language itself; and the language of desire and sexuality. Kershner's work also shows the importance of Bakhtin and his theory of heteroglossia. According to Bakhtin, novels are not monologic, but dialogic in that they contain a dialogue among diverse styles. According to Kershner,

> On the one hand Gabriel's experience is shaped by the series of outwardly manifest dialogical encounters with others, culminating in his dialogue with his wife; on the other, his perceptions are increasingly dominated by an internal dialogue between his everyday inner monologue and the disturbing, unwonted inner voice that calls him lyrically to the outdoors, to the snow, to the west, and to the dead. (139-40)

---

19) M. M. Bakhtin, *The Dialogic Imagination,* ed. Michael Holquist, trans. Caryl Emerson and Michael Holquist (Austin: U of Texas P, 1981) 291-92.

As Kershner explains,

> For Bakhtin, both written and spoken language and inner monologue are made up of a great variety of conflicting variants—"languages" of officialdom, vernaculars, occupational jargons, technical, literary, and subliterary languages, all polyphonically resounding. (15)

In a recent interesting essay, which combines Bakhtinian aspects with the Aristotelian focus on how narration persuades readers, "Distant Music: Sound and the Dialogics of Satire in 'The Dead,'"[20] Bruce Avery argues that while "most critics argue that the story creates a perspective that invites some kind of judgment of Gabriel, one that the narrator makes and seeks to implicate the reader in: either Gabriel achieves transcendence or he does not," he also argues that "we need to look at Gabriel and the narrator differently, because the narrator does not implicate us in a judgment of Gabriel for the simple reason that by the end of 'The Dead,' he is unable to make any judgment of his own for fear that in so doing he would invite the same fate for himself" (473). At the ending, the narrator shifts attention:

> Whereas before the narrator's discourse concentrated on its dialogue with the discourse of Gabriel and the other characters, taking for granted, as it were, its position relative to the listeners, now it has entered a new dialogue, this time attentive to its distance from the *listener.* Having constructed a discourse which says that the petty elitism of Gabriel results in both self-deception and isolation from everyone else, including Gretta, the narrator has aligned himself and his listener (or reader) with a specific conceptual horizon—one which condemns elitism....
>
> ...We are left pondering whether perhaps, in these final pages of "The Dead," Joyce heard in the echoes of his "moral

20) Bruce Avery, "Distant Music: Sound and the Dialogics of Satire in 'The Dead,'" *James Joyce Quarterly* 28.2 (1991): 473-83.

> history" a voice too much like his own sounding too much like the voice of judgment—too much, in fact, like Gabriel. Perhaps then he began to see and hear Dublin in a way that would stir him to write the more compassionate history he would come to call *Ulysses.* (Avery 481-82)

With the development of women's studies in the past decade, Joyce's view of women and heterosexual relationships has come in for considerable reevaluation. As Richard Brown has pointed out, "the story of Gabriel Conroy seems tailor-made for feminist interpretation. Gabriel's evening consists of a succession of significant encounters with women."[21] In an insightful study, "Joyce and Lacan: 'The Woman' as a Symptom of 'Masculinity' in 'The Dead,'" Garry Leonard applies the theories of the French psychoanalyst Jacques Lacan—theories that have become increasingly influential in literary studies in the past decade—to "The Dead." Lacan has argued that for males, women are a function of their phallic sexuality, and women are reinvented by males to fill an absence they experience in their consciousness. Of the ending of "The Dead" Leonard writes,

> Gabriel believes the time has come for him to set out on his journey westward: away from the Dublin / fictional self that he thought he knew, towards the Galway / want-in-being that he has refused to acknowledge. He must read the censored chapters of his history, the ones that refute the unity of his subjective consciousness and are therefore not consciously know. Joyce ends "The Dead" with Gabriel adrift between the "lumber room" of the unconscious and subjective consciousness: his fictional unity, what a woman is a symbol of, cannot, for the moment, be found.[22]

Important feminist studies include the collection *Women in Joyce,*

---

21) Richard Brown, *James Joyce and Sexuality* (Cambridge: Cambridge UP, 1985) 92.
22) Garry Leonard, "Joyce and Lacan: 'The Woman' as a Symptom of 'Masculinity' in 'The Dead,'" *James Joyce Quarterly* 28.2 (1991): 451-72

edited by Suzette Henke and Elaine Unkeless (1982) and Bonnie Kime Scott's *Joyce and Feminism* (1984). An example of recent feminist criticism is Ruth Bauerle's "Date Rape, Mate Rape: A Liturgical Interpretation of 'The Dead,'" *New Alliances in Joyce Studies*, edited by Bonnie Kime Scott (113-25), which examines biographical evidence, including the relationship between Joyce's father and mother. She sees Gabriel as betrayer, seducer, and even rapist. Stressing the role of women in "The Dead," Kershner writes, "The paradox of 'The Dead'—that within a society in which women are disempowered there should arise an opposing imaginative scenario in which women are omnipotent—is wholly parallel to the original paradox of courtly love to which Lacan points in an analysis of the phenomenon's historical rise" (147).

In recent years, critics have been more aware of the continuity of Joyce's major works—*Dubliners, A portrait of the Artist as a Young Man, Ulysses,* and *Finnegans Wake*—and of how *Dubliners* anticipates these later, more experimental texts. Recent work on "The Dead" has reflected the theoretical explosion of the past two decades. Indeed, recent critics stressed the text as an example of theoretical models. Colin MacCabe's work demonstrates the influence of deconstruction: "Language introduces us to an existence which can never be satisfied, for, as a condition of our speech, something is always missing."[23] MacCabe makes the further point that "in Joyce's text the division between signifier and signified becomes an area in which the reader is in (and at) play—producing meaning through his or her own activity."[24]

In *Joyce Between Freud and Jung* (1980) and a subsequent study of Joyce and Lacan, *The Veil of Signs: Joyce, Lacan, and Perception* (1991), Sheldong Brivic has written compellingly of the importance of seeing Joyce in the context of twentieth-century psychology. Suzette A. Henk

---

23) Colin MacCabe, *James Joyce and the Revolution of the Word* (New York: Harper, 1979) 2.

24) MacCabe 2.

in "James Joyce and Women: The Matriarchal Muse,"[25] was among the first to discuss the possibilities of Lacan for Joyce studies.

V

Much of the criticism has focused on the ending. The debate is whether Gabriel can escape the sterile and paralyzed world of Dublin or whether he remains locked in his narcissistic prize. One can locate two basic strands of the first argument, the dominant one that Gabriel achieves heroic transcendence and achieves a new level of self-knowledge as he transcends his material circumstances. A somewhat different version of the argument that Gabriel escapes his confining world is that he moves to a more authentic awareness of his material existence rather than to an epiphanic revelation. In an influential study, *A Reader's Guide to James Joyce*, William York Tindall focuses upon symbolic paterns of imagery and speaks of Gabriel's "enlargement" and moral expansion: "Gabriel, facing reality at last, goes westward to encounter life and death."[26] Ellmann focuses on the westward journey to "the place where life had been lived simply and passionately" (249). But on occasion even a humanistic critic demurs from either version of this optimistic reading; Charles Peak, in *James Joyce: The Citizen and the Artist*, believes that Gabriel's "swooning surrender" is not a "vision of reconciliation."[27] And Edward Brandabur argues that "Gabriel anticipates the paralysis which will befall him.... Throughout the story, personal encounters disturb his poise until he finally gives in to the annihilation he has not only anticipated but invited."[28] Phillip Herring argues that

25) Suzette A. Henk, "James Joyce and Women: The Matriarchal Muse," *Work-in-Progress: Joyce Centenary Essays,* ed. Richard Peterson, Alan M. Cohn, and Edmund L. Epstein (Carbondale: Southern Illinois UP, 1983) 117-31.

26) William York Tindall, *A Reader's Guide to James Joyce* (New York: Farrar, 1959) 46.

27) Charles Peake, *James Joyce: The Citizen and the Artist* (Stanford: Stanford UP, 1977) 53.

28) Edward Brandabur, *A Scrupulous Meanness: A study of James Joyce's Early Work* (Chicago: U of Illinois P, 1971) 116.

"Isolated by education, temperament, and egotism, Conroy is defeated by forces that conspire against him, and by his ultimate awareness of inadequacy as a man."[29)]

Vincent P. Pecora stresses uncertainty in "The Dead." Contrary to most prior criticism, in "'The Dead' and the Generosity of the World," Pecora argues that

> In fact, however, Gabriel in no way overcomes or transcends the conditions of his existence. Rather, he merely recapitulates them unconsciously in this self-pitying fantasy.... Moreover, he appears completely assured of the sincerity of his gesture. That is, Gabriel has reproduced in himself, like his vision of Michael Furey, the most fundamental structuring device for heroism, generosity, self-knowledge, and spiritual transcendence in his culture: the story of Christ.... If Gabriel fools himself, if in the very process that we accept as self-discovery he only reimplicates himself blindly in the cultural conditions he longs to transcend, then we may simply be doing the same thing, in our reading, in our lives. And if it is the Christlike "hero" who is "the bloodiest imposter of all," then we are forced to question one of the most deeply embedded institutions of his entire culture—and ours. Gabriel may see "mystical" union with all humanity as the only possible escape from the real humiliation of his Dublin life. The question remains, Must we escape with him?[30)]

Pecora's work is also symptomatic of placing readings in the context of the intellectual tradition of modernism:

> My reading of "The Dead" is grounded in Nietzsche's response to Schopenhauer's "ascetic ideal" and the Christian tradition as simultaneously powerful negations and unconscious preservations of suffering existence (see esp. third essay in *On the Genealogy of Morals,* "What Is the Meaning of Ascetic Ideals"

---

29) Phillip F. Herring, *Joyce's Uncertainty Principle* (Princeton: Princeton UP, 1987) 71.

30) Vincent P. Pecora, "'The Dead' and the Generosity of the World," *PMLA* 101:2 (1986): 243.

97-163). (243-44)

Pecora idenfies himself with what he calls "Joseph Buttigieg's anti-humanist reappraisal of Joyce's work, with lenses provided by Nietzsche."[31] His is an example of a deconstructive reading which, rather than confine itself to the text, traces an elaborate pattern of inter-textual relations that establish a rhetorical argument in opposition to the usually construed reading of the central agon.

John Paul Riquelme has written an excellent response to Pecora in "Joyce's 'The Dead': The Dissolution of the Self and the Police."[32] Requelme takes issue with Pecora's view that "the self in 'The Dead' is dissolved into exhaustion and incoherence." He believes that Pecora attributes thoughts to Gabriel that might be more adequately assigned to the narrator:

> The death signaled in Joyce's story by the dissolving of the self and by the intensified use of free indirect style tends to reverse rather than to reinforce some conventional attitudes. As the vehicle for communication and transferring the reversal to the reader, free indirect style is central to the effect that "The Dead" has on the living. (Riquelme 489)

Influenced by the work of Stephen Greenblatt—especially his *Renaissance Self-Fashioning: From More to Shakespeare*—the New Historians have emphasized the micropolitical implications of texts and have stressed how texts both reveal and conceal hidden power relations among socioeconomic groups and genders. New historicism and its critical companion, cultural criticism, focus on the suppressive and repressive role of the church; the relationship between rural Ireland and Dublin; and the debate between Joyce's view that Ireland

31) See Joseph Buttigieg, "The Struggle against Meta (Phantasma)-physics: Nietzsche, Joyce and the 'Excess of History,'" *Boundary* 2.10 (1981): 187-204.

32) J. P. Riquelme, "Joyce's 'The Dead': The Dissolution of the Self and the Police," *Style* 25.3 (1991): 489-505.

should be a European country and Yeats's view that it should be a separate Celtic country. In this mode Gabriel is a dominating male in a sexist exploitive society, and the culture of Dublin is examined in terms of failed capitalism. Thus Riquelme contends that "Gabriel has the disposable income and the time to purchase goods and engage in activities intended to promote health, fitness, and longevity. He participates in cultural mythology about improving and prolonging life that includes a denial of death" (489). As I argue in my essay in this volume, Gabriel's fortunes in his own mind are interconnected with his fears about the economic fortunes of his extended family: the three spinsters who run the music school and who are hosting an annual party, a party that is really an advertisement.

VI

Critics have differed over the meaning of the snow. David Daiches argued in *The Novel and the Modern World* (1939) that the snow represents "Gabriel's new sense of identity with the world, of the breakdown of the circle of his egoism."[33] For Allen Tate, snow stands for "Gabriel's escape from his ego in a larger world of humanity" (409). He argues for the centrality of the snow imagery:

> The snow is the story.... At the beginning, the snow is the cold and even hostile force of nature, humanly indifferent, enclosing the warm conviviality of the Misses Morkan's party. But just as the human action in which Gabriel is involved develops in the pattern of the plot of Reversal, his situation at the end being the opposite of its beginning, so the snow reverses its meaning, in a kind of rhetorical dialectic: from naturalistic *coldness* it develops into a symbol of warmth, of expanded consciousness; it stands for Gabriel's escape from his own ego into the larger world of humanity, including "all the living and the dead." (282)

33) David Daiches, *The Novel and the Modern World* (Chicago: U of Chacago P, 1939) 99.

For Kenneth Burke the snow is a mythic image by which he transcends Gabriel's conditional and materialistic world: "We return to the topic of snow, which becomes the *mythic image,* in the world of conditions, standing for the transcendence above the conditioned" (150). For William York Tindal it represents life and death. In his *The Literary Symbol,*[34] he discusses how the story occurs during Christmas season, "a season of birth and of the year's death" (225). Snow thaws to become water, a traditional image of life, suggesting life and hope despite its death-like whiteness and coldness. Gabriel's vision of the falling snow becomes, for Tindall, "an acceptance of death as a part of life" (227). Somewhat in agreement with Tindal, Richard Ellmann believes that the snow represents "mutuality" between the dead and the living, "a sense of their connection with each other, a sense that none has his being alone" (251), and he stresses that "The snow does not stand alone in the story. It is part of the complex imagery that includes heat and cold air, fire, and rain, as well as snow" (251). By contrast, Charles Peake contends that snow represents "Dublin as a moribund city" and argues that it is an image for "a people who have allowed their lives to be annexed by the dead" (53). For Hugh Kenner, Gabriel's desire to be alone in the snow is a longing for death indicated by the fact that he "pursues the 'wayward and flickering existence' of the dead."[35]

VII

To conclude: "The Dead" is among the most read short novels in English. It has wide appeal to students because it dramatizes emotions that most of us share: love, hope, passion, insecurity, jealousy, a sense that our lives are not turning out as we wish, and a fear that our dreams will end in failure and compromise. For high school and college students, Gabriel is an example of a man who

---

34) William York Tindal, *The Literary Symbol* (New York: Columbia UP, 1955) 224-28.

35) Hugh Kenner, *Dublin's Joyce,* (1956; Boston: Beacon, 1962) 68.

has compromised in both his career and personal aspirations. "The Dead" has brought pleasure and insight to generations of readers, and it has provided food for critical speculation and hermeneutical exercises. Its multiple perspectives, dense linguistic texture, and complex unity remind us that "The Dead" was written as Picasso was experimenting with his great study of sexuality, *Les Demoiselles d'Avignon*(1907) and remind us, too, that Thomas Mann would soon write *Death in Venice*(1912), his tale of debilitating repression. That each critical approach finds a rich source in "The Dead" is testimony to its complexity, subtlety, and appeal as a human story.

from Daniel R. Schwarz, ed,. *James Joyce: The Dead* (Boston and London: Bedford Books, 1994) 63-82.

"The Dead"에 나타난 자아의 완성[1)]

Ⅰ. 서론

모더니즘 소설의 대가인 제임스 조이스(James Joyce)의 첫 소설인 『더블린 사람들』(*Dubliners*)은 15편의 단편 소설들의 모음집이다. 더 정확하게 말한다면 14편의 단편과 중편소설인 "사자들"(The Dead)로 이루어진다. 마지막 소설인 "사자들"은 이 단편 모음집 전체를 집약하고 보편화시키는 에필로그와 같은 역할을 한다. 작가는 애정과 증오의 상반된 두 가지 감정을 동시에 가지고 있는 조국 아일랜드와 그 심장부인 더블린의 정신적 도덕적 마비 상태를 죽음과 암흑의 상태로 통찰한다. 이 소설 전반에 만연된 어둠은 "아일랜드 국민들의 고뇌 the plight of the Irish people"[2)]를 상징하며, 그것은 물리적 암흑뿐만 아니라 종교적, 정치적, 문화적 암흑을 포함하며, 무엇보다도 더블린 사람들이 생동하며 살아있는 중요한 일체의 것들부터 스스로를 소외시키는 정신적 암흑 상태를 나타낸다. 작가는 "마비된 도시라기보다 사경의 도시 a city moribund rather than paralysed"[3)] 속에서도 긍정적이고 적극적인 비전과 가능성을 발견한다. 더블린과 더블린 사람들의 생중사의 암흑 상태는 인간의 삶에 보편적으로 확대되어 적용될 수 있는 인식으로서, 조이스가 이러한 삶의 조건에 대해서 "사자들"에서 제시하는 희망의 가능성은 인류 전체에게 긍정적 가치를 부여해 준다.

조이스는 『더블린 사람들』에 나오는 단편들의 원고를 1904년부터

---

1) 졸고, "The Dead"에 나타난 자아의 완성," 『경성대학교논문집』 제19집 2권 (1998.8), 55-68.

2) M. W. Murphy, "Darkness in Dubliners," *Modern Fiction Studies*, Vol. XV, No. 1 (Spring, 1969), 100.

3) C. H. Peake, *James Joyce: The Citizen and the Artist* (Stanford: Stanford University Press, 1977), p. 45.

1906년까지 써서 런던의 출판업자인 그랜트 리차즈(Grant Richards)에게 보내서 출판을 의뢰했으나 원고를 반송 당하고 내용을 수정하도록 요청을 받는 등 많은 우여곡절을 겪은 후 10여년이 지난 1914년에 출판을 하게 된다. 그는 "사자들"을 1907년에 완성하여 단편집에 추가하기 전인 1906년 5월에 리차즈에게 편지를 보내어 이 작품의 창작 동기를 분명하게 밝히고 있다.

> 내 의도는 우리나라의 도덕사의 한 장을 쓰는 데 있었다. 나는 그 무대로 더블린을 골랐는데, 그것은 이 도시가 나에게는 마비의 심장부로 보였기 때문이다. 나는 무관심한 대중들에게 어린 시절, 사춘기, 성년 시절, 공공생활의 네 단계로 이를 제시하려 애썼다.
>
> (My intention was to write a chapter of moral history of my country and I chose Dublin for the scene because that city seemed to me the centre of paralysis. I have tried to present it to the indifferent public under four of its aspects: childhood, adolescence, maturity and public life.)[4)]

조이스가 밝힌 마비는 중압적인 외부적 환경과, 정신적 도덕적 타락과 부패의 내면적 요인으로부터 야기된다. 더블린 사람들을 억압하는 외부적 힘은 아일랜드를 지배하는 영국의 권력과 로마 카톨릭 교회, 그리고 가정 등이다. 그리고 내면적으로는 더블린 사람들이 여러 가지 악덕에 사로잡혀 있는 것으로 그려진다. 문제는 마비에 사로잡힌 사람들이 그 상태에서 벗어나고자 하나 제 자리를 맴돌고 마는 원형의 상태에 머물러 있다는 것이다.

본고는 앞의 열 네 단편들에서 보여주는 답답한 마비의 상태에서 벗어나 "사자들"에서 작가가 제시하는 적극적인 결말을 고찰해 보려고 한다. 그

4) Richard Ellmann, ed., *The Letters of James Joyce*, Vol. 2 (New York: Viking Press, 1966), p. 132.

리하여 문학이 가질 수 있는 보편적 주제로까지 논의를 진전시켜서 "사자들"이 갖는 진정한 가치와 메시지를 심층적으로 이해하는 데에 목적을 두고 있다. 가브리엘과 그레타가 직면한 상황은 그들만의 특별한 상황이 아니라 보편성을 가질 수 있는 상황이라는 것이다. 자아와 타자의 구별이 분명하고, 주관과 객관의 의식이 확고한 좁은 이기의 세계에서 어떤 계기와 어떤 이유들로 인하여 인간애의 열린 세계로 성숙하고 변모해 가는가를 가브리엘(Gabriel)을 중심으로 고찰할 것이다.

Ⅱ. 본론: 이기에서 인간애로

1. 이기의 닫힌 세계

주인공인 가브리엘 콘로이(Gabriel Conroy)는 대학에서 강의를 하며 더블린의 『데일리 익스프레스』(*The Daily Express*)라고 하는 보수적인 친 영국적 성향의 신문 문필란에 매주 수요일에 글을 기고하는 고정 집필자이다. 그에게는 사랑하는 아내 그레타 콘로이(Gretta Conroy)와 아들 톰(Tom)과 딸 에바(Eva)가 있고 외견상 행복한 삶에 필요한 모든 외적 조건들이 갖추어져 있다. 사회적 지위와 부와 명성을 어느 정도는 다 누리며 살고 있다고 할 수 있다.

가브리엘이 이모 모칸(Morkan) 여사 댁에서 연례행사로 개최되는 무도회에 아내와 함께 참석하면서 이 소설은 시작된다. 정확한 시점이 제시되지는 않지만 가브리엘이 관리인의 딸 릴리(Lily)에게 동전을 건네주며 "크리스마스 때"라는 표현을 사용하고 소설 후반부에서 파티를 마치고 돌아가는 장면에서 마부가 가브리엘에게 "번성하는 새해가 되시길"하고 인사를 하는 것으로 보아 이 무도회는 연말에 열린 것으로 생각된다. 주최자는 가브리엘의 고인이 된 어머니 엘렌(Ellen)의 독신 동생들인 케이트(Kate)와 쥴리아(Julia) 이모와 그들의 오빠 팻(Pat)의 외동딸인 메리 제인(Mary Jane)이며, 참석한 손님들은 가브리엘 부부, 아이브스 양(Miss Ivors), 프레디 멀린스(Freddy Malins)와 그의 노모, 브라운 씨(Mr. Browne), 바텔 달시 씨(Mr. Bartell D'Arcy) 그리고 메리의 여러 제자들이다. 이 만찬회는 매번 "큰 행사"였으며, "단 한 번도 지루하게 된 적이 없는" 멋진 것이었다.

그러나 첫 장면에서 손님맞이를 도와주는 릴리의 발길이 분주한 가운데 가브리엘 부부의 도착이 늦고, 해마다 술에 취해 늦게 오던 프레디가 아직 오지 않아서 모칸 자매는 몹시 초조해 하고 있다. 마침내 가브리엘 부부가 도착하는데 이들의 말과 모습에서 이 작품의 전체적인 분위기를 우리는 알 수 있다. 가브리엘은 지각의 이유를 아내가 준비를 하는 데에 무려 "지긋지긋한 세 시간(three mortal hours)"[5]이나 걸렸기 때문이라고 말한다. 벌써 여기서 "지긋지긋한 mortal"이란 단어는 밝은 기쁨의 잔치여야 할 잔치가 그렇지만은 않을 것임을 암시해준다. 요컨대 어둠과 죽음의 그늘이 드리워져 있음을 생각하게 만들어준다. 뿐만 아니라 강설과 추위를 뚫고 온 그레타에게 이모들이 "얼어 죽을 뻔 했겠구나(she must be perished alive.)"(23)라고 인사를 건넴으로써 이 파티에 등장하는 사람들이 다시 말해 더블린 사람들이 생중사의 상태 즉 살아 있으나 실상은 죽은 것과 다름없는 삶을 살고 있다는 것을 강하게 시사하고 있다.

이러한 도입부의 분위기 속에서 가브리엘은 덧신(goloshes)의 화제에서 보여지듯이 문약한 인물로 그려진다. 대륙 사람들이 신는다고 해서 덧신을 신을 것을 권유하여(26) 대륙지향적인 그의 성향을 보여준다. 아울러 아내에게 눈과 추위를 피하기 위해서 덧신을 신으라고 강요하는 그의 행위는 아내를 한 인격체로 보지 않고 자신의 소유물로 보려는 태도의 반영이며, 그의 허약성과 현실성의 반영이다. 이 덧신과 관련하여 그가 지나치게 조심성이 많은 사람으로 비난을 받는데 이것은

---

5) James Joyce, "The Dead," *James Joyce: The Dead*, ed. Daniel R. Schwarz(Boston and New York: Bedford Books of St. Martin's Press, 1994), p. 22.(앞으로 본 작품의 인용은 인용문 뒤에 면수만 표시함)

얼마든지 달리 볼 수도 있는 특징이다. 아들 톰의 시력을 보호하기 위해 밤에 전등에 녹색 갓을 씌울 것을 주장하고 건강을 위해 덤벨 운동을 하게 한다. 그리고 딸 에바로 하여금 강제로 죽을 먹게 만든다. 이러한 부분은 자상한 긍정적인 면도 될 수 있는 성격이라 하겠다. 또한 그는 무척 꼼꼼하고 실질적이고, 정확한 사람(as right as the mail)(23)이며 준비성이 뛰어난 사람이다. 이처럼 세심하고 꼼꼼하고 자상한 가브리엘의 성품에 대해 그레타가 털어놓는 이야기는 자기와는 상이한 삶의 방식에 지쳐서 늘어놓는 깊은 내면의 불만일 수도 있지만, 아내로서의 행복한 푸념일 수도 있는 것이다. 그런데 이것은 작품의 결말을 보면 아내가 결코 만족해하는 덕목들은 아니지만 가브리엘이 유연성 있게 변모할 수 있는 가능성의 기초가 되는 것들이라 할 수 있다.

그는 다른 손님들의 신발 끄는 소리, 옷이 스치는 소리를 들으며 교양이 없다고 생각한다. 그리고 만찬회 후에 하게 될 연설문 내용을 검토하면서 가브리엘은 지적 교만과 오만함을 보인다. 로버트 브라우닝(Robert Browning)의 시귀를 인용할 것인지 여부로 고심한다.

> 그는 손님들이 이해할 수 없는 시를 인용함으로써 자신을 우스꽝스럽게 만들뿐이리라. 그들은 괜히 우수한 교육을 받았음을 자랑한다고 생각하리라.
>
> (He would only make himself ridiculous by quoting poetry to them which they could not understand. They would think that he was airing his superior education.)(24)

가브리엘의 이기와 오만의 견고한 담장은 첫 장면에서 릴리와의 만남에서 약간의 상처를 입는다. 릴리에게 "조만간에 너의 결혼식에 참석하게 되겠구나 we'll be going to your wedding one of these fine days with your young man, eh?"(24)라고 그가 건네는 인사말은 별로 깊은 애정과 관심을 지니지 못한 겉치레의 말일 뿐이다. 그는 릴리가 졸업한지 일 년이 넘었는데도 아직 학교에 다니는지를 묻고 있으니 평소에 관리인의 딸인 그녀에 대하여 진지한 관심을 기울이지 못하였음이 분명하다. 이런 인사말을 건넨 후 당연히 그는 신랄한 말대꾸를 듣게 된다. 당돌하게도 릴리는 가브리엘을 포함한 당시의 모든 남성들을 향하여 "요즘 남자들은 감언이설만을 일삼으며 여자들에게서 무엇을 빼어낼 것인가만 생각한다. The men that is now only all palaver and what they can get out of you."(23)고 반박을 한다. 난처한 국면에 처한 가브리엘은 반강제로 동전 한 닢을 그녀의 손에 쥐어준 채 위층으로 올라가 버린다.

그는 심기가 불편해진 가운데 위층으로 올라가게 되고 의례적인 인사말들을 교환하며 메리 제인이 피아노 연주를 하는 동안에 혼자만의 몽상에 젖어든다. 그는 가문의 체통을 중시하며 자기와 형 콘스탄틴(Constantine)의 이름을 지어주신 어머니를 회상한다. 그리고 아내 그레타와 결혼할 당시 두 사람의 결혼을 반대하며 그레타를 영악한 촌뜨기라고 어머니께서 모욕을 주던 장면도 기억한다. 그러나 가브리엘은 몽크스타운(Monkstown)의 집에서 어머니가 마지막 투병생활을 할 때 그레타가 정성으로 돌보았음을 생각하며 어머니의 결혼반대와 그레타에 대한 과소평가는 부당한 것이었음을 가슴 아프게 느낀다.

"가브리엘의 이기의 원을 깨뜨리려는 첫 시도 the first attempt to break down the circle of Gabriel's egotism"[6]로 해석되는 릴리와의 해프닝으로 약간의 상처와 동요를 겪은 후, 만찬에 앞서 열린 무도회에서 가브리엘은 파트너가 된 몰리 아이브스 양(Miss Molly Ivors)으로부터 심한 공격을 당한다. 그녀는 가브리엘이 친영국 성향의 신문에 기고했다는 사실을 못마땅하게 여긴다. 그녀로부터 "당신이 영국의 앞잡이라고는 생각하지 않았는데. I didn't think you were a West Briton."(31)라고 공격을 받자 가브리엘은 당황하며 자신의 순수성을 확인하며 다음과 같은 내

6) David Daiches, *The Novel and the Modern World*(Chicago and London: The University of Chicago Press, 1960), p. 75.

부독백에 빠진다.

> 수요일마다 『데일리 익스프레스』지 문예란에 글을 썼던 것은 사실이었다. 고료로 15실링을 받는다. 그러나 그렇다고 해서 그가 분명 영국의 앞잡이가 된 것은 아니었다. 서평을 쓰기 위해 그가 받는 책들은 얼마 안 되는 고료보다 반가웠다. 그는 새로 인쇄된 책의 표지를 만지고 책장을 넘기기를 좋아했다.
>
> (It was true that he wrote a literary column every Wednesday in *The Daily Express*, for which he was paid fifteen shillings. But that did not make him a West Briton surely. The books he received for review were almost more welcome than the paltry cheque. He loved to feel the coversand turn over the pages of newly printed books.)(31)

그는 문학은 정치를 초월하는 것이라고 항변하고 싶었지만 아이브스 양이 오랜 지기(知己)이며 같은 대학을 나오고 함께 교직에 있는 등 비슷한 길을 걸어 왔기에 더 이상 거론하지 않는다. 춤을 추면서 다시금 두 사람이 마주하게 되자 그녀는 농담이었을 뿐이라고 말하고 이번에는 오는 여름에 애란 섬(Aran Isles)[7]으로 여행을 함께 떠나자고 제안을 한다.

아일랜드의 서부로의 여행은 단순히 문자적 의미를 넘어서는 중요한 상징적 의미를 갖는다. 열렬한 민족주의자로서 조국의 언어와 문화를 부흥시키고 발전시키기를 원하는 아이브스 양과 대륙 지향적 사고와 기질을 가지고 마비된 좁은 더블린을 떠나고자 하는 가브리엘 사이에 격렬한 언쟁이 벌어진다. 가브리엘은 서부로의 여행을 거부하고 이미 계획된 대륙으로의 여행을 가려고 한다.

---

7) Off Galway on the West Coast, they were regarded as an ideal by the Celtic Renaissance because Irish was spoken and the denizens lived, supposedly, a utopian agrarian life.

"그럼 당신은 접촉할 모국어가 없다는 겁니까? 아일랜드의 말말입니다." 아이브스 양이 물었다.

"그 점에 대해서라면," 가브리엘이 말했다. "아시다시피 아일랜드 말은 나의 말이 아니요."...

"그렇다면 당신은 찾아볼 조국도 없고," 아이브스 양이 계속했다. "당신이 거기에 대해서 잘 모르는. 민족도 없고 나라도 없나요?"

"아, 사실을 말하자면," 갑자기 가브리엘이 쏘아붙였다. "나는 내 나라가 지겹소. 지겨워요!"

(—And haven't you your own language to keep in touch with—Irish? asked Miss Ivors.

—Well, said Gabriel, if it comes to that, you know, Irish is not my langauge....

—And haven't you your own land to visit, continued Miss Ivors, that you know nothing of, your own people, and your own country?

—O, to tell the truth, retorted Gabriel suddenly, I'm sick of my country, sick of.)(32)

이 소설에 강하게 나타난 자전적 요소들을 볼 때 이 장면의 가브리엘의 조국관은 작가 자신의 것이라고 보아도 무리가 없을 것이다. 스스로 망명자(exile)의 삶을 선택하여 일찍이 조국을 떠나 대륙에서 산 조이스는 물리적으로는 조국을 떠나 있었지만 정신적으로는 항상 조국의 품안에서 살았다고 볼 수 있다. "조이스의 조국애는 긴 세월 동면상태에 있었으나 결코 사라지지 않았다."[8] 그가 선택한 대륙 지향성은 "아일랜드가 나아갈 적절한 길은 유럽의 지적 문화적 공동체에 참여하는 것이라"[9]고 그가 믿었기 때문에 갖게 된 태도였다. 조국의 현실을 마비와 죽음의 상태로 진단한 조이스는 아일랜드에 관해 글을 쓰기 위해서, 같은 동포로서가 아니라 한 예술가로서 아일랜드의 삶에 대해

8) Harry Levin, (ed.), *The Portable James Joyce*(Harmondsworth: Penguin Books Ltd., 1979), p. 6.

9) Daniel Schwarz, p. 6.

글을 쓰기 위해 조국을 떠났다.[10] 환언하면 예술가인 조이스에게는 객관적 거리의 확보가 중요한 관심사였다. David Daiches는 다음과 같이 기록하여 아이브스 양이 가브리엘에게 쏟아 붙는 공격의 공허함을 드러나게 한다.

> 하지만 그의 전 작품이 더블린과 관계가 있고, 그의 등장인물들은 더블린 사람들이며, 배경도 분위기도 더블린이다. 그리고 상징적 리얼리즘의 방대한 소재들이 젊은이로서 그가 등을 돌렸던 더블린의 본질과 실체를 언어로 창조하려는 데에 사용되었다.
>
> Yet all his work is concerned with Dublin; his characters are Dubliners, his background is Dublin, his atmosphere is Dublin, and all the tremendous resources of his symbolic realism were employed in creating in language the essence and reality of the Dublin he turned his back on as a young man.[11]

조이스 혹은 가브리엘의 이러한 입장은 물론 많은 공격을 받을 취약성을 지니지만, 인간적인 관점에서 본다면 자신의 이기적 입장만을 너무나 고집하기 때문에 생겨난 것이라고 볼 수도 있다. 지나친 자기 우월감, 자신만이 전적으로 옳다고 하는 확신감, 사고의 유연성의 결여, 상대방의 공격에 자신의 감정을 적절하게 절제하지 못하는 미성숙 등으로 인하여 가브리엘은 자신의 이기의 좁은 테두리 안에 살고 있다고 하겠다.

서부로의 여행 계획에 관한 소식을 듣자 그레타는 자신의 고향도 그쪽의 골웨이(Galway)이기도 하기에 반가워하며 함께 가기를 원하나 가브리엘은 일언지하에 거절한다. 따라서 아이브스 양, 애란 섬, 골웨이, 그레타, 민족주의, 아일랜드 문화 등으로 묶여지는 하나의 범주가

---

10) David Daiches, p. 64.
11) *Ibid.*, p. 63.

가브리엘을 반대 축으로 하여 형성이 된다.

가브리엘이 보는 문제점은 지나치게 협소한 국수적 민족주의에 집착하는 것이다. 많은 파티 참석자들이 이런 관점에서 편견을 보이며, 전통과 과거를 과장하고 미화시킨다. 쥴리아 이모가 30년 전에는 괜찮은 목소리를 가졌었다고 헛된 몽상에 빠지고, 가장 훌륭한 테너 가수가 누구인가 하는 논란이 벌어졌을 때 카루소(Caruso)의 가치가 무시되기도 한다. 그러나 가브리엘은 만찬 후 연설을 하는 가운데 아일랜드가 자랑할 만한 환대(hospitality)의 전통을 지니고 있음을 인정하면서 그러나 파티장에서 그간에 세상을 떠난 사람들을 생각하며 서글픔을 느낀다. 하지만 그는 과거에 집착하지 않겠다고 하는 진취적 자세를 보인다. 그리고 국수적, 보수적, 민족주의적인 편협된 입장을 배격한다. 그의 사고와 성품이 변모할 수 있는 가능성도 이 장면에서 암시된다.

> "오늘 같은 모임엔 늘 우리 마음속에 과거와 젊음과 변화와 이 밤에 우리가 볼 수 없는 얼굴들에 대한 생각 같은 서글픈 생각들이 떠오릅니다. 우리의 인생길엔 그런 많은 슬픈 기억들이 뿌려져있습니다. 그런데 우리가 늘 그런 슬픔만을 곰곰이 생각한다면 우리는 살아서 용감하게 우리가 할 일을 해나갈 수 없을 것입니다. 우리 모두에게는 마땅히 우리의 끈질긴 노력을 필요로 하는 의무와 애정이 있습니다."
>
> "따라서 저는 과거 속에서 머뭇거리지 않겠습니다."
>
> —...there are always in gatherings such as this sadder thoughts that will recur to our minds: thoughts of the past, of youth, of changes, of absent faces that we miss here tonight. Our path through life is strewn with many such sad memories: and were we to brood upon them always we could not find the heart to go on bravely with our work among the living. We have all of us living duties and living affections which claim, and rightly claim, our strenuous endeavours.— Therefore, I will not linger on the past.(44)

2. 애타의 열린 세계

가브리엘의 자기만족적이고 현실 속에 안주하는 이기적 삶에 릴리의 말대꾸와 아이브스 양의 공격에 이어 변화의 결정적 계기를 마련해 준 것은 아내로부터 듣게 되는 뜻밖의 사연 때문이었다. 본 장에서는 소설 후반부의 내용을 중심으로 가브리엘이 새롭게 자기 인식을 하며 폭 넓은 인간으로 변모해 가는 과정을 상술할 것이다.

파티가 마무리되어가고 위층에서 누군가가 피아노를 치며 노래를 부르는 가운데 현관에서는 집으로 돌아가려는 사람들의 작별인사와, 마차를 잡으려는 소란 등으로 어수선하다. 가브리엘도 예약해둔 호텔로 돌아가기 위해 일층 거실에서 아내를 기다리나 그레타가 나타나지 않는다. 그는 여기서 돌아가신 조부 패트릭 모칸(Patrick Morkan)의 접착풀 공장에서 일하던 말 자니(Johnny)가 원형의 제자리 운동을 하다 봉변을 당했던 에피소드를 들려준다. 어느 날 조부께서 공원에서 열리는 군대의 사열식을 구경하기 위해 자니에게 마구를 채우고, 최상의 옷으로 차려 입고 조상들로부터 물려받은 저택을 나섰다. 자니가 빌리왕(King Billy)[12]의 동상 앞에 이를 때까지는 아무런 일도 없었으나 그 말이 동상을 보자 왕이 탄 말에게 사랑에 빠져서인지 아니면 풀 공장으로 돌아왔다고 생각한 연유인지는 알 수 없었으나 그 동상을 빙글빙글 돌기 시작했다는 것이었다. 이런 기행으로 인하여 자니는 수난을 당하였다. 가브리엘이 들려준 이 이야기 속에서 빌리 왕의 동상은 "영국 속박의 상징 symbol of the English yoke"[13]이며, 이 동상을 선회하는 말은 영국의 굴레를 벗어나지 못하고 제자리걸음만 하고 있는 마비된 더블린 사람들을 상징한다.

---

12) William of Orange, a Protestant king who won the Battle of the Boyne in 1690 and suppressed the Irish independence movement. The statue of Billy in College Green, like the statue of Lord Nelson in front of the post office, and the Wellington Monument were major irritations to Irish Catholics.

13) Sydney Bolt, *A Preface to James Joyce(*London and New York: Longman, 1981), p. 42.

한편 아직 떠날 차비를 않는 그레타는 층계 위에서 우아하고 신비로운 모습으로 희미하게 들려오는 음악에 귀를 기울인다. 파티 동안 줄곧 심한 감기를 이유로 노래 부르기를 거부하던 달시 씨가 "오그림의 처녀"(The Lass of Aughrim)[14]라는 슬픈 사연의 노래를 부른다. 층계 위에서 노래에 귀를 기울이고 있던 아내의 모습을 바라보며 가브리엘은 자기가 화가라면 "은은한 음악 Distant Music"(48)이라는 제목으로 그 감동적인 모습을 그림으로 그렸을 텐데 하고 안타까움을 느낀다. 그는 아내의 모습이 무엇인가 다른 의미를 갖는다고 느낀다.

> 그는 마루의 어두운 곳에 가만히 서서 누군가 부르는 노래를 이해해보려고 애를 쓰며 아내를 올려다보았다. 마치 무엇의 상징인 것처럼 아내의 모습 속에는 우아함과 신비스러움이 들어 있었다. 그는 멀리서 들려오는 은은한 음악을 들으며 어둠 속 층계 위에 서있는 여인은 무엇을 상징하는가를 자문해보았다. 만일 그가 화가라면 그녀의 그런 모습을 그림으로 그릴텐데.
>
> (He stood still in the gloom of the hall, trying to catch the air that the voice was singing and gazing up at his wife. There was grace and mystery in her attitude as if she were a symbol of something. He asked himself what is a woman standing on the stairs in the shadow, listening to distant music, a symbol of. If he were a painter he would paint her in that attitude.)(48)

Tilly Eggers는 가브리엘이 아내의 정체성에 대해서 이처럼 의문을 품는 장면은 사회적 상황에서 개인적 경험으로 전이되는 전환점을 이룬다고

14) "The Lass of Aughrim," a sad ballad about a young woman from a little village in the west of Ireland not far from Galway. The song relates how she is seduced and later abandoned with her baby in her arms. She visits Lord Gregory, the father-lover, who asks her a series of questions but does not allow her to visit him. After the lass is rejected by Lord Gregory, she and her son are drowned.

주장하였다.[15] 소유의 대상에 지나지 않던 그레타가 개체성을 지닌 한 인격체로서 인식되기 시작한다는 것이다. 가브리엘에게 자신의 아내가 아닌 다른 그 무엇의 상징으로 아내가 비쳐지는 것은 그의 외로움과 예술적 통찰의 표현이라는 것이다. 그는 계속해서 이 층계 장면 이전에는 어느 누구도 그레타에 대해서 관심을 기울이지 않았다고 말한다. 가령 이모들은 "가브리엘의 아내"에게 키스를 하며, 그녀를 하나의 아내와 어머니로서만 인식한다.[16] 서술자도 그녀를 "그의 아내"로 지칭한다.

가브리엘 역시 그녀를 자신의 소유물로 생각한다. 볼이 발그레하게 상기되고 눈이 반짝이는 아내의 모습을 보며 환희의 물결과 아내의 육체에 대한 욕망을 느낀다. 너무나 연약해 보이기 때문에 보호해주고 싶은 강한 욕망을 느낀다. 이모 집을 떠나 호텔로 돌아오기까지 가브리엘은 우아하고 아름다운 아내를 소유하였다는 사실에 자부심과 행복감을 느끼며 아내를 향한 성적 욕망에 들떠 있다.[17] 그러면서 한편으로는 아내와 그녀가 경청하던 음악 사이에는 무슨 연고가 있을까 궁금하게 생각한다.

마침내 그레샴(Gresham) 호텔의 자신들의 숙소에 도착한 두사람은 중요한 대화를 하게 된다. 그레타가 갑자기 눈물을 왈칵 쏟으며 자기는 "오그림의 처녀"라는 노래를 생각하고 있다고 말한다. 이어서 그 노래를 부르곤 하던 오래 전의 어떤 사람을 생각한다고 털어놓는다. 그는 소녀 시절 골웨이의 할머니 댁에서 살 때 사귀었던 마이클 퓨어리(Michael Furey)라는 아주 섬세하고 예민한 성격의 노래를 잘 부르던 사람이라고 밝힌다. 충격을 받고 분노심과 질투심을 느끼던 가브리엘은 마이클은 이미 고인이 되었으며 가스 공장의 직공이었다는 말을 듣

15) Tilly Eggers, "What Is a Woman...a Symbol Of?," in James Joyce's *Dubliners,* ed. and with an introduction by Harold Bloom(New York and Philadelphia: Chelsea House Publishers, 1988), p. 23.

16) *Ibid.*, p. 30.

17) 본문 p. 53을 참조. He had felt proud and happy then, happy that she was his, proud of her grace and wifely carriage.

자 갑자기 자신의 우스꽝스러운 모습을 성찰하게 된다.

> 가브리엘은 자신의 비꼼이 실패로 돌아갔으며 가스 공장의 소년을 죽은 자들에게서 불러낸 것이 수치스러웠다. 그의 가슴은 그들 내외 간의 비밀스런 추억으로 가득 차 있었고, 애정과 기쁨과 욕망으로 가득 차 있었던 반면, 아내는 마음 속으로 다른 남자와 그를 비교하고 있었던 것이다. 자기 자신의 존재에 대한 수치스러운 의식이 그를 엄습했다. 그는 이모들을 위하여 한 푼짜리 심부름꾼 노릇을 하는 우스꽝스러운 인물, 속인들에게 열변을 토하며 자기 자신의 광대 같은 욕정을 이상화하는 신경질적인 선의의 감상주의자, 조금 전 거울 속에서 언뜻 보았던 애처롭고 바보 같은 자신을 생각했다. 그는 자신의 이마 위에서 불타는 수치를 아내가 보지 못하도록 본능적으로 등을 더욱 불빛 쪽으로 돌렸다.
>
> (Gabriel felt humiliated by the failure of his irony and by the evocation of this figure from the dead, a boy in the gasworks. While he had been full of memories of their secret life together, full of tenderness and joy and desire, she had been comparing him in her mind with another. A shameful consciousness of his own person assailed him. He saw himself as a ludicrous figure, acting as a penny boy for his aunts, a nervous well-meaning sentimentalist, orating to vulgarians and idealising his own clownish lusts, the pitiable fatuous fellow he had caught a glimpse of in the mirror. Instinctively he turned his back more to the light lest she might see the shame that burned upon his forehead.)(56)

아내의 고백은 계속해서 이어진다. 열일곱의 이른 나이에 소년이 죽은 것은 자기 탓이라는 것이다. 그레타가 할머니 댁을 떠나 수녀원으로 가려고 할 즈음, 때는 겨울이었는데 그는 병을 앓고 있었고 면회는 허용되지 않고 있었다는 것이다. 두 사람이 시골에서 순박하고 아름다운 순애보적인 사랑을 했었는데 마침내 그레타가 더블린으로 떠날 날이 임박하자 여름에 다시 돌아올 것이며 그때는 병세가 호전되기를 기

원한다는 내용의 편지를 보낸다. 그런데 할머니 댁을 떠나기 바로 전날 밤에 그 불쌍한 소년이 비를 맞으며 찾아와 뜰에서 자기를 부르더라는 것이다. 그 후 일주일 만에 결핵이 더욱 악화되어 그는 죽게 되어 친척들이 사는 우터라드(Oughterard)에 묻혔다는 것이다. 그레타는 그 소년이 창밖에 와서 부르곤 하던 슬픈 사연—사랑에 버림받고 아기와 함께 익사한 내용—의 "오그림의 처녀"를 듣고 마음 속 깊은 곳에 한으로 쌓여 있다가 북바쳐오르는 감정을 남편에게 이렇게 다 털어놓은 것이다.

아내의 고백을 들은 가브리엘은 깊은 잠에 빠져든 아내의 모습을 바라보며 남편인 자기가 아내의 삶 속에서 얼마나 하찮은 역할밖에 감당하지 못하였나 하는 생각이 들어도 괴로워하지 않는다. 마치 그레타와 부부로서 함께 살아오지 않았다는 느낌까지도 갖는다. 아내를 향한 이상한 연민의 감정을 느끼며 자신의 인생이 너무나 소유와 아집에 집착한 편협된 것이었음을 생각한다. 쥴리아 이모가 죽어 돌아가신 조부 패트릭 모칸과 함께 있는 모습이 떠오른다. 파티가 열린 바로 그 이모 집의 거실에 상복을 입고 장례식에 참석하는 자신의 모습도 그려보게 된다. 가브리엘은 방안 공기의 한기를 느끼며 아내 옆에 나란히 누워 이불을 덮는다. 사랑에 절망하고 그레타를 찾아와서 나는 더 이상 살고 싶지 않다고 말할 때의 마이클의 눈초리, 그 연인의 눈초리를 어떻게 그레타가 오랜 세월 동안 결코 잊을 수 없었는가 하는 생각을 하며 그는 사랑과 용서의 눈물을 쏟는다.

> 관용의 눈물이 그의 눈을 가득 채웠다. 그는 어떤 여인에 대해서도 자기 스스로 지금까지 그와 같은 감정을 결코 느껴보지 못했으나 이러한 감정이야말로 사랑임을 알았다. 눈물이 더 많이 눈에 고였고, 희미한 어둠 속에서 빗물이 뚝뚝 떨어지는 나무 밑에 서 있는 한 소년의 모습을 보고 있는 것 같았다. 다른 형상들도 다가왔다. 그의 영혼은 수많은 사자(死者)의 무리들이 살고 있는 지역으로 점점 다가갔다. 그는 그들의 걷잡을 수 없이 깜박이는 존재를 의식했으나 붙잡을 수가 없었다. 자신의 정체는 회색

> 의 불가사의한 세계 속으로 사라져갔고, 이러한 사자들이 한때 자라면서 살았던 실질적인 세계 그 자체가 허물어지며 줄어들고 있었다.
>
> (Generous tears filled Gabriel's eyes. He had never felt like that himself towards any woman but he knew that such a feeling must be love. The tears gathered more thickly in his eyes and in the partial darkness he imagined he saw the form of a young man standing under a dripping tree. Other forms were near. His soul had approached that region where dwell the vast hosts of the dead. He was conscious of, but could not apprehend, their wayward and flickering existence. His own identity was fading out into a grey impalpable world: the solid world itself which these dead had one time reared and lived in was dissolving and dwindling.)(59)

눈송이가 창문에 부딪치는 소리를 듣고 그의 시선은 창문으로 향한다. 마침내 그가 서부로 여행을 떠날 때가 되었다고 생각한다. 눈은 아일랜드 전역에 내려서 모든 것을 덮어 버린다. 우주 전체에 부드럽게 내리는 눈 소리, 그들의 최후의 내림처럼 모든 산 자와 죽은 자 위에 사뿐히 내리는 눈 소리를 듣자, 가브리엘의 영혼은 무의식의 상태로 빠져든다.

이 마지막 장면의 강설은 작품의 대단원을 완결지어 주는 대단히 아름답고 감동적인 장면이다. 이 장면의 강설의 의미는 축복과 용서와 융화와 몰개성의 상징이다. 이 소설 전반에 걸쳐서 눈(snow)은 아주 효과적인 상징으로 사용된다. 첫 장면에서 내리는 눈은 가브리엘이 덧신을 신고 막아내야 하고 이모 집에 도착해서 털어 버려야 하는 성가시고 귀찮은 차가운 것이었다.(23) 두 번째로 눈은 가브리엘의 상상 속에서 등장한다. 그는 파티에서 아이브스 양의 격한 공격을 받고 흥분된 마음을 억제하며 강변과 공원 속을 산책하면 무척 즐거울 텐데 하는 생각을 하며 나뭇가지 위에 그리고 웰링턴 기념비 위에 쌓여 있을 눈을 상상한다. 여기서 눈은 파티가 열리고 있는 집안의 편협하고 답답한 분위기로부터 탈출할 수 있는 가능성과 희망을 암시한다고 볼 수 있다. 눈은 메리 제인이 전해준 “30 년만의 큰 눈이 왔으며, 아일랜드 전국에 걸쳐 내린다.”(50)고 하는 말과, 호텔로 돌아가는 장면에서 “눈이 덮여있는 동상”(52)을 가브리엘이 가리키는 곳에서 다시금 언급된다. 마지막 장면에서 눈이 내려 온 세상을 다 덮어버림으로써 개성과 이기의 와해와 융해를 가져온다. 가브리엘이 다시 부활하고 재생하기 위해서 기독교의 예수 그리스도가 십자가의 형벌을 받을 때 창과 가시에 찔리는 고통을 당했는데 “사자들”의 마지막 장면에서도 창과 가시(spears and thorns) 위에도 눈이 내림으로써 효과적인 연상을 가능하게 해준다. Florence Walzl은 “창과 가시에 나타난 그리스도의 수난에 대한 회상은 자아의 희생이 재생의 조건이라고 하는 사실을 환기시킨다”[18]라고 이 점을 지적하고 있다.

주인공 가브리엘의 변화와 재생을 불러온 아내 그레타는 단순히 하나의 기능적 인물에 머물고 마는 것인가? 소설 후반부에 이르기까지 그녀에 대한 관심이 충분히 나타나 있지는 않지만, 소설 모두에서 덧신에 대해 왈가왈부하는 가운데 남편이 그레타에 대해서 “내버려두면 호텔까지라도 걸어갈 여자”(25)라고 이모들에게 말하는 장면에서 그녀의 성격을 우리는 짐작할 수 있다. 이 말은 그레타가 고집과 열정을 지니고 야생화 같은 강인한 생명력을 소유하고 있음을 암시한다. 그리고 호텔에서 남편에게 고백한 소녀 시절의 연애담이 신뢰성과 개연성을 갖도록 만드는 일종의 복선의 역할을 하는 말이다. 가슴속에 남모르는 비밀을 가진 그레타가 마비된 인물이라고 보기는 다소 무리일 것이다. 그것은 얼마든지 현실 속에서 가능한 일이기 때문이다. 단지 아쉬움을 표한다면, 일반적으로 이기적인 인물로만 평가되는 가브리엘의 장점들을 그레타가 진작에 주목했었더라면 더 진실한 사랑을 하며 결혼생활을 하지 않았을까 생각해본다. 그녀가 소홀히 한 가브리엘의 장점은 보기에 따라 단점이 될 수도 있겠지만 사회적 경제적으로 안정된 지위 외에 다음과 같이 요약할 수 있다. 비가 올 때나 눈이 올 때나 그녀의

18) Requoted from Schwarz, p. 70.

발이 젖지 않도록 덧신을 신도록 한다. 물론 그레타가 덧신을 신기 싫어하지만 그녀를 위해서라면 심지어 잠수복까지도 사 입힐 것이다. 지난 해 파티를 마치고 늦은 시간 마차로 귀가하다가 그레타가 심한 감기에 걸렸기 때문에 올해는 호텔에서 하룻밤 묶기로 한다. 가브리엘의 어머니는 그녀와의 결혼에 반대하고 그녀를 영악한 촌뜨기라고 불렀는데 그런 말은 그녀에게 맞지 않고, 그러한 것을 생각하면 여전히 가슴이 아프다. 파티에서 돌아온 가브리엘은 그녀에게 강한 욕정을 느끼지만 그녀가 다가올 때까지 기다린다.

비평가 Eggers는 그레타의 역할과 위치를 다음과 같이 설명한다.

> 그레타는 맡는 역할에 유연성을 갖는다...그녀는 눈 속을 멋대로 걸어가려고도 하나 또한 눈으로부터 자신을 보호할 것이다. 소설에서 그녀의 위치는 희생적 사랑으로 비를 맞고 죽음을 불사한 마이클과, 자기애로 자신을 눈으로부터 보호하나 진정한 삶의 경지를 모르는 가브리엘 두 사람 사이 어딘가에 있다.
>
> (She possesses a flexibility in the roles she plays...Gretta would walk freely into the snow, but she will also protect herself from the snow; her position in the story is somewhere between Michael, whose selflessness leadshim into the rain to death, and Gabriel, whose self-possession protects him from the snow and from life.)[19]

그러나 위에서 그레타가 보편적 인간상이 될 수 있다고 했듯이 가브리엘 역시 우리가 부정적인 입장에서만 보아서는 안 될 것이다. 그는 작품 후반부에서 보여주는 자기 인식과 자아 완성에 도달할 수 있는 잠재적 자질들과 가능성을 애당초 가지고 있었기에 변화할 수 있었던 것이다. 그리고 전적으로 자신의 아내로만 생각하고 살아온 그레타가 정신적으로는 좌절된 사랑의 추억에 몰입한 채 자신과는 형식적이고

---

19) Eggers, p. 32.

의무적인 결혼생활을 해온 것을 알고 자기 자신의 모습을 적나라하게 새롭게 발견하는 가브리엘의 자기 인식은 가볍게 볼 수 없는 인간적 행위일 것이다. 그리고 가브리엘이 최종적으로 사랑과 용서의 눈물을 흘리며 자아의 완성 상태에 도달 할 수 있었던 것은 모든 인간에게 보편적 운명으로 다가오는 죽음에 대한 인식을 했기 때문이다. 죽음의 인식 앞에서 산 자와 죽은 자, 자아와 타자, 주관과 객관, 이기와 인간애, 사랑과 미움의 상반된 모든 것들이 허물어지고 녹아져버리는 것이다. 가브리엘이 서부로 여행을 떠나려고 하는 것은 "삶과 죽음을 조우하기 위한 것"[20]이며, "소박하고 열정적인 삶이 있는 곳"[21]으로의 여행이기 때문에 서부적 가치 즉 그레타, 아이브스 양, 골웨이, 애란섬을 수용하는 행위이다.

Ⅲ. 결론: 자아의 완성

지금까지 우리는 제임스 조이스의 첫 소설인 『더블린 사람들』에서 단편 소설 모음집인 이 작품을 마무리하는 작품이면서 후기작들의 면모를 예견케 해주고, 독립된 하나의 작품으로 본다 하더라도 그 자체로서 완결성과 통일성을 지니고 세계 문학의 범위에서도 가장 훌륭한 소설 중의 하나로 평가되는 "사자들"을 자아의 완성이라는 관점에서 자세히 살펴보았다.

부부간의 사랑의 부재가 주제라고 본 사람[22]도 있으나 본고에서는 조이스 소설에 공통적으로 나타나는 특징인 "자아 혹은 이기의 죽음으로의 움직임 a movement toward the death of the ego"[23], "담으로 둘러싸

20) William York Tindall, *A Reader's Guide to James Joyce*(New York: The Noonday Press, 1959), p. 46.

21) Requoted from C. H. Peake, p. 51.

22) Phillip F. Herring, *Joyce's Uncertainty Principle*(New Jersey: Princeton University Press, 1987), p. 71.

23) Robert Kiely, *Beyond Egotism: The Fiction of James Joyce, Virginia Woolf, and*

인 가브리엘의 이기주의에 대한 공격 the assault on the walled circle of Gabriel's egotism"[24], "오만과 사랑의 갈등, 이기와 인간애의 갈등 the conflict of pride with love, of ego with humanity"[25] 등의 주제에 주목하며, 인간에 보편적인 주제를 추적해보려고 노력하였다.

릴리의 신랄한 말대꾸로 상처를 입고 민족주의자 아이브스 양의 모욕적 언사의 공격을 받은 가브리엘은 뜻밖에도 내면적으로 다른 세계에 살고 있었던 아내 그레타의 마음을 알고 나서 충격을 받는 동시에 중요한 각성을 하게 된다. 자기 자신은 이기와 현실에 안주하며 모든 것을 다 가지고 부족함이 없는 행복한 삶을 누리고 있다고 생각해온 가브리엘의 삶의 방식과 그의 인생 자체가 흔들리게 된다. 아내의 깊은 내면을 전혀 알지 못한 채 지적 우월감과 만족감에 빠져 아내를 향한 육체적 사랑을 꿈꾸던 모습이 한낱 가스 공장에서 일하던 열일곱의 마이클 퓨어리가 죽음을 불사하고 그레타를 사랑한 그 열정적 사랑 앞에서 빛을 잃는다. 가브리엘은 사랑은 헌신적이고 아낌없이 주어야 하는 것이며 머리가 아니라 가슴으로 정열로 불꽃처럼 하는 것이어야 함을 인식한다. 위선과 체면과 가식과 우월감, 오만함의 껍질을 뒤집어쓴 사랑은 진실한 사랑이 아니며 깊고 고귀한 사랑도 아니다.

가브리엘은 외부 세계의 수용, 나와 다른 생각이나 관점을 용납, 다양성을 인정, 타자성을 인정 즉 다른 사람을 한 인격체로 인식하는 등의 엄청난 변화를 겪는다. 그는 사랑의 위대함과 죽음의 불가피성을 인식하고 결점을 용서하는 너그러운 마음과 모든 사람을 다 사랑할 수 있는 넓은 열린 마음을 가지고 부활하기 위한 잠에 빠져든다. 가브리엘이 성취하는 초월적 비전과 열린 희망의 가능성은 죽음과 어둠과 마비의 도시 더블린과 더블린 사람들의 구원의 가능성을 보여주는 결말이다. 비록 종교적 의미의 구원은 아니지만 인간 전체의 구원의 가능성도 유추해볼 수

D. H. Lawrence(Cambridge: Harvard University Press, 1980), p. 8.

24) Daiches, p. 75.

25) Tindall, p. 49.

있는 낙관적 결말이다. 사람이 세상을 살아가면서 사랑하고 미워하며 가슴에 응어리진 것들이 쌓여 있기에 이 소설을 읽으며 우리는 마음의 카타르시스를 느낀다. 또한 "사자들"이 사랑과 죽음의 근본적 주제를 다루기에 우리의 영혼에 진한 반향을 불러일으키게 된다.

Bibliography

Text:

Joyce, James. "The Dead," *James Joyce: The Dead* ed. by Daniel R. Schwarz. Boston and New York: Bedford Books of St. Martin's Press, 1994.

References:

Bolt, Sydney. *A Preface to James Joyce.* London and New York: Viking Press, 1966.

Chambers, Ross. "Gabriel Conroy Sings for His Supper, or Love Refused ("The Dead")," *James Joyce's Dubliners* ed. by Harold Bloom. New York and Philadelphia: Chelsea House Publishers, 1988, pp. 97-119.

Daiches, David. *The Novel and the Modern World.* Chicago and London: The University of Chicago Press, 1960.

Doherty, Gerald. "Undercover Stories: Hypodiegetic Narration in James Joyce's *Dubliners*," *The Journal of Narrative Technique*, Vol. 22, No, 1. Winter, 1992, pp. 35-45.

Eggers, Tilly. "What Is a Woman...a Symbol Of?," *James Joyce's Dubliners* ed. by Harold Bloom. New York and Philadelphia: Chelsea House Publishers, 1988, pp. 23-38.

Ellmann, Richard ed. *The Letters of James Joyce.* New York: Viking Press, 1966.

Herring, Phillip F. *Joyce's Uncertainty Principle.* New Jersey: Princeton University Press, 1987.

Kiely, Robert. Beyond Egotism: *The Fiction of James Joyce, Virginia Woolf, and D. H. Lawrence.* Cambridge: Harvard University Press, 1980.

Levin, Harry ed. *The Portable James Joyce.* Harmondsworth: Penguin Books, 1979.

Murphy, M. W. "Darkness in *Dubliners*," *Modern Fiction Studies,* Vol. XV, No. 1. Spring, 1969, pp. 97-104.

Peake, C. H. *James Joyce: The Citizen and the Artist.* Stanford: Stanford University Press, 1977.

Schwarz, Daniel R. ed. *James Joyce: The Dead.* Boston and New York: Bedford Books of St. Martin's Press, 1994.

Tindall, William York. *A Reader's Guide to James Joyce.* New York: The Noonday Press, 1959.

편주자
나병우

서울대학교 영문학과 졸업
서울대학교 대학원 영문학과 석사, 박사
육군사관학교 교수 역임
한국버지니아울프학회 부회장 역임
미국 버지니아대학교 영문과 객원교수 역임
경성대학교 영문학과 교수

명작영미단편선
Famous Short Stories
with Essays in Criticism

1판 1쇄 발행 _ 2008년 8월 20일
1판 4쇄 발행 _ 2018년 8월 30일

편 주 자 • 나 병 우
발 행 인 • 정 현 걸
발 행 • 신 아 사
인 쇄 • 대명프린팅
출판등록 • 1956년 1월 5일 (제9-52호)
주 소 • 서울특별시 은평구 통일로 59길 4 2F
전 화 • 02)382-6411 • 팩스 02)382-6401
홈페이지 • www.shinasa.co.kr
E-MAIL • shinasa@daum.net

ISBN 978-89-8396-294-2 (93840)

정가 *13,000* **원**